Australian Sport: Better by Design?

Australians have invested an enormous amount of emotional and physical capital in their sporting systems and structures. While Australian sport has mostly been dissected from a historical and cultural perspective, there is little detailed analysis of sport's relationship with government.

This book focuses on sport policy, and examines the ways in which government has impacted on the development of Australian sport since 1920. The text identifies the political, economic and cultural context in which the policies were set, and examines critical policy shifts. The book also provides a strong theoretical foundation by discussing first, the underlying principles of policy formulation, and second, the rationale for government intervention in national sport. It includes a number of sport policy case studies, with particular attention to the following topics:

- Assistance to high performance sport
- Tensions between elite and community sport development
- Trends in participation and sport fan preferences
- Problems in attracting young people to sport
- Improving the management systems of sporting bodies
- Sport broadcasting and pay television
- Fair play in sport
- Tools for evaluating sport policy.

Providing a unique blend of theory, history and practice this text provides an essential foundation for sport policy analysis and will be read by students of sport studies and sport management as well as professionals with an interest in sport development.

Bob Stewart is Associate Professor and Manager of the Sport Management and Policy Division, Victoria University, Australia.

Matthew Nicholson is Lecturer in Sport Media and Management at Victoria University, Australia.

Aaron Smith and **Hans Westerbeek** are Associate Professors of Sport Management at La Trobe University, Australia, and co-Directors of the consulting firm *Manage to Manage*.

Australian Sport: Better by Design?

The evolution of Australian sport policy

Bob Stewart, Matthew Nicholson, Aaron Smith and Hans Westerbeek

Routledge
Taylor & Francis Group

LONDON AND NEW YORK

First published 2004
by Routledge
2 Park Square, Milton Park, Abington, Oxon, OX14 4RN

Simultaneously published in the USA and Canada
by Routledge
270 Madison Avenue, New York, NY 10016

Routledge is an imprint of the Taylor & Francis Group

© 2004 Bob Stewart, Matthew Nicholson, Aaron Smith
and Hans Westerbeek

Typeset in Goudy by
Integra Software Services Pvt. Ltd, Pondicherry, India
Printed and bound in Great Britain by
TJ International Ltd, Padstow Cornwall

British Library Cataloguing in Publication Data
A catalogue record for this book is available from the British Library

Library of Congress Cataloging in Publication Data
A catalog record for this book has been requested

ISBN 0–415–34046–2 (hbk)
ISBN 0–415–34047–0 (pbk)

Contents

Figures

Tables

Acknowledgements

We would like to first thank the members of the Sport Management and Policy Division at Victoria University for their encouragement and advice during the writing of this book. We also appreciate the professional guidance and support provided by the staff of the Centre for Privatisation and Pubic Accountability in the Monash University Law School. We also wish to thank Archery Australia, Athletics Australia, the Australian Football League Commission, Cricket Australia, Hockey Australia, Gymnastics Australia, Tennis Australia, and Women's Golf Australia for giving us access to valuable case study information. Finally, we want to thank the staff of the Australian Sports Commission who provided generous support and advice throughout the project. We also wish to note that the views and opinions contained in this book are solely those of the authors.

Preface

Australia has a tradition of sport participation, and of taking sport seriously. In turn, Australian sport followers use their sport experiences to construct a sense of both personal and national identity. Moreover, this heavy emotional investment in sport has been complemented by an ongoing investment in sporting infrastructure, which was traditionally the responsibility of local government. However, since the 1970s the Commonwealth Government has taken a leading role in developing the Australian sports system.

Despite the crucial importance of government sport assistance, there is very little written on sport policy in Australia. This book aims to fill this gap, and in doing so provides a detailed examination of sport policy and how it has impacted upon Australian sport development. This will be achieved by discussing Australian sport policy from four perspectives: first, the policy context, second, the evolution of sport policy, third, the implementation of policy into practice, and finally an evaluation of contemporary sport policy. These perspectives have been used to divide the book into a context section, an evolution section, a practice section and an evaluation section.

In the context section, Australian sport will be set within a historical, cultural and political framework. This will begin with an examination of Australia's sporting traditions, and why Australians have taken sport so seriously for so long. This will be followed by an analysis of Australia's sporting preferences, and the current standing of Australian sport. The context section will also re-visit the concept of sport, and the different ways that it can be defined and practised.

Importantly, this section will provide a theoretical foundation for exploring sport policy, an examination of the different forms that policy takes, and how policy operates at the general political level. The policy process will be highlighted, together with the view that policy making combines rational and evidence-based decision with decisions that are bound up in values and ideology. This will be done in the context of Australian sport development.

The context section will round off with a discussion of the ways in which governments defend and justify their involvement in sport. This will include an analysis of market failure, the problem of externalities, sport as a public good, and the extent to which sport provides external and social benefits.

In the evolution section, the long-term development of the Commonwealth Government's sport policies and programmes will be reviewed. The analysis will begin just after the end of First World War when Australia set about re-invigorating its sports system and preparing itself for the 1920 Antwerp Olympic Games. It will end with Australia's loss to England in the Rugby World Cup and its win against Spain in the Davis Cup in 2003, and its continued preparation for the 2006 Commonwealth Games to be held in Melbourne.

The evolution of sport policy will be broken down into four stages. The first is a benign indifference stage running from 1920 to 1971; the second is a crash-through stage, running from 1972 to 1982; the third is an augmentation stage running from 1983 to 1996; and the final one is a consolidation stage running from 1996 to the present day. Sport policy will be seen as an evolutionary process strongly influenced by not only changes taking place in the sport-world but also changes in society and the economy. These changes will be linked to the emergence of sport-related problems that in turn led to policy statements and subsequent action. A detailed model of sport policy is developed in Chapter 2, and this problem-based model will be used to frame the subsequent analysis of the Commonwealth Government's sports policies and programmes.

In the practice section the focus will be on contemporary sport policy and its delivery. It will begin with an assessment of current Commonwealth Government sport policy, which is titled *Backing Australia's Sporting Ability*, and will include an examination of the assumptions and values that underpin its operation. These policy strands will be divided into the following categories. There is *sport development*, which includes elite and high-performance sport at one end of the continuum, community sport and junior sport at the other end of the continuum, and sporting pathways as a bridge between the two extremes. There is *management improvement*, which includes programmes aimed at establishing more business-like structures in sport, programmes to improve the skills of professional managers and volunteer officials, and programmes that optimise the social and economic impacts of sport on the broader community. Finally, there is *fair play in sport*, which includes anti-doping programmes, anti-discrimination policies, anti-harassment policies, and policies aimed at eliminating severe disadvantage.

The practice section will examine cases that reveal the ways in which the Commonwealth Government sport policy strands have been implemented. The cases will begin with a discussion of their links to specific policy statements, and the ways in which these policy statements were translated into strategies. The bulk of the case discussion will centre on their operational outcomes, with a particular focus on the relationship between the Australian Sports Commission (ASC) and national sporting organisations (NSOs). These cases will also be used to assess the extent to which Commonwealth Government sport policy has been successfully implemented. The cases in this section will centre on elite development, targeted participation, junior development, management improvement through performance measurement, fair play, and sport broadcasting regulation.

The evaluation section will provide an overall assessment of Australian Government sport policy. This will be done in a number of ways. It will begin with an examination of the ideologies, values, and assumptions that underpin these policies and programmes. The policies and programmes will then be analysed in terms of their start-up and operational costs, and the private and social benefits that flowed from their implementation. This will be followed by an assessment of the extent to which the policy statements were effectively translated into operational polices and programmes at the level of the Australian Sports Commission, the sport-governing bodies, and clubs.

Running through this book will be a number of fundamental themes. There will be a strong focus on the ways in which the Commonwealth Government sets the policy agenda, seeks advice from key stakeholders, uses the Australian Sports Commission to implement policy, and shapes the policies and practices of all the other sport organisations. There will also be a constant reminder of the values and ideologies surrounding the development of policy, and the ways in which they compete with the more rational, evidence-based approaches in formulating sport policy.

Part I
Context

1 Sport and Australian society

Australian profile

Australia is an island continent that contains a relatively small population of 20 million within a landmass of around 7.7 million square kilometres. In contrast, Indonesia, a close northern neighbour, has a significantly smaller landmass of 1.9 million square kilometres, but sustains a population of just over 216 million. Australia has been inhabited by aboriginals for at least 40,000 years, but has only 216 years of permanent European settlement. It is an English-speaking country, having been established as a British penal colony in 1788. Since then it has grown into a cosmopolitan and wealthy western-style society governed by a democratically elected parliament and the rule of law.

In some respects, Australia is an archetypal post-modern nation in that it contains many contradictions and ambiguities. For example, while it covers an enormous land-mass, a large part of the country is dry and sparsely populated. Most of its 20 million inhabitants live on the coastal fringes. It has been traditionally mythologised as a land of laconic bushmen who live on small farms, but in reality over 70 per cent of all Australians live in cities. In fact, Australia is one of the most urbanised countries in the world (Salt, 2003).

Australia's shifting identity is also apparent when it tries to define itself in relation to its region. It occupies a strategic place in the Asia-Pacific region but has a weak cultural connection to many of its Asian and Pacific neighbours (Figure 1.1). It is caught between its Anglo-Irish origins and a desire to integrate into the wider Asian community. At the same time, it has augmented its British colonial roots with millions of migrants from Continental Europe, and more recently Asia and South America. However, the broadening of Australia's migration base did not come easily, and for much of its early history Australia opposed migration from non-western European countries. During the 40 years immediately after its Federation in 1901, Australia had a white-Australia policy, which meant that Asian migrants were often denied entry (Rickard, 1988). Moreover, it has treated its indigenous aboriginals poorly over many years, and they are still the most disadvantaged ethnic group in the country.

Australia's economic development has also taken many twists and turns. It was traditionally an exporter of primarily rural products and raw materials, and until

Figure 1.1 Australia in the Asia-Pacific region.

the 1950s it was often said that Australia rode on the sheep's back. However, in recent times Australia has relied extensively on its service sector to fuel its growth. Primary industry has ended up supporting less than 10 per cent of the workforce, and the most recent United Nations human development index ranks Australia as the third most-developed country in the world. This was achieved through a combination of 'explosive productivity growth', low inflation, a rapid expansion in the finance, business and communication industries, and a growth in global trade (Edwards, 2000: 10). Despite the chronic disadvantage suffered by aboriginal communities, Australia has also used a system of industrial conciliation and arbitration and progressive taxes to ensure an even spread of wealth and income between workers and households. However, the income gap between rich and poor has been progressively widening in recent years, and the egalitarian myth that has been projected to the world is under threat (O'Connor *et al.*, 2001).

Australia's global image also contains a shifting mix of contradictory features. On one hand, it is internationally known for its medical research, opera singers, quality educational system, and early adoption of technology. On the other hand, it is probably even better known for its relaxed lifestyle, open spaces, surf beaches, television (TV) soap operas, and laconic, apparently dim-witted, but street-smart movie stars like Paul Hogan and Steve Irwin.

Australia's enigmatic history has created a diverse society, but it has also produced many social fractures and cultural tensions. Australia is divided in all sorts of ways, with the main tensions being economic, religious, racial, and gender-based (O'Connor *et al.*, 2001). At the same time, there are many occasions when Australians are strongly united, and for the most part this occurs when the nation is represented in major sporting events. Indeed, one thing that seems to define Australia's global image is sport. Sport has, more than any other cultural practice, the capacity to unite Australians, whatever their background. Sport's nation-building capacity has been a feature of Australia's development, and reached its zenith over the last 10 years in the wake of Olympic and Commonwealth Games successes. It has been embedded into the national psyche through a national sport policy that has focused on international sport achievement.

The British tradition

Australians take their sport very seriously, but this immediately begs the question as to why they value it so highly. The answer can be partly located in the nation's history and culture. The sporting values and preferences of British settlers moulded the cultural practices of sport in Australia, which affected the nation's desire for sporting success and the path it has carved towards that goal (Adair and Vamplew, 1997).

Sport in the pre-Victorian period was developed within a rigid British social structure (Cashman, 1995). Consequently, sport was constrained by strict behavioural parameters based on chivalry, gentlemanly conduct, and moral development. However, this romanticised perception of sport was exclusive to the aristocratic class, whose time and money afforded them the luxury of pursuing athletic contests. In contrast, there were few opportunities for the working class to participate in any sporting activity. The British 'gentleman amateur' was born of the pre-Victorian era and became the epitome for the definition of manliness (Booth and Tatz, 2000: 50). Sport, which combined strict standards of play with class-based privileges, served to further distinguish aristocrats from common men and women.

By the time of first white settlement in Australia in 1788, sport was becoming prominent in the lives of the majority of British people (Cashman, 1995). While class barriers were still firmly erected, sport of the less gentle type had permeated through to the commoners in various forms. The sports that arrived in colonial Australia were from three different cultural origins: English national sports like cricket and horse racing; traditional sports that were distinctively Scottish or Irish, namely shinty and hurling; and local versions of British sports such as wrestling and football. These sports became as prominent in the lives of colonial Australians as they were in the lives of their originators.

The pursuit of sport was widely encouraged, with colonial values advocating that sport created more rounded individuals, subsequently leading to a better society. Sport was the cure-all for social deviance and dysfunction. According to colonial administrators it developed character and elevated national worth. The belief that sport should be 'socially productive' remains a stalwart of government motivation for sporting development (Stoddart, 1986: 22–23). The success of the colonies in the eyes of its pioneers could only be measured by direct comparison with the Motherland. As a result there were frequent sporting competitions between settlers and members of the parent stock.

Gaming and betting became important pastimes during the early colonial period particularly among ex-convicts and working people (Adair and Vamplew, 1997). Gaming with coins, dice and cards was practised in the colonies from their inception. Public house practices, such as betting on tests of drinking prowess, were also popular, while other forms of betting evolved with the establishment of colonial sport. Allied with the development of gaming, betting, and drinking standards, was the maturation of what contemporary Australian society refers to as mateship. This boisterous camaraderie provided the social glue and cohesion that 'bonded the colonies together' when they participated in sporting pursuits against British-bred opposition; a proclivity that is just as fervent today (Mandle, 1976: 46).

Sport consequently provided the opportunity for the colonials to beat their masters at their own game, and this became a significant measure of achievement (Dunstan, 1973). It was during this pioneering period that Australians adopted an intemperate pride in their sporting prowess, one that is still evident in Australian society today. It must be remembered that there were two distinct constituents in colonial society: the convict settlers, and the ruling and free settler group. Recreational pastimes were largely denied to the convicts, but the free members of society could participate in whatever they wished (Booth and Tatz, 2000). When sport was introduced into the convict ranks as both a recreational pastime and a character-building exercise, it was adopted with fervour by an opportunity-starved community. Having been denied their freedom, sport became a form of emancipation, and one into which they zealously threw themselves. This fierce passion for sport is evident in contemporary Australian society.

The evolution of a sporting culture

By the 1820s the wealthy and the gentry began to play cricket in organised clubs, while horse racing was formalised by the establishment of the Sydney Turf Club in 1825 (Cashman, 1995). Fist-fights and gaming were thriving as well, but these activities were clearly associated with the so-called lower classes. The one common denominator was that they all took sport seriously.

The economic development and social status of sport was bolstered by the gold rush of the 1850s. Successful miners, with their newfound wealth, created substantial demand for goods and services. With the influx of capital came substantial social infrastructure development, which had a generative effect on the already firm social institution of sport. Groups that had prospered during the economic expansion adopted games such as tennis and lawn bowls. At another level, the gold fever indirectly introduced new sports and games into Australia, not the least of which were baseball and basketball, imported by American miners (Stoddart, 1986). This constituted the first significant non-European influence on Australian sport.

The late nineteenth century saw sport create a diverse and robust following. Sport developed as a 'social metaphor for national development', with sporting accomplishments synonymous with social improvement (Stoddart, 1986: 27). This attitude was crucial in the eventual disposition of Australian attitudes towards sport. Perhaps the most influential catalyst of this social metaphor lay in private school education, where British traditions of fair play, amateurism, and character building through sport were strictly upheld (Adair and Vamplew, 1997). Rowing, cricket, football and rugby were especially cultivated as 'character-building sports' (Stewart, 1992: 40–45). In addition, in all schools, physical education became compulsory, which stimulated many schools to measure their success on the field rather than in the classroom. On the other hand, females were explicitly discouraged from participation in any type of vigorous activity that would diminish their femininity, and were relegated to spectator and supporter roles (Booth and Tatz, 2000).

Twentieth-century sport development

Australian sporting culture progressed uneventfully during the early part of the twentieth century. Notably, sport became increasingly formalised during this period. A bureaucratic codification of sport was taking place that laid the foundation for the club system of sport participation that is evident today. By 1910 there were national governing bodies in Australian football, cricket, cycling, golf, lawn bowls and rifle shooting (Shilbury and Deane, 2001). Governing power was not, however, evenly distributed. A division existed between upper- and middle-class administrators, who exercised control and power in the sporting organisations, and the working-class players and participants, who enjoyed the rough and tumble, but had little influence over the management of clubs and leagues.

Following the Second World War, Australia's sporting culture, propped up by a hero-worship mentality, began to diversify with the inflow of migrants. European and American sports began to gain popularity, although competitive British team sports were still dominant (Stewart, 1990). The next decades were transformational for Australia as a nation, with sport leading the way. Until that time, the Australian economy was based on farming communities that created their prosperity through the wool trade. However, Australia began to emerge as an industrialised and urbanised society with a 'strong consumer culture' (Whitwell, 1989: 29–31). By 1980, there was growing professionalism in the sport and exercise industries, which pushed the old amateur-ideal to the margins. There was an increasing realisation that sport was a legitimate and lucrative vehicle for entertainment, sponsorship, and large-scale TV broadcasting (Stewart and Smith, 2000).

Women also occupied more sporting space during the 1970s and 1980s. Shane Gould took women's swimming to new levels of performance, the women's field hockey team became world champions, and Glenis Nunn and Debra Flintoff-King won Olympic Games gold medals in track and field. Australian women road athletes also achieved strong international prominence when Kerry Saxby broke a number of world walking records, and Lisa Martin secured a silver medal at the 1988 Seoul Olympics. However, despite their successes, women athletes still found it difficult to attract large-scale sponsorship and media attention (Stell, 1991).

Contemporary Australian sporting culture

By the 1990s many sports organisations had embraced many of the characteristics of business enterprises (Stewart and Smith, 1999). The influence of modern communication technologies has been profound, with international sporting broadcasts and results now as readily available as their domestic equivalent. Australian sporting organisations have begun to realise that in order to remain competitive they must provide entertainment value that equals or exceeds their overseas competitors. Consequently, levels of professionalism and sponsorship revenue have increased. One visible change to the Australian sport landscape has been the proliferation of corporate boxes that line major sporting venues, where company executives can wine, dine, and entertain clients. These developments mirror the hyper-commercialisation of Australian sport in which Australian football, basketball, cricket, golf, rugby union and league, soccer, and tennis support a core of professional players and administrators (Stewart and Smith, 2000). In 2003, the annual turnover of these sport enterprises ranged from AUS$300 million for Australian Football League (AFL) to AUS$100 million for Cricket Australia (CA). Even lower profile sports like athletics and swimming now sustain solid organisational structures and well-paid athletes.

The hyper-commercialisation of Australian sport was accompanied by an apparently insatiable need for sporting heroes. According to Australian sporting folklore, heroic individuals emerge from the rank and file of the population, and because they are in some way seen to be extraordinary, become symbols of their time and embodiments of idealised moral and cultural values (Jobling, 1987). However, not all Australia's contemporary sporting heroes fit the archetypal mould. Cathy Freeman does because she is unassuming, dedicated, courageous, and a great spokesperson for the Aboriginal community (Bruce and Hallinan, 2001). Lleyton Hewitt did not fit the mould for a long time because he was seen to be too competitive and opinionated, and not as modest as we like our heroes to be. The player who best fitted the archetype was Pat Rafter. He was not only an outstanding tennis player, but also good looking, self-depreciating, close to his family, every mother's ideal son, and one of the boys. Sporting heroes are an important part of Australia's sporting landscape and are used to not only promote their sport, but also endorse all sorts of consumer products. It is also worth noting that 25 per cent of all people who won the Australian of the Year award over the last 30 years were sportspersons, while the last three Australian cricket team captains have all become Australians of the Year.

Australians also like their sporting heroes to be extra-ordinary in the sense that they should both win against the world's best, and symbolise sport's working-class traditions and tribal relations (Cashman, 1984). Australian sporting larrikins are revered for their indifference to authority, loud humour, and 'heavy drinking' (Lalor, 2003: 16; Stoddart, 1986: 110). There is, however, a downside to this hyper-masculine and blokey sporting ethos. In addition to its tendency to marginalise the participation of women, it can produce chronic displays of poor sportsmanship and crass behaviour. While sporting larrikins are quintessentially Australian, they also reveal an ugly and anti-intellectual side of the Australian sporting culture, where boisterous good humour degenerates into personal abuse, racist taunts, and physical violence. At the same time, larrikinism is a strong reminder that the Australian passion for sport is buried deep in the national psyche.

Australia's sporting obsession

Australia not only has a strong culture of sport participation and sport watching, but also uses sport to establish a sense of collective identity, self-respect, and national 'sense of self' (Stoddart, 1986: 71). A recent nationwide survey found that 92 per cent of respondents felt proud of Australia's international sport achievements. Another survey found that 'seven of the ten most inspirational moments' in Australian history were sport-related (Oakley, 1999: 53–55). These survey results can be interpreted in a number of ways. On one hand, they indicate that Australia's white history is short and that Australia's social and political institutions are not very inspirational. On the other hand, they confirm that sporting success has a unique capacity to unite Australians and help construct a sense of community. These survey results also show that in an increasingly globalised world, sport has become the primary vehicle for expressing national legitimacy, pride, and independence. For a small country with only 20 million inhabitants, and geographically isolated from the rest of the world, sporting success is a highly visible and potent way of achieving global media exposure and international awareness. By any account, sport is highly valued by Australians.

Australians also value sport because they are good at it. Australian athletes have achieved numerous international sporting successes over the last 50 years. Australia's level of sport performance peaked in the late 1990s when a number of unexpected wins were achieved. Between 1996 and 1999 Australia produced world champion teams in women's hockey, netball, under-23 men's basketball, rugby league, rugby union, men's test cricket and one-day cricket, and women's cricket. Australia's men's and women's basketball, men's hockey, and women's softball were ranked in the world's top ten. World championship medals were gained in cycling, rowing, and track and field. In men's and women's triathlon, five of the ten top-ranked competitors were Australians. In 1998, Michael Doohan won his fifth consecutive world 500-cc motorcycle championship, while Grant Hackett, Michael Klim, and Ian Thorpe demonstrated that they were just about the three best freestyle swimmers in the world. Susie O'Neil was easily the best butterfly swimmer, and Layne Beachley and Mark Occiluppo won the world women's and men's surfing championship respectively.

Australian golfers were also amongst the world's best and Karrie Webb became the world's leading female golfer. In late November 1999, the Australian under-17 soccer team reached the final of the world championships for the first time, being narrowly defeated by Brazil. The nation was even more surprised when, at around the same time, the Australian baseball team won the Intercontinental Baseball Cup by defeating Cuba in the final. In late 1999, Australia defeated France to win the Davis Cup, the premier team tennis competition. At the same time, many of Australia's best male athletes rarely competed overseas, and instead played Australian football. These achievements came from a population of just under 20 million.

Australians not only like watching their athletes beating the world's best, but also enjoy watching and playing at home. Over the last 30 years there has been sustained growth in professional and spectator sport. The Melbourne Cup horse racing carnival now attracts more than 500,000 visitors, while the Australian Open Tennis Championships has increased its annual aggregate tournament attendance to nearly 500,000. The AFL, Australia's most popular spectator sport, generated a total attendance of 6.5 million for its winter competition in 2003, while the National Rugby League (NRL) drew a cumulative attendance of nearly 3 million. Melbourne has a particular passion for professional sport, and was judged to be the sporting capital of the world on the basis of its ability to attract a minimum average weekly spectator audience of more than 320,000, easily beating London. Overall, just over 7 million or 47 per cent of adult Australians attend sporting events on a regular basis, the most popular of which are listed in Table 1.1 (Australian Bureau of Statistics, 1999b).

These attendance figures strongly reflect Australia's British colonial traditions, although the most popular spectator sport is Australian football, which was invented in Melbourne in the middle of the nineteenth century. Surprisingly, horse racing has the second highest attendance levels, closely followed by motor racing. On the other hand, it is not surprising that apart from tennis, the most popular sports are dominated by male players, although in the case of Australian football, cricket, and horse racing a significant minority of women regularly attend major events and games. It has been calculated that women constitute more than 40 per cent of total attendance at elite Australian football games (Australian Bureau of Statistics, 2003).

Australians also watch a lot of sport on TV. The two most popular TV sports are Australian football and rugby league, which also happen to be the strongest national sport leagues. Each sport is broadcast on both free-to-air and pay TV networks over their entire season that can be anywhere between 20 and 25

Table 1.1 Attendance at major sporting events

Sport	Total attending per year (million)	Percentage of adult population
Australian football	2.5	16.8
Horse racing	1.8	11.9
Motor sports	1.6	10.6
Rugby league	1.5	10.1
Cricket	0.94	6.3
Final	0.62	4.2
Harness racing	0.53	3.6
Basketball	0.53	3.6
Rugby union	0.45	3.0
Tennis	0.45	3.0

Sources: Australian Bureau of Statistics (1999b), Cat. 4174.0, Australian Bureau of Statistics (2003), Cat. 4156.0.

Table 1.2 Most watched sports on TV 2002–2003

Sport	Total national viewing audience (million)
Rugby Union World Cup Final 2003	3.9
AFL Grand Final 2003	2.9
Soccer World Cup Final 2003	2.7
Cricket World Cup Final 2003	2.5
Rugby Union World Cup 2003	2.5
Melbourne (horse race) Cup 2002	2.5
Rugby League Grand Final 2003	2.3
Commonwealth Games 2002	2.2
Pan Pacific Swimming Championship 2002	1.9
Home cricket internationals	1.8
Formula 1 Grand Prix 2003	1.7
Australian Swimming Championship 2003	1.4

Sources: The Age (2003) and The Australian *Media* (2002–2003).

weeks. The grand finals for each league usually attract a nationwide audience of more than 2 million people. Cricket is the other dominant TV sport, and over the summer period can regularly attract nationwide audiences of between 1.5 and 2 million fans (Table 1.2).

Australians also play sport on a large scale. For example, a 2002 Australian Sports Commission survey found that 11.7 million, or 78 per cent of adult Australians participated in some form of sport exercise or physical activity. The most popular forms of sport and physical activity are listed in Table 1.3.

Although there is still a hard-core of non-participants (22 per cent of adult Australians are physically inactive), the Australian participation rate is high by world standards. For example, the Canadian sport and physical activity

Table 1.3 Participation in Australian sport and physical activity

Sport	Number of participants (million)	Percentage of adult population
Walking	4.4	28.8
Swimming	2.4	16.0
Aerobics and fitness	1.9	13.0
Cycling	1.4	9.5
Tennis	1.3	9.2
Golf	1.2	8.2
Running	1.1	7.2
Bushwalking	0.79	5.5
Soccer	0.72	4.9
Cricket	0.59	4.0
Weight training	0.45	2.9

Source: Australian Sports Commission (2002b).

participation rate is now 34 per cent, having fallen from 45 per cent in 1992 (Sport Canada, 1998).

However, these surprisingly high figures must be tempered by the high degree of informal engagement. That is, most of this participation involves casual unstructured activity like walking to the park, swimming at the beach, cycling along a bike path, or exercising in the backyard. When sport participation is confined to organised and competitive sport activities in a club setting, the participation rates are much lower. According the ASC report referred to above, the overall participation rate for structured, competitive sport was 39.9 per cent or just over 6 million adult Australians. The most popular structured, club-based sport activities are listed in Table 1.4.

Table 1.4 Participation in structured and competitive sport

Sport	Number of participants (million)	Percentage of adult population
Aerobics	1.10	6.4
Golf	0.99	4.3
Tennis	0.92	3.6
Netball	0.52	3.5
Soccer	0.49	3.3
Cricket	0.39	2.6
Basketball	0.36	2.4
Touch	0.34	2.3
Tennis	0.32	2.2
Australian football	0.27	1.8
Lawn bowls	0.27	1.8
Dancing	0.22	1.4

Source: Australian Sports Commission (2002b).

These figures are interesting for a number of reasons. First, the four most popular structured activities (aerobics, golf, tennis and netball) have a high female participation rate. Second, contact and collision sports like Australian football and rugby, which have high levels of attendance, have relatively low participation rates. Third, a number of Olympic sports, which the Australian government generously funds (track and field, cycling, field hockey, rowing, sailing and water polo in particular), have very low participation rates. The participation rates for Olympic sports will be discussed in more detail in later sections of the book.

Despite the low participation rates in many competitive sports, the above figures indicate that a sizeable majority of Australians have an interest in sport and physical activity, and use it to fill in large slabs of their spare time. Indeed, most sport writers and commentators have concluded that Australians are obsessed with sport. For example, Australians 'have a consuming desire to conquer at sport' (Dunstan, 1973: xii), its 'international tag and self image as a sporting nation is undeniable' (Stoddart, 1986: 4), it has been the 'cornerstone of Australian life' and at one level is a 'paradise of sport' (Cashman, 1995: 205). However, these conclusions have been tempered by subsequent analysis of Australian sport. While it is no longer disputed that Australians are highly 'sport-minded', Australians may be no more fanatical than 'Americans, Britons, Brazilians and New Zealanders' (Adair and Vamplew, 1997: 8).

To some critics, sport is too much a part of Australia's national character and culture and, as a result, Australia has become culturally dysfunctional. One critic noted that in the run-up to the Sydney 2000 Olympic Games, Australia's sporting obsession had become 'frenzied and hysterical'. Moreover, the resultant collective euphoria concealed a deep-seated anxiety and tension about issues like racism, social inequality, foreigners, 'and irrational fears about our Asian neighbours' (Kell, 2000: 9–11). Other critics acknowledged the Australian passion for sport, but found 'little to celebrate in the Australian sporting character'. This obsessive interest in sport was used to hide many unpleasant realities like 'aboriginal living conditions, urban sprawl, water and air pollution, forest clearance, and overgrazing' (Booth and Tatz, 2000: 210, 218).

Why so much success?

It is one thing to be obsessed with sport. It is another thing to compete successfully in so many different sports. How is it then that Australian athletes have been able to achieve so many international successes in sport?

There are a number of things to be said here. First, as was indicated in the early part of this chapter, sport has been an important part of Australia's social and cultural fabric since the early colonial period. The early British administrators were quick to establish sporting activities and clubs, and effectively transplanted most of the their own pastimes, which included horse riding, fox-hunting, boxing, and emerging team games like cricket and rowing (Stoddart, 1986). By the middle of the nineteenth century, the Australian colonies had a strong sport club system, and inter-colonial sport became increasingly popular (Cashman, 1995). By the beginning of Australia's federation, in 1901, sport had become a taken-for-granted part of its popular culture.

Second, the rapid economic growth of Australia from the 1850s provided the resources for sport activities. Public space was allocated for a range of sports and games in all the main cities, a strong middle-class set up clubs and organised inter-club competitions, and local municipalities were quick to provide a base of sport grounds and venues (Cashman, 1995). Australia's continued economic growth throughout most of the twentieth century not only enabled its sporting infra-structure to expand in line with its population growth, but also provided most people with the time and money to play sport.

Third, Australian sport has traditionally run itself without too much govern-ment interference. Apart from the role local government played in funding com-munity sport infrastructure, sport clubs, associations, for most of the twentieth century governing bodies were left alone to set their own plans and programmes (Adair and Vamplew, 1997). It also meant they had to find their own funds, administrative resources, and volunteer officials. This system had both its strengths and weaknesses. On the positive side, it meant that communities were always quick to establish sporting clubs, and both cities and country towns had a tradition of providing a solid foundation of sport facilities. It also made Australian sport self-reliant, and athletes had to be resourceful to compete internationally. Success subsequently came from a strong club-based sport system that valued competition and collective initiative.

Fourth, these successes can be linked to a broader society that valued the expression of one's physical self. According to one commentator, Australians 'worshipped' the physical (Bloomfield, 2003: 31). While Australians did not always adhere to the monosyllabic stereotype that Australia's critics purveyed to anyone who would listen, the Australian media had a tendency to give more space to people who were physically impressive or intimidating, than those with intellec-tual weight. The perfect vehicle for displaying one's physicality was sport (Cashman, 1995). It is therefore not surprising that most of Australia's national heroes have been sportsmen.

Fifth, this emphasis on physicality was sustained by a warm, stable climate that enabled outdoor activity to be engaged throughout the year. Moreover, most Australians live within close proximity of the coast, and the beach has been a pivotal part of most people's lives (Rickard, 1988).

Sixth, as indicated in the early part of this chapter, sport has become the dominant vehicle for the expression of national pride and self-esteem. Sport has given Australians an international profile, and the success of its athletes has allowed Australians to claim a central place on the world stage. It helps Australians to define who they are as Australians. The expression of nationalism through sport has a long history in Australia (Mandle, 1976).

Concluding comments

Despite the natural and socially constructed advantages listed above, Australia's international sporting image was progressively tarnished during the 1960s and early 1970s. As a result of the growing commercialisation of sport in Europe and the USA in the 1960s, international sporting success became more difficult to achieve for Australia. A subsequent loss of collective confidence and national sports pride coincided with a change in the way governments saw sport and its role in society. In the early 1970s the Commonwealth Government became increasingly interested in sport development. The state governments also began to create significant sporting infrastructure from this period. Historically, local government had been the dominant provider of community sport facilities, but by the end of the twentieth century, the Commonwealth Government was the major government player in sport, and set the sport agenda. This ranged from regional sport to national development and elite training and coaching. One of the themes running through this book is the contention that Commonwealth Government sport policy has been central in driving sport and ultimately re-shaping the Australian sporting landscape.

2 Sport policy foundations

Introduction

Over the last 25 years there has been some serious discussion about the state of Australian sport and the strengths and weaknesses of Commonwealth Government sport policy (Armstrong, 1987; Baka, 1984; Semotiuk, 1987; Toohey, 1990). However, for the most part, there has been little analysis of the ways in which the policies were framed, and the processes that produced the on-the-ground strategies and programmes. In this chapter this sport policy gap will be filled by exploring the background to the sport policy-making process. First, the concept of sport and identity will be re-visited, with attention to the different ways sport can be defined, and how these different definitions impact on scale and scope of sport policy making. Second, a conceptual framework will be designed, within which the nature and scope of sport and sport policy can be discussed. Third, the policy-making process will be examined, and subsequently used to locate the development and practice of sport. Finally, the rationale for government involvement in sport will be explored, which will include an analysis of how sport policy can be used to enhance the welfare of society in general and specific communities in particular.

The scope of sport

In order to contextualise and frame sport policy, it is important to develop a clear understanding of just what sport involves, and the different meanings it has for different people. Therefore a useful first step is to de-construct its meaning and scope. In other words, what exactly does sport mean and what does it embrace? While sport is superficially easy to define, it can encompass an array of related, but distinctive activities. It is frequently assumed that all sport analysts, policy makers, and participants agree on what sport is, and what activities it includes and excludes. However, this is not always the case. In practice, sport means different things to different people.

In the previous chapter a distinction was made between competitive and highly structured sport played in a club setting, and more informal and recreational sport that is less competitive and more spontaneous. This begs the question as to what exactly the sport experience involves, and if being physically active by walking and cycling for pleasure is really sport, or just a way of vigorously filling in spare time. From a policy perspective it is important to agree on what makes up the sport experience, since funding and assistance will be dependent on whether or not an activity can be categorised as a sport. It is generally agreed that darts is a sport but that chess is not. However, even in this apparently clear-cut instance, the distinction can be disputed. For example, in some Eastern European countries chess is classified as a sport. So, if chess is a sport, then a vigorous activity like recreational swimming surely fits into the sport category. However, here again, there is room for interpretation, since some rigid definitions of sport suggest that if it does not have a competitive dimension, it is something other than sport.

Defining sport

There have been many attempts to categorise sport, and to distinguish it from related activities like play, games, contests, and athletics (Pearson, 1979: 159–183). When the various theories of sport are conflated, three defining themes emerge (Guttmann, 1978). First, it must have some physical dimension to it. It has to involve some running, jumping, kicking, hitting, throwing, some form of gross bodily movement, or fine psycho-motor skill. Archery and shooting are not vigorous activities, but because they both involve good hand–eye coordination they qualify as sports. By this criterion, darts and lawn bowls are also clearly sports, but chess, scrabble, and blackjack are not. Second, it should normally have a competitive element to it. That is, there is a contest in which there are winners and losers. In other words, vigorous physical activities like recreational swimming and bushwalking do not qualify as sports, but less strenuous activities like competitive golf and curling do. Third, the activity has to be structured. That is, there will be an agreed-upon set of rules that govern the way the game is played and conducted. These rules will also prescribe the nature of the playing arena and what equipment may be used. Social tennis qualifies as a sport under this criterion, but a daily exercise regime does not. In short, sport is usually seen as a regulated, rule-bound physical activity played in a competitive setting (Loland, 2002). The permutations and combinations of these three criteria are represented as a typology in Table 2.1.

According to the three defining themes listed below, only category 1 qualifies as a sport since it is the only one that features all of active, competitive and structured. While it clearly illuminates the ideal or traditional view of sport's essential nature, it is an unnecessarily restrictive definition. If it was used to identify levels of sport participation in Australia, it would reveal that just under 40 per cent of adult Australians play sport, a relatively low rate by international standards. In order to be as inclusive as possible, sport analysts, policy makers and participants have increasingly cast a wide net and focused on the physical dimension rather than the regulatory and competitive dimensions. In this way, they emphasise the physical nature of the activity, and include a wide variety of pastimes that may not be structured or involve two or more competing teams,

Table 2.1 Typology of physical activity and sport

Category	Active	Competitive	Structured
1	✓	✓	✓
2		✓	✓
3	✓		✓
4			✓
5	✓		
6			
7	✓	✓	
8		✓	

Source: Adapted from Snyder and Spreitzer (1983) *Social Aspects of Sport.*

but nevertheless have a strong physical dimension. On this basis we can include disparate activities like snowboarding, bushwalking, skateboarding, recreational swimming, and walking for pleasure. The use of this broader and more inclusive definition of sport produces a much higher participation rate. In Chapter 1 it was noted that the Australian Sports Commission found that 78 per cent of adult Australians engage in some form of recreational, spontaneous, or competitive sport. Depending on which figures are used, Australians can be described as either very sedentary or very sport-active. These contrasting conclusions can not only be very confusing for policy analysts and researchers, but also create quite different images about the Australian sports culture.

As a first step in getting a more systematic grip on how sport can be defined, it is essential to examine different ways people actively experience their sport. While working definitions of sport have become increasingly broad and inclusive, some fundamental distinctions can be made. The classification system detailed in Table 2.2 uses the four categories in Table 2.1 that feature physical activity to not only distinguish between the competitive, recreational, exercise, and remedial aspects of sport, but also highlight their linkages.

Table 2.2 shows that sport, broadly defined, is a multi-dimensional activity that embraces both high-performance athletes who perform on a global stage, and weekend players who confine their performance to a suburban playing field. It includes players who take their sport seriously, and where winning is

Table 2.2 Sporting categories and practices

Sport category	Sport type	Examples
1	Elite competitive sport	National sports league, Olympic Games, National championships
1	Community competitive sport	Suburban and regional tennis competitions
7	Spontaneous/pick-up sport	Street basketball or soccer
3/5	Recreational sport	Cycling and bushwalking for pleasure
3/5	Exercise sport	Aerobics and remedial exercise

everything, as well as those players who go out of their way to avoid competition. It also includes players who demand structure and clearly agreed upon rules, and those who prefer their sport to be informal and fluid. Importantly, the table should be read as a constantly shifting sport-scape where players can move between categories depending on their ability, motivation, and sporting preferences. As we shall see in later chapters of the book, this assumption underpins sport policy that aims to establish a mutually reinforcing link between elite athlete development and grass-roots participation.

Implications for sport policy

While for the most part we will focus our discussion on category 1 sports, category 3, 5 and 7 sports are also addressed at various stages. In particular, sport analysts and policy makers often take the broader view of sport, but often do it implicitly, and without making their intentions clear. The Australian Sports Commission, which will be examined in detail in the following chapters, continually shifts from less to more restrictive definitions. When it launched its *1800 Reverse Street Active* initiative in 2002, which focused on unorganised community skateboarding, it took a broad view of sport. However, when deciding on which organisations are eligible for Commonwealth Government sports grants, the parameters of sport are more tightly prescribed. In this instance sport is described as a 'human activity capable of achieving a result requiring physical exertion, and a physical skill which by its nature and organisation is competitive and generally accepted as being a sport' (Australian Sports Commission, 2003b).

In practice these different sporting categories are both connected and distinct. Figure 2.1 divides sport practice into five segments, and illustrates the relationship between them. The first thing to note is that there is a core of competitive sport that begins with community, school and local sport and culminates in elite sport, which includes national sport leagues, national championships, and international sport events. There is a strong link between these segments as young talent is channelled into the elite end of the competitive sport core, while retired elite athletes frequently return to the community and local core. There is also a constant shift between recreational, or non-competitive sport and community sport as older players become less competitive, and new entrants want more intense competition and structure. The same fluidity applies to spontaneous and 'pick-up' sport where children in particular may decide to move into more organised systems of sport as their skill and commitment strengthens. The exercise sport segment is probably more self-contained than the others since the participants here mostly have an instrumental and goal-directed focus to their activity.

These different types of sport practice will be fleshed out in the remaining chapters, and their relevance to sport policy-making addressed. While most of the Commonwealth Government funding goes to the competitive sport area, there are instances where important initiatives have focused on recreational and spontaneous sport practices. Definitions of sport are also crucial in deciding who

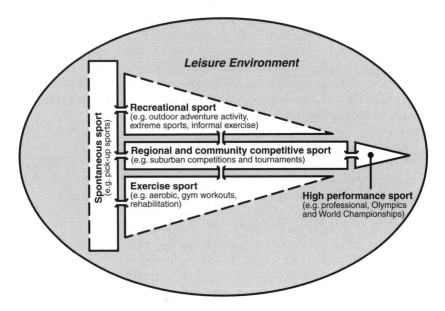

Figure 2.1 A typology of sport practice.

is in and who is out when it comes to things like who is eligible for grants and assistance. The essential lesson to be learnt from the above discussion is that any analysis of sport policy should, as a first step, provide a clear and concise indication of exactly which of the above categories are being referred to, and why.

Conceptualising sport policy

Like sport, policy is a superficially simple term, but in practice means different things to different people. Policy is an integral part of the political process (Bridgman and Davis, 2000: 3). However, it is also a slippery term, since it is often confused with planning, and frequently used as a synonym for strategy. It is fundamentally important to have a clear picture of what policy involves, because it assists in understanding how government goes about setting agendas, and making decisions on a raft of economic, social, and cultural issues.

A policy is similar to a plan, but is not usually as precise or detailed. Policy is often no more than a stance or a position, which provides the context for future decisions (Parsons, 1995: 13–14). For example, the Commonwealth Government may have a policy of attracting more young people into sport refereeing and umpiring, but have no immediate or specific strategy or programme for making it happen. Policy can also be viewed as a web of decisions and actions that allocate values (Colebatch, 2002: 2). The Commonwealth Government anti-doping policy is a good example of values-driven policy, since it is founded on the premise that sport is all about fair play, playing within the rules, and not getting an unfair advantage. According to this view, athletes who take drugs are cheats whose behaviour undermines their own credibility, and the integrity of the sport experience. Or, being slightly more obtuse, policy can be seen as a course of action or inaction. In the case of sport, the lack of any clear government guidelines on pregnancy and sport participation during the 1990s was a good example of policy being defined by the absence of a clearly articulated position or view.

In general, though, policy is an instrumental and 'goal directed' activity that emerges from a political issue or problem (Bridgman and Davis, 2000: 4). Policy is also hierarchical and authoritative, since it involves decisions and instructions being made by a clearly designated authority figure like a 'minister, general manager, or executive committee' (Colebatch, 2002: 8–10). Finally, policy comprises both major 'directional choices' and more specific 'operational decisions and programs' (Stewart and Ayres, 2001: 21).

Policy as process

Policy is also a process in which the final policy outcomes are influenced by an array of political parties, politicians, government bureaucrats, and interest groups, who all have an impact on its formulation (Edwards, 2001: 5). For example, policy is usually more than a simple matter of government having a rush of blood to the head, coming up with a clever idea, and then deciding to take a particular course of action by putting it into a policy statement. It is a far more complex process, and involves a number of actors and players who aim to influence the people who actually formulate the policy (Hill, 1997: 111). The actors and players will aim to occupy as much stage time or space as they can, with a view to persuading the policy formulators that their proposals will be socially beneficial, politically attractive, or both. It is also important to note that these actors and players can congregate into distinct groupings. First, they can form 'policy communities', with each community having its own political agenda, primary interests, or similar way of doing business (Parsons, 1995: 184–191). Second, they can form issue networks, which come together in response to some dispute or problem. In both of these instances, governments have a vested interest in fostering their formation and consolidation since they 'facilitate consultation' and create more predictability and continuity (Houlihan, 1997: 14–20).

Underlying values and assumptions

Government policy can often seem inconsistent, at best, and irrational and 'ideological', at worst (Hylton *et al.*, 2001: 5). One reason for this is that many of the underlying assumptions and rationales are not explicitly stated. In other instances, the policy may be the result of a strong ideological stance pushed by a powerful interest or lobby group. In many cases, a particular set of arguments and assumptions frequently become the rationale for the development of government policy.

At the same time, policy has a rational side to it. If it can be demonstrated that the provision of a sporting service, or the construction of a sport facility provides social and private benefits that comprehensively exceed the cost of providing them, it makes sense to fund them, since society will be better off as a result. Of course, stakeholders and interest groups intent on pushing their own values and agendas can complicate the policy-making process. This is particularly so in sport, where many of the arguments for social benefits are often backed by exaggerated claims and flimsy evidence (Long and Sanderson, 2001).

Because of sport's potential to deliver significant social benefits, there are a number of sound reasons for government wanting to invest in it. However, government resources and taxpayer funds are always scarce, and sport is one of many institutions that wants to claim part of the government budget. As a result, sport assistance cannot always be guaranteed. Sport must compete with defence, health, policing, social welfare and education, and as is demonstrated throughout this book, it was a low priority of Australian national governments until the 1970s.

Political ideologies

The formation of sport policy cannot always be explained by reference to strong supporting evidence, a logical appraisal of its economic and social benefits, or the force of an argument by a stakeholder. It can also arise out of a political party's ideology (Hylton *et al.*, 2001). For the purposes of this book, political ideologies have been divided into three working categories.

The first ideology is conservatism. A conservative ideology values tradition and customary ways of doing things. Conservative governments have a tendency to regulate the social lives of people, and therefore want to censor works of art and literature they find offensive. They also want to control the distribution of legal drugs like alcohol, and generally act to protect people from themselves. On the other hand, they believe that business should be left to its own devices, where the combination of individual self-interest, the profit motive, and market forces will ensure a favourable outcome. However, because conservative governments believe a strong private sector is the key to progress, they are prepared to assist and protect industry when the need arises. For conservative governments, sport policy is not so much a blind spot as a vacant space. While on one hand they recognise sport as an integral part of the social life of most people, they do not want to assist or protect it since it is not part of the world of business. Indeed, for many conservatives, it is another world altogether that should be best kept at a distance from business. This 'sport world' is underpinned by the romantic belief that sport fulfils its function best when it is done for its own sake, played by amateurs, managed by volunteers, and generally left to look after its own affairs.

The second ideology is reformism or, as it is also known, welfare statism or social democracy. Reformism is primarily concerned with social justice and equity. While reformists recognise the necessity of a strong private sector, they believe it cannot be trusted to deliver fair and equitable outcomes. It therefore needs to be strictly managed. This could take the form of additional state-owned enterprises, or tight regulations on business behaviour. Reformists share the conservative view that assistance and protection may be necessary in the public interest. Unlike conservatives, though, reformists believe primarily in social development, which not only means legislating for social freedom, but also for social justice. Income redistribution to disadvantaged groups is important, and is done by ensuring that wealthy individuals and corporations are taxed most heavily. Government spending is also crucial to reformists, since it is used to stimulate the economy when demand and spending is low. Reformist governments tend to be more centralist, and aim to use this centralised power to engineer positive social outcomes. It is therefore not surprising that reformists generally see sport as a tool for social development, and aim to make sport more accessible to the whole community. In particular, programs are established to cater for the needs of minority groups like aboriginals, the disabled, non-English speaking migrants, and women. In short, reformist government policy focuses on community rather than elite sport.

The final ideology is neo-liberalism. Neo-liberals believe that society is at its most healthy when people can run their daily lives without the chronic intrusion of government regulation. The rule of law is important but beyond that, people should be free to choose how they organise their social lives, and business should be free to organise their commercial lives as they see fit. Neo-liberals see little value in state-owned enterprises, and argue that the privatisation of government services produces greater efficiency and higher-quality outcomes. Moreover, deregulated industries are seen to run better than tightly controlled ones. In short, neo-liberals believe government should not engage directly in most economic activity, but rather provide only base-level infrastructure, and legislative guidelines within which private business can thrive. Sport is valued as an important social institution, but should not be strictly controlled. However, neo-liberals also believe sport can be used as a vehicle for nation-building and economic development, and should be supported in these instances. This produces a sport policy that focuses on elite sport rather than community sport.

Each ideology contains not only quite different assumptions about the proper role of government, but also different ideas about what sport can do to improve the welfare of society (Hylton *et al.*, 2001). As a result, each ideology will produce different sport policy outcomes, strategies and programmes, and the ideology often overrides the claims of interest groups and stakeholders. The three ideologies described provide a simplified typology and, in practice, governments can contain elements of each ideology. At the same time, most governments will be characterised by more of one, and less of another ideology. These ideologies will be used to frame the analysis of sport policy evolution in the following chapters of this book.

Sport policy formulation

Specific sport policies, like other aspects of government policy, also arise out of the identification of some economic issue or social problem that requires attention

(Edwards, 2001: 4–5). In sport, these issues and problems have covered a wide range of matters. They include factors as disparate as poor international performances, the taking of performance enhancing drugs, and run-down facilities, to the increasing prevalence of preventable diseases, declining rates of physical activity, low sport participation rates for minority groups, and growing levels of discrimination and harassment in sporting clubs. While these issues and problems are generally given form and substance by government, their origins usually lay often elsewhere in the sports system. An important sport policy question is therefore how an issue or problem becomes a core policy agenda item.

In the Australian sporting context, the drivers of sport policy are multi-faceted (Bridgman and Davis, 2000). Firstly, a major source of sport policy formation is the political parties when in opposition, whose election policies frequently form the basis of subsequent government policy. The Whitlam policy of 1972, the Hawke policy of 1983 and the Howard policy of 1996 are good examples of opposition parties using an election victory to implement a clearly defined sport policy. A second source of policy formation is the government of the day, which can shift policy in response to changing conditions. In a later section of this book it will be demonstrated how the Commonwealth Government's *Active Australia* programme was modified in the light of stagnating participation rates for organised sport for children. A third source of policy formation is the major agencies, stakeholders, and interest groups. They include the Australian Olympic Committee, the Commonwealth Games Association, major sport leagues, national and state sporting bodies, the Australian Sport Drug Agency, the digital, electronic, and print media, elite athletes, sport scientists and physicians, health and physical education professionals, and volunteer sport officials. Another influential body is the Australian Sports Commission, which is responsible for implementing government policy as well as managing the Australian Institute of Sport (AIS). As previously noted, these stakeholders, interest groups, and sport-related organisations are sometimes described as policy communities, with each community having its own political agenda, primary interest, and similar ways of doing business (Hill, 1997). Governments have an interest in fostering policy communities since they facilitate consultation, make the policy process more predictable, and 'often reduce policy conflict' (Hill, 1997: 73). A schematic representation of the Australian sport policy community is illustrated in Figure 2.2 (adapted from Oakley, 1999: 62–63).

The initiative for a policy can also arise from any number of crisis events that create either a benign level of public interest, or a more serious level of community anxiety. An instructive example occurred in 2001 when the governing body of netball, Netball Australia, controversially resolved to ban pregnant players from participating in competitive games. This produced an immediate outcry from netball players around the nation, and a rash of commentary from sport lawyers. It in turn forced the Minister of Sport, through the Australian Sports Commission, to establish guidelines to assist other sports bodies to design rules that were both fair and legal.

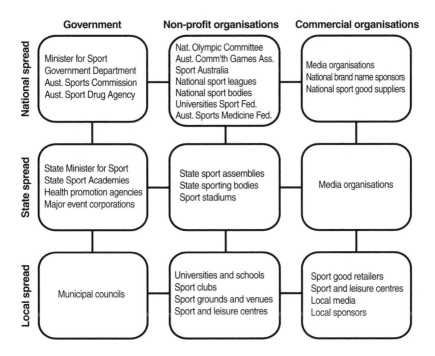

Figure 2.2 Australian sport stakeholders.

Once an issue or problem has been identified and illuminated, the next step is to undertake a detailed analysis of all key and related matters. This will include a review of the context in which the issue or problem arose, the factors that precipitated the problem, its various dimensions, and the possible options for managing it, or indeed solving it. Underpinning this stage is the desirability of consulting with all stakeholders and interest groups to get a broad range of opinion and evidence. Once the analysis is complete, government is then in a position to make a policy decision and implement it. The policy process is completed when the policy is reviewed, re-examined, and possibly re-made. In the end, government in general, and the appropriate Minister in particular, is solely responsible for making, stating, and changing policy. A typical framework for policy development is listed in Table 2.3.

The stages identified in Table 2.3 have been used to create a policy cycle where 'policy develops through a standard sequence of tasks that can be framed as activities or questions' (Bridgman and Davis, 2000: 23–24). This view of the policy highlights its key operational components, and illuminates the ways in which each stage is both conceptually and practically linked to the others. It also provides a model of what good policy-making looks like and how successful policy outcomes may be achieved (Bridgman and Davis, 2000: 25; Edwards, 2001: 2–3).

Table 2.3 Stages in the policy development process

Policy step	Key participants
Issues and problems identified and illuminated	Political parties, Government departments, policy communities
Policy options analysed through data collection and consultation	Government departments and agencies, committees, task-forces
Policy decision made and communicated	Government departments and agencies
Policy decision implemented through strategies and programs	Government departments and agencies
Policy monitored and reviewed	Government departments

Source: Adapted from Bridgman and Davis (2000), Edwards (2001).

Policy messiness

In practice, though, sport policy processes, like other policies, are not as routine, rational, and linear as the above idealised model suggests. First, policy means different things to different people. It can range from a broad statement of intent, a grand vision, or legislation, to a specific proposal, strategy, or programme (Stewart, 1999: 52). Second, the construction and interpretation of the problem can be ambiguous and subjective. For example, drug use in Australian sport can be viewed from many perspectives. It can be seen as a cheating problem, a health problem, a criminal problem, an equity problem, or even a problem of declining international sporting performance. Third, the extent to which a problem becomes a core government agenda item is the result of a complex array of pressures and influences. Some of the influences reside in the government and its departments, but others reside in stakeholder groups with a 'vested interest in having the item addressed' (Hill, 1997: 116). Fourth, once an item has been placed on the policy agenda it can be subject to many political processes. For example, a policy option may be marginalised by an antagonistic government attacking its proponents and undermining its credentials. Alternatively, stakeholders and interest groups that support the preferred policy option may be given additional places on a committee or task force, or provided with more grant money or assistance. Finally, the policy decision may not be the most rational or theoretically effective one, but instead be one that symbolises the victory of one interest group over another, is the least offensive to major interest groups, or has the most electoral appeal. In short, policy formation can involve a mix of rational decision-making, political opportunism, a lot of muddling through, and frequent incremental change (Lindblom, 1959).

A policy-making process for sport

As Figure 2.2 illustrates, Australian sport has become a complex enterprise comprising networks of not-for-profit and voluntary organisations, community sport facilities, large-scale sport stadiums, elite athlete training centres, commercially driven sport leagues, and mega-sport events. All these organisations, activities and facilities are surrounded by a sport culture that has to balance the traditions and history of sport with its commercial imperatives.

Sport policy in Australia has to consequently deal with a disparate number of competing values. While on one hand, sport policy has to deal with the economic and commercial implication of a particular course of action, it also has to deal with the culture of sport and, in particular, issues related to gender, race, equity, and tradition. There is also the need to deal with the ongoing tension between policy that assists the elite athlete and the sports that have an international profile, and policies that enable local communities to participate in a broad range of sport activities.

Sport policy is also problem-centred. There are numerous cases, as indicated earlier, where policies were developed in response to a crisis, failure, or problem in sport. The most significant policy development resulting from a crisis and failure was the national trauma caused by Australia's dismal performance at the 1976 Montreal Olympic Games. Another instructive example of problem-induced policy occurred in the late 1980s when a number of critical incidents forced sport officials and the Commonwealth Government to act on the drugs-in-sport problem. In addition, sport policy comprises a mixture of incremental change and transformative change. The establishment of the Australian Sport Drug Agency in 1990 was indicative of a transformative policy change, while the recent programmes aimed at educating parents about fair play in sport were more reflective of incremental policy change.

When the 'rational–ideological' continuum is combined with the 'transformative–incremental' continuum, four policy decision options become available, as illustrated in Table 2.4.

As Table 2.4 reveals, policy decisions can take one of four different forms. It highlights the fact that both transformational and incremental shifts in policy can be driven by either ideology or evidence. It also provides a useful way of classifying sport policy decision-making by linking the scale of the anticipated change to the arguments and values supporting the change.

In the light of the Commonwealth Government's ongoing concern about the healthy development of sport, and the theory and practice of policy making, a policy process model has been designed, and is described in Figure 2.3. The model, which is based on the policy cycle of Bridgman and Davis (2000), aims to highlight the problem-based foundations of sport policy, and the importance of implementation to successful policy outcomes. It also highlights the crucial

Table 2.4 Sport policy decision options

	Ideology	Evidence-based
Transformational	1	3
Incremental	2	4

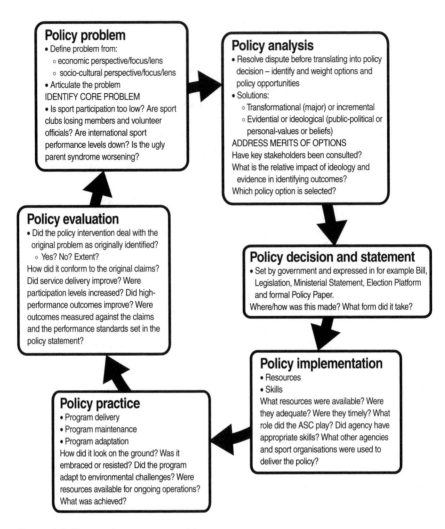

Figure 2.3 Sport policy process model.

importance of policy analysis, and the role played by political parties, individual politicians, and sport industry interest groups and stakeholders. The model also notes the fact that policy can be driven by either rational and evidence-based factors, or ideology, emotion, and values. This part of the model is particularly important for sport policy in view of the passionate beliefs many people have about the value of sport, and its role in society. The model also distinguishes between policy that is gradual and incremental, and policy that is large-scale and transformative. This again is important for sport policy since it has comprised a mix of the two policy types over recent years.

The primary feature of the model illustrated in Figure 2.3 is that it operates as a cycle. In other words, policy is never complete, but is continually being evaluated and assessed, and re-invented. This is particularly applicable to Australian sport development, where there has been adjustment, refinement, and prioritising for 25 years. While there has been general agreement that sport policy should embrace both elite and community sport, there has been ongoing dispute over the balance to be struck, and the appropriate funding arrangements for each policy strand. There have also been many changes in sport policy implementation and practice as some sporting bodies and programmes are found to be either more or less successful than others in achieving the stated policy outcomes.

Sport, policy and government

Prior to the 1970s there was general agreement that sport was somehow separate from government, and that apart from local government provision of grounds and venues, government had no significant role to play in sport development or assisting talented athletes to achieve international success. Sport policy was not on the government agenda, and the term was effectively an oxymoron. However, 30 years later there is a taken-for-granted acceptance that government should assist sport in a variety of ways. So, why has there been such a dramatic change in government and community attitudes to government involvement in sport, and why has sport policy become such an important issue for many Australians? In order to answer these questions, it is crucial to: first, understand how government works in Australia; second, appreciate how it goes about defending and justifying its involvement in sport; and finally, understand the ways in which government policy is revealed in policy documents and statements.

Sport as industry

Australian sport has been often referred to as an industry, and there are good grounds for this claim. It has a large participant base, with 78 per cent of adults involved in some form of sport or physical activity (Australian Sports Commission, 2002b). There are 14,000 playing fields and indoor sport centres, supported by 1.5 million volunteer administrators and officials. The sport industry provides paid employment for 275,000 people and includes approximately 4,000 businesses. Households spend more than AUS$7 billion a year on sport-related services and goods, while corporate sponsorship accounts for AUS$300 million. When AUS$430 million of sport exports are added to the national sport accounts, the total contribution of the sport industry to Gross Domestic Product is approximately 1 per cent (Australian Sports Commission, 2002a: 7). It is also a complex industry, since it comprises an array of government-owned facilities, not-for-profit clubs and associations, and privately owned businesses. It specifically includes sporting competitions that range from small amateur country competitions to fully professional national sport leagues, commercial operators, consultants, and sport product manufacturers and retailers.

The three tiers of government

The institutional framework for Australian sport development is underpinned by a three-tier federalist system of government that was established in 1901. Under this model, power is shared between the six States and two Territories and the Commonwealth or Federal Government. The Constitution was structured to give the Commonwealth Government a number of specific and limited powers centred on defence, foreign relations, and customs. Tax matters were initially left to the States. However, taxing powers were handed over to the Commonwealth Government during the Second World War and since then it has taken over full responsibility for all major economic management, financial, and revenue-raising matters. States became dependent on the Commonwealth Government for the funding of key services like transport, policing, health and, to a lesser extent, education and sport. States also created local authorities whose responsibility was to provide local community services like roads, rubbish collection, libraries, and sporting infrastructure and facilities. The structure of Australian government and the traditional allocation of responsibilities are illustrated in Table 2.5.

Local government has been the dominant provider of funds for sport development, with most of it being used to set up infrastructure and facilities for local communities. State governments have increasingly funded state sporting bodies, talent development programmes, and sport stadia, while over the last 25 years the Commonwealth Government has guided the development of national sporting organisations (NSOs) and high-performance sport. Recent estimates show that local government accounts for 50 per cent of total government spending on sport, with 95 per cent of these funds going to the building and maintenance of sport venues, grounds, and facilities. State Governments account for an additional 30 per cent of spending, of which 80 per cent is spent on venues, grounds, and facilities. Finally, the Commonwealth Government contributes 20 per cent to sport, with most of the funds going to the AIS and NSOs via the Australian Sports Commission (Australian Bureau of Statistics, 2003).

The public, private, and not-for-profit sectors

The other important institutional feature of Australian society is the clear division between the public and private sectors. The public sector comprises government, its agencies and infrastructure. The private sector comprises a variety of shareholder-based corporations, owner-operated businesses and not-for-profit entities

Table 2.5 Levels of government in Australia

Level of government	Core responsibilities
Commonwealth	Economic management, trade, defence, welfare, and health
State	Health, welfare, education, transport, and police
Local/municipal	Community and leisure services

like welfare organisations, community support groups, associations, and clubs. Economic, cultural, and recreational activities are generated and supported by both sectors, although the balance has shifted from time to time.

When the three tiers of government are combined with the private and not-for-profit sectors, a broad range of service and infrastructure delivery options become available. First, services and infrastructure can be delivered centrally by the Commonwealth Government, or nationally based corporation, community agency or association. Second, the services and infrastructure can be delivered at local level by state government, the local authority, business, association, community groups, or commercial operators. The different delivery modes are detailed in Table 2.6, and like the tiers of government, the relative importance of each sector in delivering sport has varied from time to time.

Market failure

Governments, even in relatively wealthy countries like Australia, never have enough resources to satisfy every community's demand for more facilities and financial assistance. And in any case, in capitalist countries like Australia, resources are in the main allocated in markets through the interaction of demand, supply, and prices. However, there are often cases where markets do not operate in the best interests of the community or nation. This is known as market failure. Market failure can occur when the full benefits of markets are not realised because of an under-supply of socially desirable products or, alternatively, an over-supply of less desirable products (Cooke, 1994: 104).

Market failure and under-supply arise in situations where there are significant external or social benefits in addition to private benefits (Gratton and Taylor, 1991: 55). Private benefits are the values consumers obtain from the immediate purchase of a good or service and are measured by the prices people are prepared to pay for the experience. In sport, private benefits arise from attending a major sport event, working out at a gymnasium, playing indoor cricket, or spending time at a snow resort. Social benefits are the values that society, or the community

Table 2.6 Structures for delivering sport experiences

Service delivery structures	Cases and examples
Government department	State government departments of recreation/sport
Government agency	Sport institutes and academies
Private not-for-profit agency	Learn to swim organisations
Private not-for-profit national association	National sport governing bodies (NSOs)
Private not-for-profit state association	State and regional sport governing bodies (SSOs)
Private not-for-profit league	National, regional, and local competitions
Private not-for-profit member-based club	Sporting clubs (netball, golf, tennis, etc.)
Commercial operator	Indoor sports and leisure centres

in general, obtains from the production of a good or service. These social benefits are over and above the private benefits. In cases where social benefits can be
established, society would be better served by allocating additional resources
into those activities. However, private investors will not usually do this because
of a lack of profit incentive. Consequently, it will be left to government to fill
the breach, and use taxpayers' money to fund additional sporting infrastructure
and services.

A number of arguments have been mounted to support the view that sport
provides significant social benefits, and consequently deserves government
assistance to ensure that the welfare of the whole community is maximised.
According to the proponents of sport assistance, social benefits can arise from
both active participation, and elite and spectator sport (Australian Sports Commission, 1999b; Cooke, 1994; Gratton and Taylor, 1991).

In the case of active participation, the benefits include improved community
health, a fall in medical costs, a reduction in the crime rate, the inculcation of
character, the development of ethical standards through the emulation of sporting heroes, greater civic engagement, and the building of social capital (Australian
Sports Commission, 1999b; Cameron and MacDougall, 2000; Gratton and
Taylor, 1991; Long and Sanderson, 2001; Oakley, 1999).

Recent research into social capital building suggests that it not only expands
social networks, but also produces 'safer neighbourhoods and healthier and
happier communities' (Productivity Commission, 2003: 17–19). Moreover, the
social benefits linked to social capital are extended when sport groups and clubs
'look outward and encompass people across diverse social cleavages' (Putnam,
2000: 22). This bridging or inclusive social capital can be contrasted with
bonding social capital, which characterises sport groups and clubs with a narrow
ethnic, social or occupational base.

In the case of elite and spectator sports, the benefits include tribal identification with a team or club, social cohesion, a sense of civic and national pride,
international recognition and prestige, economic development, and the
attraction of out-of-town visitors and tourist dollars (Cooke, 1994; Gratton and
Taylor, 1991; Houlihan, 1997). When these social benefits are aggregated, the
results are quite extensive, and are listed in Table 2.7. At the same time, they are

Table 2.7 Social benefits of sport development

Arising from active participation	Arising from elite athlete successes
Improvement in community health and productivity	Tribal identification and belonging
Fall in medical costs	Social cohesion
Reduction in juvenile crime rate	Civic and national pride
Development of character and sense of fair play	International recognition and prestige
Building of social capital, social cohesion, and civic engagement	Economic development and tourism

often difficult to quantify, and in some cases the evidence to support the claims is weak.

Public goods

A case can also be made for government assistance to sport on the grounds that sport is often a public or collective good. Public goods are those goods where one person's consumption does not prevent another person's consumption of the same good. For example, a decision to walk in the park, visit a surf beach, or identify with a winning team or athlete, will not prevent others from doing the same. Indeed, the experience may be enhanced by others being in proximity. This is a non-rival feature of the good. Public goods are also goods where, in their purest form, no one can be prevented from consuming the good. Again, a walk in the park, a visit to the beach, and identifying with a winning team meet this criterion. This is a non-excludable feature of the good. Public goods can provide substantial benefits throughout the whole of society, and are usually not rationed through high prices. However, they are not attractive to private investors since there is no assurance that all users will pay the cost of providing the benefit. Where the number of free-riders exceed the number of paying consumers, there is no incentive for private operators to enter the public good market (Gratton and Taylor, 1991). In this instance it is argued that government should again take up the slack.

Equity

Finally, there is also an argument for government funding of sport on equity grounds. For example, there may be instances where the whole community benefits from being fit and healthy, and where people feel good about their bodies and use this feeling to develop a positive sense of self. In these cases, the optimal outcome can only be achieved if everyone has access to those facilities that enable them to improve their health and fitness, enhance their self-image, and build the community's social capital. In order to improve accessibility, and ensure equality of opportunity, government can either establish their own low-cost service, or subsidise existing sport activity providers (Gratton and Taylor, 1991).

Concluding comments

Sport policy is a seductively simple term that easily rolls off the tongue. However, in many respects it is a conceptual and practical minefield that requires careful analysis in order to understand its underlying principles and assumptions. Deciding what constitutes sport is in itself a challenging exercise, since its definition constantly shifts in response to changing government and sport industry expectations. Neither is there always agreement on what constitutes policy, nor the ways in which policy is best formulated and implemented. Finally, there is never a complete agreement on how government can best involve itself in sport, or what forms of assistance and regulation will produce the best outcomes. This then is the challenge of analysing sport policy. There are so many grey areas where assistance is provided because it a good idea, or where some traditional beliefs about the social value of sport are accepted with little supporting evidence. At the same time, there is no longer any dispute that sport is an important part of the Australian cultural and commercial fabric, and government support can potentially provide significant social benefits.

Part II
Evolution

3 Benign indifference: sport policy 1920–71

Australia's sporting foundations

Most studies of Australian sport development state that Commonwealth Government sport policy was not a serious issue until 1972, when the Whitlam reformist Government was elected with a mandate to change both the economic and social conditions of Australian society (Adair and Vamplew, 1997; Booth and Tatz, 2000; Cashman, 1995; Houlihan, 1997; Mckay, 1991; Shilbury and Deane, 2001). While there is some truth in this statement, there is also evidence that the Commonwealth Government provided intermittent, if limited, support for sport since 1920.

Both the Australian economy and sport grew strongly between 1901, when the colonies were federated into the Commonwealth of Australia, and 1939, when the Second World War began. Boxing and horse racing were highly commercialised largely due to the ability of the public to wager or bet on the outcome of matches and races. Australian football, rugby league, and tennis also attracted a large spectator base, while golf, rugby union, soccer, and netball attracted many players, but were less popular spectator sports (Cashman, 1995).

At the same time, Australia had a strong beach culture. Bathing and swimming were popular sporting leisure activities at the turn of the century, and gained broad acceptability when daylight bathing was permitted at beaches and women were invited to compete in swimming carnivals. Soon after, surf-bathing associations were formed to promote swimming and surf bathing, and were later expanded to take on a lifesaving role. State water-safety associations were established, and in 1923 the Australian Surf Lifesaving Association was formed to coordinate programs and activities at the national level. The New South Wales and Western Australian State Governments, being 'well aware of the cost effectiveness of voluntary organisations', provided funds to the state water-safety and lifesaving bodies, but the Commonwealth Government did nothing for the national body at this time (Booth, 2001: 147).

During the 1930s, cricket consolidated its position as Australia's national sport. The 1937–38 cricket tour of Australia by England drew some of the largest crowds in the history of the game. The test matches alone attracted 900,000 spectators at an average of 35,000 per day. The 1936–37 series confirmed Donald

Bradman's status as the world's greatest cricketer, as well as cricket's ability to engender widespread national pride and 'form a uniquely Australian identity' (Hutchins, 2002: 17). It was all achieved without Commonwealth Government support.

Local government infrastructure

Throughout the first 40 years of federation, local government was an important contributor to the success of club-based sport. It traditionally provided playground facilities, which comprised slides, swings, hoops, and bars. These facilities were usually located in public parks and gave children the opportunity to not just play, but also develop their confidence and motor skills. In addition, local government constructed sports grounds and pavilions. Australia's community sporting infrastructure was therefore dependent upon local councils, particularly when large open space was required for the activity. In this respect, the football codes, cricket, swimming, tennis, and netball benefited substantially from local government support (Cashman, 1995).

Clubs and associations

Between 1901 and 1939 the delivery of sport services was mainly done through the non-profit part of the private sector. The foundation of sport was the member-based club that centred on a single sport activity. The club provided the playing facilities, and fielded teams that participated in local and regional competitions. This system supported a successful array of amateur and semi-professional sports. The most popular activities during this period were Australian football, cricket, golf, lawn bowls, netball, tennis, and to a lesser extent, athletics, rugby league, rugby union, and soccer (Australian News and Information Bureau, 1962). Every suburb, district and country-town club offered most of these activities. Regional associations comprising member clubs managed the competitions. In turn, State sport governing bodies coordinated regional competitions and organised State championships, while national sport governing bodies organised national championships and sent national teams overseas. The club-based sport system provided an inclusive structure for sport participation where competitions were graded by ability. It consequently provided for the social, recreational, low skill player as well as the ambitious, elite performer. Sport was seen to be available to anybody and everybody, all with a minimum of Commonwealth Government support (Daly, 1991).

Selective government assistance to the Olympics

While the Commonwealth Government had no formal relationship with NSOs, it understood the ways in which international sport successes could assist the nation-building process. Soon after the establishment of the Australian Olympic Federation (AOF) in 1919, the AOF sought assistance from the Commonwealth

Government for the travel and accommodation expenses of the 1920 Antwerp Olympic Games team. The government responded by providing a 1,000 pound grant to assist the team's travel to Europe. The AOF gratefully accepted the grant, and assured the Government that the athletes would come together 'in friendly rivalry, and be 'ambassadors of peace and men of goodwill' (Australian Olympic Federation, 1927: 1). The grants were also made with the knowledge that the Olympics were open only to amateur athletes, who were imbued with the amateur ideal of participating and playing for its own sake, and where winning was secondary to good sportsmanship and fair play.

On the other hand, the Commonwealth Government expected that the Australian Olympic Federation would raise most of the funds to enable athletes to participate at subsequent Olympic Games. For example, the Government allocated 3,000 pounds to the 1924 Paris Olympics team on condition that the Olympic Committee 'raised 10,000 pounds through public subscriptions' (Cashman, 1995: 118). The Commonwealth Government contributed 2,000 pounds to the 1928 Amsterdam team, nothing to the 1932 Los Angeles team since the AOF had accumulated surplus funds, and another 2,000 pounds to the 1936 Berlin team. Again, the grants were conditional on the AOF raising the bulk of the funds (Prime Minister's Department, 1935).

The Government was far less generous to the inaugural 1930 British Empire Games team. These Games were designed on a much smaller scale than the Olympics, and comprised six sports, in contrast to the Olympic Games' thirteen. The Games were scheduled for Hamilton in Canada, but the Commonwealth Government refused to provide any financial support. The team made it to the Games only after Canada contributed 5000 pounds to travel and accommodation costs (Cashman, 1995). A small grant was provided to the 1934 London team, and it funded the outfitting of the 1938 Sydney Empire Games team. Prime Minister Lyons accepted the role of Sydney Games President, but all of the facilities and sporting venues were financed by the New South Wales Government. The meagre, but symbolically significant Commonwealth Government budget allocation to sport during this period is revealed in Table 3.1.

The Commonwealth Government recognised the nation-building value in supporting Olympic and Commonwealth Games teams, and felt some obligation to support Australia's best amateur athletes when competing at the international

Table 3.1 Commonwealth Government funding to sport: 1920–39 (selected years)

Year	Total funding (million pounds)	Major developments and events
1920–21	0.001	1920 Olympic Games in Antwerp
1924–25	0.003	1924 Olympic Games Team in Paris
1930–31	0.000	1930 Inaugural Commonwealth Games in Hamilton
1936–37	0.002	1936 Olympic Games in Berlin
1938–39	0.001	1938 Commonwealth Games in Sydney

Sources: Cashman (1995), Commonwealth Government of Australia (1935).

level. On the other hand, it had no policy on how sport in general might contribute to social or community development (Jaques and Pavia, 1976b; Shelton, 1999). Neither did it support NSOs, and nor did it provide funding for sport facilities.

Strengthening the nation

A significant shift in Commonwealth Government views on the importance of sport and physical activity occurred at the beginning of the Second World War in 1939. The ruling United Australia Party, under the prime ministership of Robert Menzies, established the National Co-ordinating Council for Physical Fitness (NCCPF) (Hamilton-Smith and Robertson, 1977). The NCCPF was established as a result of a Conference of State Ministers for Education that met under the guidance of Senator Fol, a member of the Federal Parliament with a long-standing interest in community fitness. It aimed to create a self-sustaining 'national fitness movement' that would address the perceived physical fragility of many Australians. The NCCPF had become aware of the large number of Australian men and women that had been classified as unfit for military service at the beginning of the Second World War. The NCCPF concluded that more professionally trained physical education instructors were needed to ensure strong and effective leadership in the area. To this end, 20,000 pounds a year for the following five years was allocated to the States for the support of outdoor leadership and physical education training programmes at Universities, youth clubs, and municipal centres. The States had concurrently established their own fitness councils which worked within the policy frame set by the NCCPF (Hansard, National Fitness Debate, 25 June 1941: 6).

The Australian government subsequently passed the *National Fitness Act* in 1941 in order to give legislative stability to the activities of NCCPF. The Act also established the Commonwealth National Fitness Council (CNFC), which was the body for coordinating all fitness programmes. The CNFC had the primary responsibility of improving the fitness levels of the population, particularly those youths eligible for military service (Mckay, 1991). When introducing the Bill, the Minister for Heath, Sir Frederick Stewart, also indicated that the CNFC had a responsibility to improve the general well-being of the nation. He said:

> Behind the machines, in the shops or on the battlefield, there must be fit men and women...and the provision to ensure the continued fitness of children and young folk. Whilst we are now preoccupied with fighting, we must not forget the ultimate goal of fitness in order to enjoy life. (Hansard, 1941: 6)

The CNFC's brief was consequently to not only prepare fit and strong recruits for the war-effort, but to also establish educational training programmes for fitness and recreation leaders. State government fitness councils used the Commonwealth funds to deliver on-the-ground recreational programmes, assist university faculties of physical education and teacher training institutes, and set up camp and outdoor leadership facilities (Shelton, 1999). While the formation of the CNFC signalled an acknowledgement that physical activity had significant social and national development value, it was not high on the government policy agenda.

Post-war initiatives

When the Second World War ended in 1945, a social democratic Labor Government was in power, with Ben Chifley replacing John Curtin as Prime Minister. The Government continued to underwrite the CNFC, and soon expanded its activities to include community-based programs like holiday camps, adventure leadership classes, and learn-to-swim days (Hamilton-Smith and Robertson, 1977). In effect it continued the programme of improving the standard of fitness among the youth of Australia (Semotiuk, 1987). The CNFC also continued to promote physical education in schools.

While the Chifley Government was generally interventionist, having success-fully centralised wage fixing, and rationed petrol, but been defeated on its bank nationalisation proposal, it did not embrace sport development to any great degree. In effect, it merely continued the programme established by the previous, and economically conservative, Menzies Government. It continued to give financial assistance to Australian Olympic and Commonwealth Games teams to secure travel and accommodation arrangements for the athletes. However, it was always only a small proportion of the total team expenses. For instance, the 1948 London Olympic Games attracted 77 Australian athletes, but '44 of them were required to fund their participation from private means' (Cashman, 1995: 118–120). The Commonwealth Government funding arrangements for sport during the 1940s are listed in Table 3.2.

In summary, sport was not heavily funded, nor high on the Common-wealth Government agenda during the 1930s and 1940s. This was not surprising in the light of resources needed to sustain the war-effort, and problems involved in reconstructing the post-war economy. At the same time, the CNFC, with the assistance of State Governments, delivered a nationwide active recreation programme that substantially benefited the poor and disadvantaged. While

Table 3.2 Commonwealth Government funding to sport: 1939–49 (selected years)

Year	Total funding (million pounds)	Major developments and events
1939–40	0.020	National Co-ordination Council for Physical Fitness (NCCPF) established
1941–42	0.020	Commonwealth National Fitness Council (CNFC) established
1945–46	0.020	CNFC obtains ongoing funding
1948–49	0.028	1948 Olympic Games in London

Sources: Cashman (1995), Jaques and Pavia (1976a), Hansard (1941).

competitive sport was not a CNFC priority, it vigorously promoted the individual and social benefits of outdoor physical activity. In 1949 the Chifley Government, having expanded the role of the Commonwealth Government by taking over income taxing powers from the States, lost the election. It was replaced by the newly created Liberal and Country Party, led by Robert Menzies.

One small conservative step at a time

While the Menzies Government was ideologically opposed to market intervention in economic affairs, one of its first actions was to re-introduce compulsory military training for all 18-year-olds, which in part resulted from a desire to train up young men to be both physically and mentally tough (Bolton, 1990). Menzies remembered the poor physical condition of Australian youth in 1939, and understood, like the Government did in 1941, that a nation's military strength was dependent on the quality of both its technology and people.

In 1951 the Government also resolved to support that other great icon of Australian outdoor physicality, the lifesaver. In response to persistent lobbying and a growing acknowledgment of the valuable service provided, it complemented existing state government assistance by providing annual grants for lifesaving programmes, beach patrols, and rescue services. This grant signalled a growing belief that investing in sport in general, and 'voluntary organisations' in particular, provided significant community benefits (Booth, 1991: 147). Lifesavers were not only great Australian symbols of physical strength and courage, but they also provided an essential and low cost service to bathers and swimmers.

At one level, the Commonwealth Government support of the CNFC, annual grants to lifesaving, and financial assistance to Olympic and Commonwealth Games, reflected a growing belief that the national government had a role in shaping the Australian sport culture. On the other hand, it did little to change the relationship between the Commonwealth Government and NSOs. Neither the interventionist, and more socially radical Chifley Government, nor the more market oriented but socially conservative Menzies Government, had formulated anything approaching a national sport policy, although Menzies had put a toe in the water through his lifesaving subsidies and CNFC grants (Baka, 1984). The main responsibility for providing community sport experiences rested with local government, schools, and not-for-profit sporting clubs and associations (Hamilton-Smith and Robertson, 1977). The Commonwealth Government responsibilities were more focussed on defence, trade, commerce, work and education, and less about what people did in their spare time (Jaques and Pavia, 1976a). Table 3.3 confirms the low levels of Commonwealth Government funding for sport during the 1940s and 1950s.

During the 1940s and 1950s, sport was seen as a local government responsibility, and Commonwealth government support was confined to funding support for national sport teams, water safety, and fitness leadership programmes. While the CNFC was used as an instrument for building social capital and improving the living conditions of local communities, NSOs were left to fend for themselves.

Table 3.3 Commonwealth Government funding to sport: 1949–55 (selected years)

Year	Total funding (million pounds)	Major developments and events
1949–50	0.020	CNFC funding continues
1951–52	0.050	Inaugural grant to life-saving and water-safety programmes
1952–53	0.070	1952 Olympic Games Team in Helsinki
1954–55	0.060	1954 Commonwealth Games in Vancouver

Sources: Cashman (1995), Jaques and Pavia (1976a).

Sport ran its own affairs, found its own resources, and established its own values, goals, and visions for the future. In short, sport was seen to be a 'purely private affair' (Booth and Tatz, 2000: 163).

Post-Olympics euphoria

Competitive sport in Australia developed a high profile throughout the 1950s in response to many international successes in athletics, cricket, cycling, swimming, and tennis (Gordon, 1962). Australia's reputation as a sport-loving nation culminated in the hosting of the 1956 Melbourne Olympics, which was jointly financed by the City of Melbourne, the Victorian State Government, and the Commonwealth Government. It was a complex event to stage, and at various times the organising committee, which comprised mainly volunteer sport officials, was under pressure to speed up its decision-making processes. When, in 1952, it could not decide where exactly to hold the Games (the MCG, The Agricultural Showgrounds, and Princes Park Oval were staking their claims) the International Olympic Committee threatened to take the Games away from Melbourne, and the Commonwealth Government intervened (Toohey, 1990). Neither was there enough Olympic village accommodation, and many athletes had to be billeted to private households. These incidents demonstrated that major sport events could ensure their viability if they had both financial assistance and management support from all levels of government (Cashman, 1986). Despite some continuing organisational difficulties, the Games were ultimately successful, Australian athletes won more gold medals than at any other previous Olympic Games, and bathed in the warm afterglow of Olympic achievement. It once again confirmed the importance attached to international sporting success, and showed that investment in the Olympics produced an enormous amount of 'national pride and self-confidence' (Stoddart, 1986: 27).

By the 1960s Australia had not only discontinued compulsory national military service, but had also cemented its place as one of the world's most affluent countries, and a sporting nation that valued its achievements on both the national and international stage (Caldwell, 1976). Sport dominated our cultural life so much that one visitor noted that it was a place inundated with athletes (Daly, 1991). Despite the lack of Commonwealth Government support, many international successes were achieved in athletics, cricket, cycling, rugby union, rugby league, swimming, and tennis. It was widely considered that Australia's natural advantage of 'climate and relative economic prosperity would produce world champions' (Australian Sports Commission, 1986: 27). Herbert Wind, a senior writer at the time for *Sports Illustrated*, concluded that Australia 'was the most vigorous sporting country of all time' (Wind, 1960: 83).

Australia's international sporting success at this time can be explained in part by a culture that valued sport as an instrument for building individual character, mental toughness, and social cohesion. Australian sporting practices were based on the English team-games model that put great store on sport enabling mainly men to develop their leadership and personal qualities. It also meant that school sport was dominated by a few traditional sports (Stoddart, 1986). For boys the choice was usually between Australian football, cricket, rugby, soccer, tennis, and occasionally baseball, while girls could opt for netball, field hockey, or tennis. Physical education was on the school curriculum, but was given a low priority by both teaching staff and students because of its low academic status. At the same time, many Australians were attracted to the competitive side of sport. Although they were constrained by a narrow range of sporting options, the strong local government support and club structures that were built up in the 1930s and 1940s provided many sporting opportunities for young men and women during the 1950s and 1960s.

A no-policy policy

Throughout this period the Commonwealth Government pursued the sort of sport policy you have when you do not have a sport policy. This benign indifference implied that sport needed neither financial assistance nor planning guidance. It was assumed that individual ambition and effort were the drivers of all sport achievement, whether in elite international sport or suburban recreation (Jaques and Pavia, 1976a). In other words, the market or, more specifically, local government and community sport facilities, sport clubs, sport leagues, and a foundation of volunteer officials would take care of people's sport and physical activity needs.

Commonwealth Government assistance to sport continued to be limited to the CNFC, grants to lifesaving, and assistance to national teams competing at the Olympic and Commonwealth Games (Oakley, 1999). This arm's-length relationship with sport was exemplified in the comments of Prime Minister John Gorton, when he noted in 1969 that governments 'should not enter into sport matters', and that the best group to organise sporting activities were the 'sporting bodies concerned' (Farmer and Arnaudon, 1996: 8). Gorton's predecessor, Menzies, shared his views. Although Menzies was a devoted follower of cricket, and used it to cement relations with Britain, his government rarely interfered in cricket affairs. Apart from an incident in 1950 when the Minister for Posts and Telegraphs intervened in a radio broadcast rights dispute, the Australian Cricket Board of Control, cricket's national governing body, funded and managed its operations without government involvement (Stewart, 2002). According to one critic, sport under Menzies was considered 'the exclusive domain of the individual and the private sector' (Armstrong, 1988: 164). Sport was treated differently from commerce because it was primarily about the use of leisure time, and not business. Sport was more about 'frivolous play' than serious work (Lipsky, 1981: 7). Indeed, Robert Menzies highlighted the balance to be struck between the separate worlds of work and sport when he spoke at a pre-Olympics function in 1956. He said:

> We are...an athletic and sporting nation...but we have sometimes been accused of delivering too much time and thought to such matters. Yet...it is the nation which has learned to work and play hard...which is most likely to have that sense of proportion. (Toohey, 1990: 24)

On the other hand, as the 1960s progressed, the Commonwealth Government also understood that not only was sport an integral part of Australian cultural identity, and good for the community, it might also solve the problems of growing inactivity and sedentary lifestyles. As a result it extended the activities of the National Fitness Council in the late 1960s. In 1966, the annual CNFC grant increased from 100,000 to 160,000 pounds, and additional funds were provided for capital works. The capital works money was to be used in developing camps and establishing recreation centres. At the same time, state government grants to state councils were also increased, and exceeded AUS$1 million for the first time (Commonwealth National Fitness Council, 1966: 1). State Councils were also instructed to promote sport activities more widely, and as a result coaching programmes were conducted in track and field, women's basketball, softball, trampolining, and women's Olympic gymnastics.

In 1967, Prime Minister Holt, who replaced Menzies when he retired in 1966, launched the Council's *Fitness Australia* campaign in a TV broadcast to the nation. The campaign was aimed mainly at adults since there were signs of a fall in community health levels. Tobacco consumption had risen, and cardiovascular disease had become a major problem. The CNFC obtained the financial support of the AMP Society, Australia's largest insurer, to produce a booklet titled *Keeping Fit* which was distributed to schools, sporting clubs, and households. State Fitness Councils organised promotional campaigns including mass walks, lectures and demonstrations of exercise programmes. One of the most popular promotions involved a walk-to-work morning in Sydney. The idea was so popular that at one stage the Sydney Harbour Bridge 'was jammed with walkers for over an hour' (Commonwealth National Fitness Council, 1966: 13).

Signs of trouble

This ambivalent and arms-length relationship between sport and the Commonwealth Government was increasingly questioned as Australia's international standing in sport declined in the late 1960s. By the early 1970s, Australia began to struggle at the Olympic Games, as the glory of the 1956 Olympics faded to a distant memory. These relative failures severely dented Australia's national pride and self-esteem. Moreover, in the light of its ability to generate significant social benefits, sport was increasingly seen to be under-resourced (Daly, 1991).

The *ad hoc* athlete funding of Australian sport was contrasted with the spending of some European countries on talent identification and the training of elite athletes (Cashman, 1995). Australia was particularly envious of relatively small socialist nations like Cuba and East Germany who had overtaken them in the Olympic arena. For example, while East Germany won 66 medals, including 20 gold, at the 1972 Munich Olympics, Australia won only 17 medals, including 8 gold. To some critics of the Australian sport system, Australia's international success came 'in spite of government apathy' (Daly, 1991: 13). While the success of the socialist nations was mainly the result of government-sponsored training camps and sport science facilities, Australia's international reputation for sporting excellence was more the result of a 'broad participation base, able coaching and plain hard work' (Wind, 1960: 84). The Commonwealth Government continued to provide financial assistance to Olympic and Commonwealth Games teams. Around $20,000 was allocated to the 1970 Edinburgh team, but it was microscopic by European standards. Table 3.4 shows a slight increase in the levels of Commonwealth Government sport funding for sport between 1956 and 1971. However in total budgetary terms it was in the small-change category.

It should also be remembered that Australia's international sporting successes during this period were not only achieved with little Commonwealth Government assistance, but was also organised in a strictly amateur context. Even cricketers, who generated the most spectator support, were only paid expenses to play. So too were our best tennis players who were subsidised by securing part-time employment with sport goods suppliers. Until 1968 all major international tournaments were strictly for amateurs, and players who turned professional were forced to play amongst themselves in an exhibition atmosphere. Australia's Olympic athletes were also unpaid, and unlike an increasing number of European, American, and Communist 'block' athletes, had to fund their training and travel from their own earnings. It became increasingly clear that Australian athletes were under-resourced when compared to those from other advanced industrial

Table 3.4 Commonwealth Government funding to sport: 1956–71 (selected years)

Year	Funding (million pounds)	Major developments and events
1956–57	0.700	Melbourne Olympics
1958–59	0.100	Commonwealth Games in Cardiff
1960–61	0.150	Olympic Games in Rome
1968–69	0.500 dollars[*]	Olympic Games in Mexico City
1970–71	0.500 dollars[*]	Commonwealth Games in Edinburgh

Sources: Cashman (1995), Jaques and Pavia (1976a), Australian Sports Commission (2001a).

[*] Decimal currency was introduced into Australia in 1966.

countries. The natural advantages that Australian athletes had in the 1950s and 1960s had for the most part disappeared by the 1970s.

Sport had become increasingly politicised during the late 1960s and early 1970s. In the lead-up to the 1968 Mexico Olympic Games many Mexican citizens were concerned that funds invested in sport facilities for the Games had been taken away from social development programmes, and violent protests resulted. At the same time, a number of African nations threatened to boycott the Games in response to South Africa's apartheid policy, and as a result the International Olympic Committee withdrew its invitation to the South African Olympic team. Closer to home, in 1971 the Chinese Government invited an Australian table tennis team to play its national team as prelude to re-opening diplomatic relations with Australia. In the same year, the visiting South African rugby union team was subject to vigorous anti-apartheid protests across Australia. This upset the conservative Liberal Prime Minister McMahon, who did not think sport and politics should mix, and led him to assert that the tour should be completed (Harris, 1972). Finally, in late 1971 the Australia Cricket Board of Control resolved to cancel the scheduled 1972 tour of Australia by the South African cricket team. While there was no agreement on how these sport problems could be best managed, it meant that international sport issues had been well and truly put on the government agenda, and it set the scene for a radical shift in Commonwealth Government sport policy.

Concluding comments

In the light of the above developments, the expansion of CNFC activities during the 1960s was significant. It indicated that while the Gorton and McMahon Governments of 1968–71 saw no role for Government funding of NSOs and elite sport in general, they recognised the benefits arising from more physically active communities. When combined with the lifesaving and water-safety grants, and assistance to Olympic and Commonwealth Games teams, it came some way to providing the skeleton for a national sport policy. However, the flesh for a more full-bodied policy came only with a change of government.

4 Crash-through: sport policy 1972–82

The Whitlam experiment

The institutional framework for the delivery of sport changed dramatically during the 1970s. In 1972, the Gough Whitlam Labor Government was elected with a mandate to change the political landscape (Crowley, 1986). It was both reformist and highly centralist, and believed that it should exert more control over both economic and cultural affairs, including sport. One of its first initiatives was to ban all racially selected sport teams from touring Australia. This was a significant policy shift since it overturned the Gorton and McMahon Governments' view that politics had no place in sport.

The Whitlam Government also re-visited the previous government's views on sport and leisure in the community. Despite many international successes, sport and recreation was seen to be underdeveloped and in need of government assistance. Prime Minister Whitlam believed that 'there was no greater social problem facing Australia than the good use of leisure' (Hamilton-Smith and Robertson, 1977: 180). Sport and physical activity was seen as a quality of life issue that could be used to improve the social conditions of outer-urban and regional Australia (Booth and Tatz, 2000). According to the Prime Minister, government responsibility did not terminate with finance, employment and defence. Indeed, 'governments are expected to improve the intellectual, artistic, and recreational opportunities of their people' (Shelton, 1999: 15). This policy shift was underpinned by a growing realisation that sport had the potential to improve the welfare of ordinary people, and therefore should be accessible to the whole community. In short, sport was a social issue and a legitimate focus for public policy debate (Armstrong, 1987).

Two important initiatives followed in 1973. First, the Government established a specialist portfolio under the name of Tourism and Recreation. Second, it established an inquiry under the control of John Bloomfield, a physical education professor from the University of Western Australia. The purpose of the inquiry was to examine 'The Role, Scope and Development of Recreation in Australia'. The Bloomfield report, as it came to be known, expressed concern at the fall in fitness levels, the declining interest in physical education in schools, the growing incidence of heart disease, and the increasing stresses faced by modern societies like Australia (Bloomfield, 1973). Bloomfield also noted the growing divide between those who 'can afford the luxury of a pastime or sport and those who cannot...the have-nots can barely afford the cost of petrol to drive to the beach, let alone join a sailing, golf, or tennis club' (Bloomfield, 1973: 6).

The Bloomfield blueprint

Bloomfield recommended that the Commonwealth Government implement a national recreation programme through a Recreation Division of the Department of Tourism and Recreation. This programme would have three prongs. The first would focus on the creation of community recreation centres throughout Australia, the second would raise the community consciousness about the importance of general fitness, while the third would build up Australia's elite athlete programmes and sport science research capability (Bloomfield, 1973). The Bloomfield model, which became a blueprint for future government policy on elite and community sport, is illustrated in Figure 4.1.

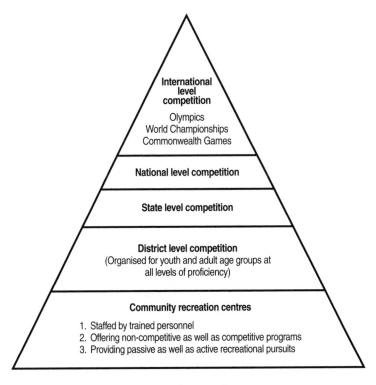

Figure 4.1 Bloomfield's recreational pyramid.

Not all of Bloomfield's 73 recommendations were implemented, but the Commonwealth Government used the report to increase funding to NSOs, and to assist local government in building additional leisure centres.

The Coles vision

The Bloomfield report was also the catalyst for the Whitlam Government to undertake another inquiry into sport. This time the brief was to examine in more detail the Bloomfield proposal to develop a high-performance unit for training elite athletes. The 1975 inquiry was chaired by Allan Coles, a sport scientist from the University of Queensland, and focused on the issue of elite athlete development, and the feasibility of establishing a sport institute (Coles, 1975). The Coles Committee quickly discovered that many European countries were far more systematic in addressing the needs of elite athletes and had developed many advanced training and conditioning regimes. The report that followed recommended that a centre of excellence be developed to 'cater to Australia's elite athletic community' (Farmer and Arnaudon, 1996: 8).

While the Bloomfield and Coles reports persuasively argued the case for greater government involvement in sport, they also revealed the problem of balancing elite sport assistance against community sport development. Frank Stewart, the minister for Tourism and Recreation, favoured the community sport model, noting that it was not the intention of his government to 'emulate the gold medal factories of East Germany'. The Commonwealth Government priority was 'mass participation' (Semotiuk, 1987: 154). Indeed, elite sport development was seen by the Commonwealth as a by-product of community participation (Cohen, 1980).

During this period the Department of Tourism and Recreation supported sport through two channels. The first channel was the Capital Assistance Program that provided tied grants to state governments for the construction of community sport facilities in designated local government areas. The second channel was the Sport Assistance Program which provided financial assistance to national sport associations 'for administration, coaching and travel' (Australian Sports Commission, 1986: 27). These schemes became the foundation for subsequent policy development by the Commonwealth government.

In order to provide state government links to these programmes, the Whitlam Government established a Recreation Ministers Council (RMC) which was a discussion forum for matters of mutual concern to Commonwealth and State Ministers. This initiative coincided with the establishment of departments of sport and recreation by the state governments, which also saw the need to assist the development of sport. Victoria, New South Wales, and Queensland incorporated their NFC state councils into sport and recreation units in 1972, and Western Australia followed in 1973. The Commonwealth Government also established a sports council to advise on emerging issues in competitive sport. The Whitlam Government's commitment to sport was accompanied by a substantial increase

Table 4.1 Commonwealth Government funding to sport: 1972–75

Year	Total funding (AUS$ million)	Major developments and events
1972–73	1.0	Munich Olympic Games
		Bloomfield Inquiry commences
1973–74	5.7	Grants to NSOs initiated
1974–75	6.9	Capital grants for community sport centres initiated
		Commonwealth Games in Christchurch
		Coles Inquiry commences

Sources: Australian Sports Commission (2001a), Semotiuk (1987).

in grant allocations. Table 4.1 reflects not only a significant increase in funding levels to sport, but also a broadening of the funding base.

While the Whitlam Government's early focus was on community sport, both the Bloomfield and Coles reports supported the establishment of some form of elite athlete training institute. However, before the Whitlam Government could respond to the Coles recommendations, it was defeated at the December 1975 election, and replaced by a more conservative political party with no clear intention to build on Whitlam's sport policy initiatives.

Downsizing sport policy

The excitement that surrounded the Commonwealth Government commitment to sport was quashed in 1975 with the election of a Liberal government under the prime ministership of Malcolm Fraser. The Liberal Party had previously supported Olympic and Commonwealth Games teams, the CNCF and lifesaving and beach rescue, but was otherwise uninterested in large-scale sport funding since it was inconsistent with its small government policy (Armstrong, 1988). Fraser also held to the view that sport should run its own affairs, and gave the impression that 'all that is required to produce a fit and healthy nation is a pair of sandshoes and running shorts' (Cohen, 1980: 5). This lack of interest in consolidating Whitlam's initiatives was reflected in the immediate dismantling of the Department of Tourism and Recreation.

Under the Fraser Government sport assistance was initially managed through the Department of Environment, Housing, and Community Development, which continued to provide grants to NSOs to improve the administrative support for elite athletes. The Whitlam Government's Capital Assistance Program was scaled down, and its Sport Assistance Program was re-shaped into a low-key Sport Performance Program that aimed to additionally secure full-time appointments to as many NSOs as possible (Australian Sports Commission, 1986). As a result, sport funding fell in the first four years of the Fraser Government. While Government spending was $7.6 million in 1976, it had declined to $3 million in

1978 (Cohen, 1980: 7). According to one critic, the Fraser Government's sport policy was 'ineffectual' (Armstrong, 1988: 139).

Government rethink

Around the same time, though, the Fraser Government became aware of an increasing incidence of a number of preventable diseases including coronary heart disease, diabetes, and lung cancer. There was growing evidence that these problems were in part linked to an increasingly sedentary lifestyle. The Commonwealth Government consequently established a national fitness promotion programme under the banner of 'Life. Be in it'. In 1976, the CNFC was absorbed into the RMC, and in the following year the RMC agreed to convert the well-known Victorian Government's 'Life. Be in it' strategy into a national programme. The national 'Life. Be in it' programme had a number of linked aims. The first aim was to increase community awareness of the benefits that flow from physical activity. The second aim was to show how local facilities could be used to engage in a variety of low cost activities. The final aim was to introduce people to sport as a way of becoming active. The Commonwealth allocated $1.8 million over three years, and the programme was launched with the distribution of information kits to Federal parliamentarians and the media. A press conference was held in Parliament House, a lunch was held at the National Press Club, and promotional material was distributed to pharmacies across the nation. A widespread advertising campaign was mounted, and as part of an integrated strategy, state governments organised family days, come and try days, and a variety of non-competitive physical activities. Later in the programme more competitive activities were introduced, one of the most popular being beach volleyball (Department of Home Affairs, 1979). While the programme successfully engineered a greater interest in outdoor recreation and sports, it only marginally increased the overall level of participation. An expenditure review committee met in 1980, and did not recommend its continuation as part of its cost cutting agenda.

The Fraser Government was also forced to reconsider its restrictive position on sport development in the light of strong lobbying from a more organised and politically astute sport system. The expectations of sport associations had been raised by the Labor Government's sport policy and, in 1977, 42 national sport associations contributed AUS$25 each to form the Confederation of Australian Sport (CAS) under the leadership of Gary Daly, a former general manager of the Lawn Tennis Association of Australia. The primary role of the CAS was to lobby government for a united case in order to achieve a better deal for sport (Stoddart, 1986: 62). One of its first tasks involved the publication of its own white paper in 1980 entitled *A Master Plan for Australian Sport*. Like the Bloomfield Report, *Master Plan* argued for government policies that would enhance both elite performance and community participation. The CAS also re-affirmed Bloomfield's call for a national sport policy that put resources into improving the management of NSOs, identifying talented athletes, improving the quality of sport venues, and making school sport a serious part of the curriculum (Daly, 1991).

A key plank of *Master Plan* called for the establishment of a national sports institute, similar to that identified by the Coles Committee. The CAS's aim of securing a better funding deal was made easier by Australia's dismal performance at the 1976 Montreal Olympic Games and the subsequent 'expressions of dissatisfaction' and crisis of confidence in the Australian sporting community (Stoddart, 1986: 69). The CAS case was reinforced by a Government discussion paper that argued for an increase in sport assistance. It cited East Germany as an exemplar of good sport policy since it funded both elite and community sport. It concluded that a national sports institute was crucial to secure Australia's strong international sporting image (Department of Environment Housing and Community Development, 1976).

These external pressures subsequently forced the Commonwealth Government to re-focus its policy on the elite end of the sport development continuum in the late 1970s. One of the first initiatives was to formalise the education and training of coaches. The Sport and Recreation Ministers Council was instrumental in setting up the Australian Coaching Council in 1978, which subsequently became the accrediting agency for all coaches at both the elite and community level. By 1979 the Fraser Government had removed its sport policy blinkers, and in the 1979–80 budget allocated AUS$2 million to the sport development pro-gramme, AUS$390,000 to lifesaving and water safety, AUS$650,000 to the national 'Life. Be in it' programme, and AUS$700,000 to the Australian Olympic Federation for the 1980 Moscow Olympic team. This spending spree also included AUS$2.5 million to the Queensland State Government for the 1982 Common-wealth Games, and AUS$750,000 to the Western Australian Government to help it build an international field-hockey stadium in Perth as part of its sesqui-centenary celebration (Cohen, 1980).

The great leap forward

The Fraser Government showed no initial interest in implementing the Bloomfield and Coles recommendations for an elite sport training academy. However, as a result of the strong leadership of the minister for Home Affairs, Bob Ellicott, and in response to community concern about Australia's erratic international sporting record during the late 1970s, it established the Australian Institute of Sport (AIS) in 1981. The failure of Australian athletes to win any gold medals at the 1976 Montreal Olympic, combined with the divisiveness resulting from the Moscow 1980 Olympic Games boycott, prompted the Commonwealth Govern-ment to re-consider its policy on elite sport development (Booth and Tatz, 2000). It 'sensed the public disquiet at the dramatic decline in Australia's Olympic performance', and began to listen to athlete grievances (Armstrong, 1988: 143). It subsequently resolved to put more resources into Olympic sport as a means of re-establishing Australia's international sporting credentials (Cashman, 1995; Daly, 1991). The electorate liked the idea, or at least the prospect that Australia might reclaim its status as a leading sporting nation, even if it meant spend-ing millions of dollars of taxpayer's money. A 1976 opinion poll found that

70 per cent of Australians believed that government should be giving more aid to sport (Australian Sports Commission, 1986: 6). This was not lost on the Fraser Government, which increasingly understood how sport could be used both as a 'symbol of national development' and a vehicle for achieving electoral popularity (Adair and Vamplew, 1997: 41). At the end of the 1982 Common-wealth Games in Brisbane, Prime Minister Fraser noted that Australia's elite athletes were the 'visible representation of a true co-operative spirit', a truly multi-cultural society, and intense national pride (Stoddart, 1986: 69).

Australia's international athletes, who felt they were at the time 'unable to compete on an equal footing with their northern hemisphere counterparts', were equally excited (Daly, 1991: 6). As a result, an impressive, high technology, training centre was established in Canberra, the national capital, with Don Talbot as its executive director. Talbot was an internationally respected swim coach, who, while not trained as a manager, was determined and tough (Bloomfield, 2003). The Institute, which was modelled on the successful East German and Chinese sport academies, not only had an elitist agenda, but also focused its resources on those Olympic sports in which international successes were likely (Houlihan, 1997). The eight sports initially selected for support were athletics, basketball, gymnastics, netball, soccer, swimming, tennis and weightlifting. The AIS facilities were complemented by a scholarship scheme that allowed selected athletes to train and compete on a full-time basis. This was a radical departure from the amateur ethos that framed Australian sport for most of the twentieth century.

The AIS was initially accused of being too centralised, failing to address the needs of state sport bodies, and ignoring the community sport model that under-pinned the Bloomfield report (Houlihan, 1997). The centralised structure was initially justified on the grounds that it provided it with 'a national character', but was soon decentralised into regional centres of sporting excellence in response to pressure from state governments and national sporting bodies. As more sports were added, hockey was relocated to Perth in 1984, diving to Brisbane in 1984, squash to Brisbane in 1985, and cycling and cricket to Adelaide in 1987. The scholarship scheme was also extended in 1982, and additional intensive training programmes were established for non-Olympic sports (Bloomfield, 2003).

Grass-roots spill-over

The AIS focussed on elite sport development, which constituted a significant shift in policy when compared to the Whitlam Government's position. However, the Fraser Liberal government argued that grass-roots participation would also be stimulated by elite sport successes. This view was succinctly put by Dick Telford, the inaugural head of the sport science unit at the AIS, when he noted that the talented performer would generate 'positive reinforcement and interest' back in the 'lower echelons of sporting achievement' (Telford, 1982: 4). In other words, the creation of national heroes would 'inspire others to emulate them' (Daly,

1991: 18). This claim was difficult to substantiate, but gained widespread accept-ance (Mckay, 1991). Despite its dubious validity, it added weight to the argu-ment that sport produced a number of benefits in addition to the immediate pleasure for players and fans (McKay, 1986). Table 4.2 highlights the funding boost to elite sport during the 1975–83 period.

The late 1970s and early 1980s in particular coincided with an increasing commercialisation and politicisation of sport. At the international level, tennis tournament prize-money escalated as global sponsors emerged. The salaries of European soccer players also rapidly increased as the major leagues secured a sub-stantial increase in broadcasting rights fees. The Olympics increasingly became a forum for government-subsidised athletes that included East German swimmers, Russian field athletes, French cyclists and skiers, and American College track athletes. Locally, Australian football, cricket, and rugby league were profession-alised through the explosive growth in revenue from sponsorship and the sale of TV rights (Stewart, 1984). The increasing commercialisation of sport in general, together with the growth in AIS scholarships, signalled a more professional approach to Olympic sports in Australia, and the demise of the amateur ethos (Cashman, 1995).

Sport also became more politically entrenched despite the myth that sport was a 'private matter separate from politics' (Booth and Tatz, 2000: 162). Countries increasingly used sport to highlight moral issues, promote grievances, and more generally to punish another country for racist or corrupt behaviour. During the 1970s, South Africa was the focal point for demonstrations and boycotts over its apartheid policy. Notwithstanding international pressures and protests, a number of sport tours went ahead, including a privately sponsored cricket tour managed by Richie Benaud, the former Australian team captain, which included players like Ian Chappell, Dennis Lillie and Mike Denness (Francis, 1989). The sport and racism problem exploded in 1976 when, against all international advice, New Zealand sent an official rugby union team to South Africa. It coincided with the Soweto uprising where nearly 600 black Africans were killed. When the

Table 4.2 Commonwealth Government funding to sport: 1975–83

Year	Total funding (AUS$ million)	Major developments and events
1975–76	9.2	National 'Life. Be in it' campaign initiated
1976–77	7.6	Olympic Games in Montreal
1977–78	5.9	Australian Coaching Council established
1978–79	3.3	Commonwealth Games in Edmonton
1979–80	3.7	National 'Life. Be in it' campaign discontinued
1980–81	8.2	Olympic Games in Moscow
1981–82	13.0	AIS established
1982–83	14.0	Commonwealth Games in Brisbane

Sources: Australian Sports Commission (2001a), Cohen (1980), Semotiuk (1987).

International Olympic Committee refused to rescind New Zealand's invitation to the upcoming Montreal Olympics, most African nations boycotted the Games (Booth and Tatz, 2000). In the following year, the Heads of Commonwealth Governments, with Malcolm Fraser taking a leading role, drafted the Gleneagles declaration which committed Commonwealth nations to withdrawing support from national governing bodies which sent sporting teams to South Africa. Sport again became immersed in politics when the United States led a boycott against the Soviet Union after it invaded Afghanistan in 1979. The Fraser Government supported the boycott, but left the decision to attend the 1980 Moscow Games to the Australian Olympic Committee (AOC). The AOC could not agree on what to do, so some teams and athletes attended, while others did not. In the meantime the Commonwealth Government compensated athletes who chose not to go, which in the eyes of some critics, amounted to bribery (Cashman, 1995). The 1982 Brisbane Commonwealth Games was also threatened with disruption when African nations protested against the inclusion of New Zealand. A boycott was avoided when Prime Minister Fraser and the Commonwealth Games Association agreed to offer athletes from developing nations AIS scholarships (Booth and Tatz, 2000).

Concluding comments

These trends further undermined the belief that sport had nothing to do with business or politics. It also meant that national government leadership could be used to not only create a more integrated and innovative sport system, but also set the parameters for its conduct. The concurrent professionalisation of NSOs, together with the establishment of the AIS, transformed the structure and day-to-day operation of Australian sport. NSOs became the focal point for Commonwealth Government sport funding, and the vehicle for identifying and nurturing talented young athletes. Both the Whitlam and Fraser Governments had crashed through the cultural and political barriers that had separated sport from the realm of government action and assistance for so long.

5 Augmentation: sport policy 1983–96

The Hawke ascendancy

In 1983, Fraser's Liberal Government was replaced by Bob Hawke's reformist Labor Government. Hawke was elected with a mandate to govern through 'consultation and consensus' (Armstrong, 1987: 168). This inclusive stance fitted snugly with its sports policy, which aimed to 'make sport and recreation available to everyone who wishes to participate' (Semotiuk, 1987: 156). The Hawke Government sport policy was based on a 1980 discussion paper prepared by Barry Cohen, a member of parliament who had been instrumental in designing the Whitlam Government sport policy. One of its earliest initiatives was to re-visit the Whitlam sport development model and establish a separate Department of Sport, Recreation and Tourism. This was followed by a report by the House of Representatives Standing Committee on Expenditure which examined the prospects for additional funding for sport. The report was titled *The way we p(l)ay* and recommended an expansion of government spending on sport. It specifically argued for more spending on tied state grants for both international standard sport facilities and recreation centres in disadvantaged regions, programmes improving the management processes of NSOs, and on facilities for disabled athletes (House of Representatives Committee on Finance and Public Administration, 1983). The Hawke Government also produced a white paper titled *Sport and Recreation: Australia on the Move*, which set the scene for an expanded sport policy with a facility development emphasis (Bloomfield, 2003).

The Department's first major decision was to both consolidate the previous government's elite sports programmes and broaden its community sport policy (Australian Government, 1983). This produced specific strategies for disabled athletes, and additional community sport facilities, as well as international standard sport venues. The Hawke Government also saw the tourist potential in sport when it allocated $30 million over three years to help develop the infrastructure for the defence of the Americas Cup in Fremantle in 1987 (Stoddart, 1986). Finally, it re-iterated the view that spending more on elite sport was good for the whole community since it stimulated participation. John Brown, the newly appointed minister for sport, tourism and recreation, argued that making more money available to our top international athletes was a 'necessary additive in getting young kids interested in sport'. He noted that 'if kids have got something to aspire to it will encourage them to participate at the base level' (Hartung, 1983: 52). However, like Telford a year earlier, he provided scanty evidence for the claim.

A coordinating commission

In 1985, not long after the early re-election of the Hawke Government, the AIS was complemented by the creation of the Australian Sports Commission (ASC). In 1984 an interim committee under the chairmanship of Ted Harris, a prominent businessman, argued that a sport system without a coordinating authority would fail to adequately meet the needs of contemporary Australian society (Interim Committee for the Australian Sports Commission, 1984). According to the Harris Committee, a sports commission would reduce fragmentation, enhance cooperation, allow for greater participation in decision-making processes by sporting groups, and broaden the financial base for sport. The Committee concluded that the commission should be set up as an independent statutory authority to both ensure the legitimacy of the Government policy-making processes, and provide leadership and direction at the national level. The Committee also wanted the commission to be mindful of its obligation to represent all sporting interests, and not just the needs of elite athletes. The Hawke Government adopted the recommendation, which was not surprising because the establishment of a commission was a plank in its pre-election platform in 1983 (Australian Sports Commission, 1986). The need to balance community and elite sport consequently became an integral part of the commission's operational philosophy. One of the first things the Hawke Government did was to use the ASC to deliver increased funding to NSOs, and to help consolidate their sport development programmes. This was linked to a Sport Talent Encouragement Program (STEP), which provided financial grants to highly ranked athletes to assist their training and competition.

The ASC also had a brief to establish a Sport Aid Foundation (SAF) whose role would be to attract funds to sport through a donation mechanism. Under this scheme all donations to the SAF would be tax-deductable, and therefore be an incentive for corporate assistance to sport.

The Australian Games

In the meantime, the Hawke Government was being persuaded that many of Australia's elite athletes in general, and Olympic athletes in particular, were disadvantaged by a lack of regular international competition. Strong lobbying by the Confederation of Australian Sport, the enthusiasm of the Victorian State Government for the idea, and the national euphoria resulting from the 1982 Brisbane Commonwealth Games and 1983 Americas Cup victory convinced the Commonwealth that it should support the concept of the Australian Games. The Games covered 22 sports, and invitations were extended to track athletes from the USA and Europe, 'gymnasts from Bulgaria, the Soviet Union and

Japan, Bulgarian and Russian weightlifters, New Zealand canoeists and rowers, Asian volleyball teams, and Brazilian and American basketballers' (*Herald Sun*, 9 June 1986). The Games were held in early 1985 in Melbourne and coincided with the State's 150th anniversary celebration. Victoria provided just over AUS$375,000, hoping that the event would generate sufficient national good-will, international exposure, and tourist dollars, to cover the investment. The Commonwealth Government injected another AUS$1.3 million, with one-third going to the upgrade of the Olympic Park running track in Melbourne. While the Games exposed Australian athletes to more international competi-tion than they would normally get in a off season, it quickly became a financial burden for the Victorian Government which had underwritten the staging of the Games. Costs escalated, and another AUS$920,000 was finally needed to pay all the event bills (*Herald Sun*, 9 June 1986). The Hawke Government resolved not to support any future Australian Games on the grounds that the money would be better spent assisting NSOs improve their coaching and international travel programmes for athletes. Meanwhile the Victorian State Government vowed not to get its fingers burnt again, and rejected an overture to stage the Games in 1987. The Commonwealth Government took the Australian Games off its pol-icy agenda, and it vanished into thin air, never to be heard of again.

However, the loss of the Australian Games did not diminish the Government enthusiasm for mega sport events. Having allocated AUS$30 million in 1983 to the Americas Cup defence in Perth, it contributed AUS$5 million to the inaug-ural staging of the Adelaide Formula 1 Grand Prix event (Department of Sport Recreation and Tourism, 1985: 67).

Managing the South Africa problem

The Hawke Government also had to deal with the problem of sporting exchanges between Australia and South African athletes. In 1984, Sport Minis-ter Brown wrote to all NSOs advising that as part of the Gleneagles declaration, the Commonwealth Government would 'vigorously combat the evils of apart-heid by discouraging contact and competition with sporting organisations, teams, or sportsmen from South Africa' (Francis, 1989: 38). Minister Brown noted that the Government had 'adhered scrupulously to the spirit and letter of the declar-ation' (Francis, 1989: 60). However, this did not stop Bruce Francis, a former Australian test cricketer, from organising a 'rebel' tour of South Africa in 1985 and 1986. The team was led by Kim Hughes, who had just been dismissed as captain of the official Australian cricket team. The tour went ahead without the endorsement of the Commonwealth Government, Australian Cricket Board, and most commentators, some of whom argued the players were taking blood money. While the tour had no official status, it captured a moderate amount of interest in South Africa, and the players were paid for their services. The tour also highlighted some of the confusion and inconsistencies involved in applying the Gleneagles declaration to Australian sporting contact with South Africa. The declaration was used by the Cricket Board, with Government support, to ban offending players from participating in any Board-sponsored events, including the local interstate competition, the Sheffield Shield. It had little impact on surfers, cyclists, golfers, squash players, and tennis players, who competed in South Africa with little comment from the Government, and no penalty from their national governing body (Francis, 1989).

AIS budget blow-out

Further controversy arose in 1985 when the AIS was accused of spending beyond its budget allocation. The AIS General Manager, John Cheffers, who replaced the inaugural CEO in 1984, was singled out for criticism. An investigation by the *Sydney Daily Telegraph* newspaper found that annual hospitality spending had increased from AUS$1,600 to AUS$42,000. An independent audit subsequently found that the Institute had exceeded its budget allocation by AUS$450,000 (Bloomfield, 2003: 80). Cheffers decided to resign and return to the USA soon after. In 1989 Sport Minister Richardson announced the merger of the AIS and ASC. The decision was made in part to ensure a closer control of the AIS, and also to eliminate administrative duplication and inefficiencies.

Children's sport

No such controversy surrounded the Commonwealth Government policy on children's sport. The community sport philosophy articulated by the Hawke Government, and implemented by the ASC, underpinned the development and launch of the Aussie Sports programme in 1986. Its vision was to contribute to the enrichment of sporting experiences and opportunities by influencing the practices of key agencies in the development and delivery of junior sport, while its basic objective was to 'improve the quality, quantity and variety of sport available to Australian children' (Vamplew, 1994). The programme was developed partly in response to growing concerns that school sport had overemphasised the competitive nature of sport, rather than elements of play, enjoyment, self-expression and individual difference. There was also concern that participation rates for children had fallen during the 1970s and early 1980s (Oakley, 1999). Aussie Sports focused on the last three years of primary school education, and also targeted coaches and teachers involved in community sport, seeking in part to foster a link between school and club sport. Programme areas within the Aussie Sports umbrella included Sportstart, Sport It!, Ready Set Go!, Sport Search, Active Girls, Sportsfun, and Challenge, Achievement and Pathways in Sport, as well as targeting school-based education, leadership programmes and public education.

The primary philosophy of the Aussie Sports programme was that sport was to be fun, and as such modified games were offered to school children in place of more traditional competitive sport. These games minimised differences in height, weight and gender, and emphasised the development of sporting and motor skills in a non-threatening sport environment. Consequently, the only competition that existed was with the individual participant, in an attempt to become a competent player, or the best that they could be.

In 1988, the year after the Hawke Government was elected for a third term, the Aussie Sports framework was broadened to include secondary school children, at a time when State Aussie Sports units within each of the State and Territory Sport and Recreation departments were established. Evaluation of the Aussie Sports programme suggests that its initiatives contributed to the improved organisation and quality of children's sport (Adair and Vamplew, 1997). In turn, this had a positive effect on the physical and social development of adolescents, as well as smoothing the transition to senior sport. On the other hand, some people opposed modified games because they compromised the opportunities for talent identification, and hindered children who might wish to specialise at an early age.

Capital grants re-visited

Around the same time the Hawke government broadened its sport participation focus by implementing a scheme that aimed to assist the expansion of community sport facilities. It was known as the Community Recreation and Sport Facility Program, and over the next six years allocated substantial grants to support the construction of community leisure centres and sport arenas across the nation. It was essentially a copy of Whitlam's capital development scheme, which was discontinued by Fraser in 1975. The programme was justified on three grounds, all of which had been argued by Whitlam in the early 1970s. First, it would reduce some of the disadvantage in low income communities. Second, it would encourage more people to participate in sport and physical activity programmes. Finally, it would expand the pool of talented young athletes with the potential to achieve elite and international status. According to sport Minister Brown, 'it is no good having an AIS in Canberra unless there is some encouragement for children at the grassroots level' (Armstrong, 1988: 238).

The expansion of junior sport development, the re-vitalisation of the capital grants programme, and the consolidation of the elite athlete support programme, all required additional Commonwealth Government funding. Table 5.1 confirms the growth in Commonwealth Government funding to sport during the 1980s.

However, by world standards, Australian sport was under-funded. A study jointly conducted by the AIS and ASC found that annual per capita Commonwealth Government spending was just over AUS$2. By contrast, the East German Government spent $20 per head, while the USA and the Netherlands spent $7 and $5 respectively on sport (Bloomfield, 2003: 92).

In summary, between 1983 and 1989 sport policy was consolidated and integrated through the establishment of the ASC. The Hawke Government also conceded that sport should be more accessible to the community. NSOs were increasingly vocal in their claim that junior sport had to be made more attractive if it was to sustain the interest of young people. Similarly, disabled people had been severely disadvantaged, and additional sport facilities were needed to

Table 5.1 Commonwealth Government funding to sport: 1983–89

Year	Total funding (AUS$ million)	Major developments and events
1983–84	23	Disabled and disadvantaged sport programme expanded
1984–85	27	Los Angeles Olympic Games ASC established
1985–86	32	Australia Games held in Melbourne
1986–87	33	Aussie junior sport group programme launched Commonwealth Games in Edinburgh
1987–88	32	Community Recreation and Sport Facility Program commences
1988–89	33	ASC merges with AIS Seoul Olympic Games

Sources: Australian Sports Commission (2001a), Going for Gold (1989).

ensure easier accessibility. On balance, though, the overwhelming majority of Commonwealth government sport funding went to the elite area. Hawke understood, like Fraser, that elite sport funding had strong electoral appeal. He also understood that commercialised sport like the Americas Cup and the Formula 1 Grand Prix, which Adelaide claimed in 1985, had the capacity to attract large audiences, and produce significant economic benefits.

By the end of the 1980s sport policy had broadened its base, and become an integral component of the Government economic and social policies. The ASC had quickly taken on a strong coordinating role, the AIS provided quality coaching and sport science advice to elite athletes, the STEP programme benefited many young athletes, and NSOs had come to rely on government funds to professionalise their operations through the sport development programme. Moreover, minority groups like women, the disabled, and aboriginals were singled out for special consideration, junior sport was supported through the Aussie sport programme, ASC support for the Australian Coaching Council continued, and a drugs-in-sport programme had been initiated.

At the same time, the Commonwealth Government began to frame its policies more strategically by linking them to the benefits they would deliver to the Australian community. In other words, policy should aim to reduce the nation's heath bill, contribute to economic growth and national development, promote national pride, develop community services, assist the pursuit of excellence, and expand Australia's international reputation and profile (Australian Sports Commission, 1986).

Structural adjustment

In 1989, the Hawke Government conducted a Parliamentary inquiry on sports funding and administration in response to the growing pressures that the professionalisation of sport was putting on those Olympic sports which provided international 'kudos', but which did not have a strong spectator or commercial base. The inquiry, which was convened by Stephen Martin, a member of parliament, resulted in two reports titled *Going for Gold* and *Can Sport be Bought?* respectively. The reports concluded that while the Commonwealth had an essential responsibility for funding the pursuit of excellence, there was also evidence that funding was uncoordinated and some of the AIS programmes were not sufficiently focused (Martin, 1989, 1990). The reports also noted that sustained excellence could only be achieved through an increase in Commonwealth Government assistance. As indicated previously, an AIS submission estimated that whereas the national governments of France and West Germany spent more than $6 a head on sport development, the Australian national government only spent AUS$2 a head (Bloomfield, 2003: 92). The Commonwealth Government consequently merged the ASC with the AIS, with the ASC becoming the core policy implementation body as well as the coordinator of all AIS programmes. This resulted in a more systematic and strategic approach to sport development. A number of initiatives were put in place, with the aim of more efficiently linking high-performance assistance and teams to schemes for producing greater community participation. Bloomfield's pyramid of sport participation was re-cast as a circle of sport structures and activities, as Figure 5.1 indicates.

Figure 5.1 highlights two consistent themes that ran through Commonwealth Government sport policy from Whitlam to Hawke. These themes were based on the proposition that elite sport development was linked to community sport development in a number of important ways. First, the more Australian athletes succeed on the international sports stage, the more likely young people will want to emulate these athletes. For example, if cyclists win gold medals at world

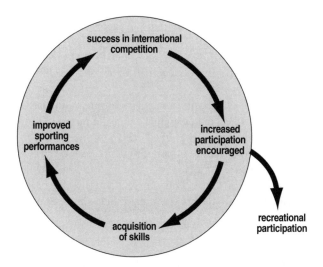

Figure 5.1 Participation and elite sport development connection.

championships and Olympic Games, then we would expect an increase in community cycle programmes and cycle club memberships. Second, the greater the pool of young athletes and players, the greater the likelihood that potential world champions will be discovered. For example, as the pool of young cyclists competing in club activities increase, we would expect more high-performance cyclists to emerge from this larger pool. However, as we have hinted in earlier sections of the book, these themes were largely unproven, but instead rested on a foundation of beliefs about the way sport systems operated.

Stepping up

Despite the lack of supporting evidence, these claims underpinned subsequent sport policy. Graham Richardson, the minister for sport, made a number of policy adjustments around these themes in 1989, which culminated in the *Next Step* policy, which ran until 1992. The *Next Step* policy entrenched sport as a major policy field for the Commonwealth Government since it not only positioned the ASC as the pivotal organisation for implementing a national sport policy, but also provided for additional funding to national sport organisations for both elite and community sport development. In addition, it successfully extended Whitlam's capital grant scheme to regional and local sport organisations. In short, the *Next Step* policy was the 'largest funding announcement that had taken place in the history of Australian sport' (Bloomfield, 2003: 93).

Acting local

First, the community recreation and sport facility programme was broadened, with just over $6 million being allocated for 1989–90. In praising the programme, Senator Richardson noted that it provided 'essential facilities at grassroots level', encouraged a healthier lifestyle, and 'enabled many projects to proceed which otherwise would have had to wait years' (*Media Release*, 6 December 1989). More than 150 grants were made in 1989, ranging from $1,000 for the Corowa Skateboard Club and $10,000 to the Birchip Netball Club, to $150,000 for the Blacktown City Soccer Club.

The main developments in the community participation programme area were the introduction of a Youth Sports Program, which aimed to get more young people into sport, and a campaign by the recently formed ASC's Women's Sport Unit to target adolescent girls. In addition, the Aussie Sport programme was broadened with the adoption of an Aussie Able scheme to support disabled athletes, a sport participation programme that focused on training activities for volunteer management was established, and aboriginal sport assistance was extended.

Thinking global

While the *Next Step* policy provided a much-needed boost to participation and community sport, most of the funds still went to the elite and high-performance area. The *Going for Gold* report revealed that Olympic athletes who competed at Seoul in 1988 were not happy with the funding arrangement for elite sport, and while they were well supported in the lead up to Games competition, had to fend for themselves for some time afterwards. In short, they were 'disillusioned and frustrated', and in their quest for excellence did not consider they were receiving sufficient support (Martin, 1989: 2). Senator Richardson aimed to remedy this problem by allocating AUS$7 million to NSOs for the preparation of athletes for the 1992 Olympic Games at Barcelona. According to Richardson, the money would allow for better planning of sport programmes, and allow more athletes to 'compete overseas and attend international events in Australia' (*Media Release*, 13 December 1989). An additional AUS$4.3 million was allocated for the year 1990, ranging from AUS$10,000 for women's volleyball to AUS$246,000 for cycling.

At the same time, AUS$3.5 million was allocated to the 1991 World Swimming Championships in Perth, a National Sport Research Centre was established in Canberra, the National Sports Information Centre was expanded, the AIS residential programme was broadened, and an Oceania Olympic Training Centre was put in place. Finally, additional funds were given to national sport organisations for management improvement, coach education, sport science, and drug education and control. In all, AUS$50 million was allocated to sport which represented a 40 per cent increase over 1988–89.

The drug problem

The drug abuse issue was very sensitive at this time, and there was growing concern that it was out of control. Drugs had become an international problem, and the International Olympic Committee had begun to strengthen its anti-doping policy. Moreover, the credibility of track and field was undermined when Ben Johnson was found to have taken anabolic steroids, and stripped of his 1988 Olympics gold medal in the 100 metres sprint. Concurrently, rumours were circulating that the AIS was being used as a distribution centre for performance enhancing drugs. This was partly confirmed by a nationwide broadcast of the Four Corners current affairs programme in November 1987, in which it was found that a number of AIS athletes had taken drugs (Houlihan, 1997). In response to increasing pressure from the wider Australian community, an inquiry was established under the chair of Senator John Black (Black, 1989, 1990). The Black Committee argued for greater drug regulation, and the Commonwealth Government subsequently established the Australian Sport Drug Agency (ASDA) in 1990. ASDA was basically set up to eliminate drug use in sport. This draconian, but visionary decision was defended on the basis that it would 'enhance the well being of individuals' and protect the 'value of sport to society' (Australian Sports Commission, 2001b: 6). ASDA was given the authority to drug-test athletes on a year-round basis, conduct research into drug use and detection, run drug education programmes, and provide government with policy advice on drugs-in-sport issues.

Great leap forward

The Hawke Government was returned for a record fourth term in 1990, and Senator Ros Kelly replaced Graham Richardson as the Minister for the Arts, Sports, the Environment, Tourism and Territories. Senator Kelly was instrumental in getting ASDA established, and strengthened the Government drug policy by requiring that all NSOs receiving Commonwealth funds develop a drug policy and provide a copy to ASDA. In the following year she presided over a quantum leap in Commonwealth Government sport policy since she not only substantially increased funding levels, but also broadened the funding base. The ASC received AUS$59 million to support its elite development, coaching, sport management improvement, and participation programmes, the Barcelona Olympic team got AUS$4 million and ASDA was allocated just under AUS$3 million. Another AUS$11 million was allocated to the Community Recreation and Sport Facility Program, water-safety organisation received just under AUS$2 million, while an array of recreation and fitness programmes were given another $1 million. The total sport budget for 1991–92 of AUS$77 million constituted a 55 per cent increase over 1989–90.

Paying the price for Olympic success

While a lot of rhetoric was used to play up the community and participation sport area, most of the Commonwealth Government funding during the early 1990s continued to go to the elite sport area in general, and Olympic sport activities in particular. The *Going for Gold* and *Can Sport be Bought?* reports were used to justify more, not less spending on elite sport. However, this generous sport policy came at a cost, since the funds were increasingly linked to the meeting of certain minimum conditions. For example, in return for getting additional government funds, NSOs were required to submit development plans that identified the scale of their management systems, development targets, and performance indicators. They were required to produce a clear and succinct vision for their sports, and design goals to make it happen. In short, they were increasingly accountable for how they spent their government-sourced money. The gold medal drive also marginalised community sport, which could only secure AUS$7 million or 12 per cent of total government funding in 1990.

AIS ten years later

The Australian Institute of Sport celebrated its tenth anniversary in 1991. In many respects the AIS had done well. It had become the centre for high-performance sport elite athlete development in 17 sports, while at the same time decentralising its residential programme around the nation. Hockey resided in Perth, Brisbane had squash, diving and rugby union, Adelaide had cricket and cycling, and the Gold Coast had canoeing. The national spread of AIS residential programmes and training centres is illustrated in Figure 5.2.

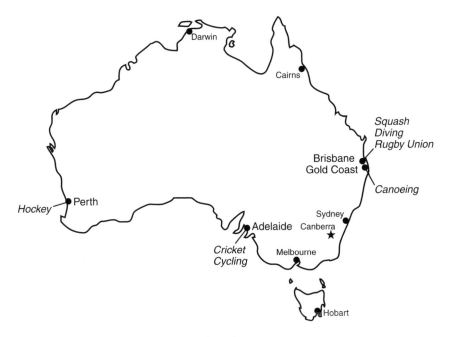

Figure 5.2 AIS residential programmes (1991).

The integration of the AIS into the ASC meant that it had to operate more strategically. As a result, its services were expanded to include not just its residential programmes, but also the ASC's elite training programmes for NSOs, intensive training and sport science support, coach education, and life skills courses for athletes. On the other hand, the AIS was criticised for focusing on a limited number of sports, and not getting a great return on its investment. The 1984 Los Angeles and 1988 Seoul Olympics produced a total of only seven gold medals, well below the number at Munich in 1972. Rob deCastella, the AIS director at the time, argued that medals should not be its sole performance indicator, but could not immediately think of a concrete alternative (*Sport Report*, Autumn, 1991: 4).

The state's response

While the AIS was broadening its base during the 1980s, the state governments were also developing programmes for elite athletes. With the establishment of sport academies in Victoria and Queensland in 1990 and 1991 respectively, every state now had centres for high-performance sport. This development had the potential to produce wasteful duplication, but was avoided in part by the state academies using university sport science facilities and seconding staff from the AIS. It also coincided with the announcement of the Commonwealth

Government's New Federalism policy that aimed to secure a more effective working relationship between the Commonwealth and the states. The Sport and Recreation Ministers Council, which had been established by the Whitlam Government to provide a forum for State and Commonwealth Ministers of Sport, was used to strengthen links between the AIS and state academies. Ros Kelly, the Commonwealth minister, noted that it was particularly important to have a 'nationally coordinated program of elite assistance' (*Sport Report*, Winter 1991: 4).

Beyond the next step

The *Next Step* policy was followed by the *Maintain the Momentum* policy, which was scheduled to run from 1992 to 1996, with an allocation of just under $290 million, or around $73 million a year on average for four years. Again the emphasis was on elite athlete development, sport science research, and coaching support, but other issues were also on the agenda. Under this policy the drug control programme was extended with the support of ASDA, professional training modules were developed for national sport organisation's staff, a volunteer improvement programme was established, and school sport was given greater attention. Sports Minister Kelly made the increasingly familiar comment that while 'we are looking after our top athletes properly' we should also 'address the base of sport as well' (*Sport Report*, Spring 1992: 3).

Re-visiting sport education

While elite and international sport was the central focus during the early 1990s, there was also growing concern about the declining status of sport in schools. In 1992, the Commonwealth government conducted a parliamentary review of Physical Education. The report, which was convened by Senator Rosemary Crowley, and titled *Physical and Sport Education*, found that there had been a significant decline in the content and quality of physical education and sport in Australian schools. The main causes of this decline were the fall in the number of specialist physical education teachers, the squeezing out of physical education from the core curriculum, and the lack of a clearly defined policy or consensus on the value of physical education to school students (Crowley, 1992). The report concluded that a number of measures should be undertaken to increase student participation in physical education and sport programmes in schools. It was recommended that a national physical education curriculum be designed, more specialist physical education teachers be recruited, stronger links be developed between schools and local sport clubs, and greater emphasis be put on skill development and less on competition. The report also warned that while Aussie Sports programmes complemented physical education activities, they should not be used to replace structured physical education classes. The Crowley Report, as it came to be known, provided a strong impetus for the further expansion of physical activity programmes in schools. In practice, though, the easy-to-organise

Aussie Sports programmes squeezed out many of the traditional physical education activities that centred on motor skill improvement, character building, and moral development (Houlihan, 1997).

Tobacco sponsorship

As the 1990s unfolded, there was also a growing concern about the amount of sport sponsorship funded by tobacco companies. The Commonwealth Government had effectively banned all tobacco advertisements on radio and TV in 1976 by amending the *Broadcasting and Television Act*. A further amendment in 1990 made it illegal to advertise tobacco products in newspapers and magazines. The tobacco companies responded to these restrictions by switching their promotional budgets into sport sponsorship. Phillip Morris, Rothmans, and WD & HO Wills subsequently poured millions of dollars into sport promotion by linking the major brands to major sport events. Rothmans sponsored motor racing, Marlboro sponsored the Australian Open Tennis Championships, Escort sponsored the Victorian Football league, Winfield sponsored Australian Rugby League (ARL), while Benson and Hedges secured the marketing rights for international cricket played in Australia. Wills also sponsored a number of major golf tournaments. Many sporting bodies did not see a problem with tobacco sponsorship, mainly because they were very generously funded by the companies. However every health agency in Australia argued that tobacco products were undermining the health of Australian society. In short, cigarettes were killing people by contributing to lung cancer and coronary heart disease. In 1992 Sport Minister Kelly introduced the Commonwealth Tobacco Advertising Prohibition Act. It not only prohibited all conventional tobacco-related advertising, but also made it illegal to use sponsorship as a promotional tool. However, agreements and contracts that had been negotiated previously were allowed to run their course. In the case of international agreements in motor sports, they sometimes ran into 2000 and beyond.

In summary the period between 1989 and 1993 was a turning point in Australian sport development (Table 5.2). The Hawke Government stepped up its support for elite athlete development, and Senators Richardson and Kelly committed themselves to strengthening the sport system in general, and NSOs in particular. Prime Minister Hawke, who was replaced by Paul Keating in 1991, was acutely aware of the need to professionalise and commercialise sport in order to make it internationally competitive. He also saw the political kudos that could be milked from international sporting success, particularly the Olympics. Although Keating, unlike Hawke, had no passion for sport, he was quick to reap the political benefits from Australia's athletic successes at the 1992 Barcelona Olympic Games. While the Hawke Government took a firm stand on drugs in sport, it was less successful in stopping sport being squeezed out of the school curricula.

Although the Hawke/Keating Governments claimed the economy in general had to be de-regulated and privatised to make it more internationally competitive,

Table 5.2 Commonwealth Government funding to sport: 1989–93

Year	Total funding (AUS$ million)	Major developments and events
1989–90	50	ASC/AIS merger complete; Martin Inquiry into sport funding and administration; *Next Step* policy commences
1990–91	68	Black Inquiry into drugs completed, and ASDA established Commonwealth Games in Auckland
1991–92	77	Crowley inquiry into sport education Tobacco Advertising Prohibition Act passed
1992–93	83	Barcelona Olympic Games *Maintain the Momentum* policy commences

Source: Australian Sports Commission (1986, 1990).

they effectively did the opposite with sport. The ASC in effect became a planning and regulatory agency for sport by setting performance guidelines and operational parameters in return for ongoing funding and support of NSOs. Through its control of the AIS it was also able to set the agenda for high-performance sport in the state sport academies. The ASC also favoured a few sports over the majority, and this angered the less-favoured sports. While 92 NSOs were funded by the ASC, 40 of them secured 90 per cent of funds. In other words, the remaining 58 per cent of sport bodies got only 10 per cent of the funds. In general, though, most NSOs had never had it so good when the 1992–93 budget allocated AUS$83 million to sport development.

The Olympic city

The *Maintain the Momentum* policy was interrupted in 1993 when Sydney was granted the right to host the 2000 Olympic Games. It was quickly complemented by the *Olympic Athlete Program* (OAP), which provided an additional AUS$135 million over the six years leading up to 2000, AUS$20 million of which was allocated to 1994–95 (Australian Sports Commission, 1994). The ASC dovetailed this programme into the AOC's Gold Medal Plan, which used a self-funded AUS$80 million high-performance pool to prepare athletes for the Olympics.

The OAP came not only with additional funding, but also with a number of goals and targets for the Sydney Olympics. First, it required appropriate funds to go to the preparation of disabled athletes to ensure a good outcome at the Paralympics, which followed on from the more prestigious able-bodied event. Second, it aimed to produce 650 athletes who were eligible to compete at the Games by meeting the qualifying standards. Finally, it wanted Australian athletes to win at least 60 medals. As it turned out, the medal target was nearly met when 58 medals were snared.

The OAP also accentuated the funding differential between Olympic and non-Olympic sports. Senator John Faulkner, the newly appointed minister of sport, argued that non-Olympic sports would not be disadvantaged, but this was clearly not the case. In addition, community sport had also been squeezed as a result of the decision to discontinue the Community, Recreation and Sport Facility Program beyond 1995.

Structural fine tuning

In 1995 the ASC, being mindful of the challenges presented by the Sydney 2000 Games, reviewed its structure and programs (Australian Sports Commission, 1996). In order to make sure it could properly prepare athletes for the Sydney Games, it restructured its policies around three activities. The first activity was elite sport and AIS services, which focused on high-performance training, sport science support, and coach education. The second activity was sport development and policy, which covered management support to NSOs, coach and athlete development, junior sport development, community sport, and overall participation. The third activity embraced business services which included revenue raising, merchandising, and the export of sport expertise to developing sport nations.

Player welfare issues

Another innovative initiative at this time was the introduction of the Athlete Career and Education (ACE) programme. The ACE programme was introduced in response to concerns that many young elite athletes had no professional or occupational skills beyond their sporting ability. It was agreed that AIS scholarship holders in particular should be given a more balanced educational experience. A pilot programme was introduced in 1995, which included training modules in public speaking, resume writing, interview skills, and media relations (Australian Sports Commission, 1996).

Access and participation

While most of the ASC's resources were directed to the Sydney Games and elite athletes, the needs of special groups were also addressed. In 1994 and 1995 a number of programmes were established to increase overall levels of sport participation. A junior sport policy was announced which centred on modified games, basic skill development programmes for children, coach and instructor education, and the provision of safe playing environments. The plight of aboriginals was also noted, and the ASC took responsibility for a new Indigenous Sport Program (ISP) which aimed to broaden sporting opportunities for aboriginal communities, particularly those in remote regions (Australian Sports Commission, 1996).

Anti-siphoning issues

The introduction of pay television in the early 1990s also posed a number of issues for the Commonwealth Government to address, some of which were sport related. One of the most pressing issues involved the implications of pay TV networks securing the rights to broadcast major sport events. The Commonwealth Government believed that it would not be in the public interest if pay TV stations could buy the broadcast rights to sport events of national significance, and consequently deny the majority of Australian TV viewers the ability to watch the event through the free-to-air stations. Whereas free-to-air stations could provide a nationwide service to more than 90 per cent of the viewing audience, the spread of pay TV was no more than 10–15 per cent. In 1994, the Commonwealth devised a set of rules that went under the name of 'anti-siphoning provisions'. The rules aimed to prevent pay TV stations from stealing, or siphoning sport events of national significance from free-to-air stations. The *Broadcasting Services Act* of 1992 was amended to include a list of sport events for which pay TV stations could not obtain exclusive rights. In other words, they could obtain the rights to only jointly televise the events. Events on the anti-siphoning list included the Melbourne (horse racing) Cup, the entire AFL and ARL competitions, the ARL State of Origin series, all international rugby union matches involving the Australian team, all international cricket matches involving the Australian team, the final of the National Soccer League, the World Cup in soccer, the World Cup in rugby union, all grand slam tennis tournaments, all international netball matches involving Australia, and an assortment of golf tournaments and international motor racing events. The appropriate Minister had the power to add or subtract from the list, and over the next few years a number of changes were made to what was a massive over-kill. The net effect, though, was to ensure that free-to-air stations had first choice on what sport events to cover. This has continued to the present, with ongoing adjustment to the anti-siphoning list.

Sport inquiries

The mid-1990s was also a busy time for sorting out a few entrenched problems in soccer and gymnastics. Soccer has played an important role in Australian sport development, and has been a strong source of ethnic identification and community building. On the other hand, it has also been chronically under-managed, and its national league has gone through many structural changes. In 1995, in response to claims of financial irregularities in the operation of national league clubs, the Senate convened a committee of inquiry chaired by the former Justice Stewart. Two reports were tabled which recommended that soccer re-structure its operations, and develop a better process for dealing with the recruitment of young Australian players by professional teams in Europe. The problem in gymnastics was different but no less serious. Around the same time, the Minister for Sport was advised of allegations that elite gymnasts at the AIS had been mistreated by the coaching staff. Hayden Opie, a leading sport lawyer, completed the inquiry and tabled a report later in the year. He found that the allegations could not be sustained, and concluded that the AIS programme provided 'a safe training environment' and a 'caring and secure residential arrangement' (Australian Sports Commission, 1996: 17). Both of these reports were not only important for resolving two crisis incidents, but also provided clear recommendations for the effective management of sport organisations.

The Keating and Kelly vanishing act

During the early part of 1996 the Paul Keating Labour Government was replaced by the John Howard Liberal Government. The main thrust of Keating's sport policy was retained by Howard, although as indicated above, the Community, Recreation and Sport Facility Program developed by the Hawke Government was discontinued. Some irregularities had been discovered in the decision-making processes, Sport Minister Ros Kelly admitted the allocation of grants had not been systematically reviewed, and there was evidence that grants were skewed in favour of marginal seats (House of Representatives Standing Committee on Environment Recreation and the Arts, 1997). Kelly stepped down as the Sport Minister, and the facilities programme became a political dead weight.

Record funding levels

As Table 5.3 indicates, Commonwealth Government funding of sport reached new heights during the mid-1990s. Despite the concern over sport in schools, levels of sport participation, and continued funding of Aussie Sports and Aussie Able, the focus was clearly on high-performance sport and the preparation of Australian elite athletes for the Sydney 2000 Olympics. Just under 80 per cent of the AUS$89 million allocation to NSOs in 1994 was for high performance and elite sport (*Sport Report*, Winter 1994: 7). Moreover, when the AOC's Gold Medal Plan was added on, a number of NSOs with Olympic medal pretensions

Table 5.3 Commonwealth Government funding to sport: 1993–96

Year	Total funding (AUS$ million)	Major developments and events
1993–94	89	Sydney wins 2000 Olympics bid OAP commences
1994–95	159*	Stewart inquiry into soccer Commonwealth Games in Victoria
1995–96	140*	Opie inquiry into gymnastics

* includes $50 million capital grant to Sydney Olympics

Source: Australian Sports Commission (1996, 2001a).

found themselves flush with funds. But again there were significant differences between sports. Whereas each of athletics, cycling, rowing, and swimming had allocations in excess of AUS$3million, archery, badminton, boxing, judo, synchronised swimming, table tennis, triathlon and wrestling could only secure AUS$300,000–500,000 each (*Sport Report*, Autumn, 1995: 14).

The 1993–96 period saw a continual strengthening of Commonwealth Government influence over the structure and direction of Australian sport. The government preference for economic rationalism and managerialism was clearly evident in the restructuring of the Sports Commission, and the signal to sporting bodies that funding for elite athlete development was contingent upon improving management systems, and delivering medals and trophies. The OAP was strongly performance oriented, with funding 'geared entirely' to athletic success and medal tallies (Australian Sports Commission, 1999b: 17). At the same time, the euphoria surrounding Sydney's winning bid to host the 2000 Olympic Games provided the ideal climate to increase Commonwealth Government funding to record levels. In 1994, the ASC received over AUS$89 million for its sport development and Olympic athlete preparation programmes, the ASDA was allocated AUS$3 million, the Community, Cultural, Recreation and Sport Facility Program was allocated AUS$14 million, while the Commonwealth contributed AUS$50 million to facility construction at the Homebush Olympic site. When the water-safety grant was added, the total sport budget for 1994–95 was AUS$159 million. This was the all-time high point of Commonwealth Government sport funding (*Sport Report*, Winter, 1994: 13).

However, the Government was also aware of criticism that its sport policy was severely biased in favour of Olympic athletes. The Community, Recreation and Sport Facility Program, ISP and Junior Sport Policy were a belated acknowledgment that the ASC also had a legislative commitment to make sport activities accessible to the whole of society. Finally, the introduction of anti-syphoning legislation illustrated the growing importance of the sport-media, and how sport had become more commercialised, professionalised, and complex, and the consequent need for government to monitor these developments to ensure full community access to major sport events.

Concluding comments

While community sport development had been frequently marginalised, the Commonwealth Government policy on elite sport development expanded rapidly and gained widespread electoral support. Australians valued sporting success, and used it to confirm their sense of national identity and pride in one's nation. In an increasingly globalised world, sport was the perfect vehicle for Australians to demonstrate its global significance and international status. Significant aspects of sport policy were framed with this nation-building process in mind, and the success of the policies were primarily, if crudely, measured by the number of world rankings and championships, and medals won in international mega events like the Olympic and Commonwealth Games. If the number of medals won at the Olympic Games are used to measure the performance of the Commonwealth Government sport policy between 1983 and 1996 then it can only be rated as an outstanding success. Whereas Australian athletes won only 9 medals at Moscow in 1980, the tally increased to 14 at Seoul in 1988, 27 at Barcelona in 1992, and 41 at Atlanta in 1996.

6 Integration: sport policy 1996–2003

The Howard victory

In 1996 the Liberal Party led by John Howard regained government after 13 years in the political wilderness. During that time sport had been transformed from a mainly dispersed recreational activity managed by volunteer officials and underpinned by the amateur ideal, into a coordinated, commercialised, and often professionally managed system of highly structured and competitive leisure activities. Moreover, the Commonwealth Government had taken on a national leadership role, and set the agenda for sport development. The Keating Government's election policy on sport, which was titled *Sporting Partnerships*, documented many of its achievements as well as its future programme. *Sporting Partnerships* modestly claimed that its support for athletes and sporting organisations over 13 years had 'delivered great benefits to the country', produced more participants than ever before and enabled Australian athletes to 'enjoy great international success' (Australian Labor Party, 1996: 3). Its election policy statement also highlighted the recent establishment of the National Elite Sports Council, comprising representatives from the AIS and state sport institutes and academies. It was established to coordinate elite sport activities across the nation, and link Commonwealth Government funding to state-sponsored programmes. To this end more than AUS$20 million was paid directly to state academies to assist in the preparation of athletes for the Sydney Games. The Keating Government's support for elite sport was vindicated by outstanding performances at the 1995 World Cycling Championships and 1996 Atlanta Olympic Games. *Sporting Partnerships* also confirmed the Labor party's commitment to nationwide assistance that gave special recognition to community level sport, women as well as men, people with disabilities, the indigenous, and both young and older people.

The Liberal Party's sport policy was entitled *Encouraging Players, Developing Champions*, and included the usual comments about 'striking a balance between elite achievers and grass roots participation' (Liberal Party, 1996: 3). The electoral importance of both Olympic success and the opportunity for participation was not lost on the Liberal party, and it confirmed its commitment to the Sydney Olympics, and agreed to maintain funding levels to NSOs and the AIS. It also made a commitment to community sport by promising to extend the Aussie

Sports program, increase assistance to aboriginals and Torres Strait islanders, consolidate the promotion of women's sport, and, through state ministries of sport, boost links between school sports, sporting clubs, local government and the community.

Active Australia

The final policy in the Liberal Party's election plank bore a striking resemblance to a 1995 government paper on the future development of community participation in sport. A working document titled *Active Australia: A National Participation Framework* was produced by a cross-portfolio working group, and circulated to major stakeholders for comment. Its grand vision was to have all Australians actively involved in sport, community recreation, fitness and/or outdoor education. The proposal fitted neatly into Liberal Party policy, and the Active Australia programme went ahead. The thrust of the programme was for the ASC to integrate sport, recreation and health strategies of the Commonwealth Government, and with the support of the Industry Science and Resources, and Health Departments, ensure effective delivery of the programmes through close liaison with state government agencies and community groups. Importantly, the input of the Health Department confirmed the relationship between health and physical activity. Research findings were used to demonstrate that an increase in physical activity would produce significant cost savings within the health sector. In other words, additional resources for sport development could be justified on the grounds that a significant health benefit would follow.

In late 1996, *Active Australia: A National Participation Framework* was launched. It was heralded as 'the first commitment by key stakeholders in the sport, recreation and health sectors to develop a strategic and cooperative approach to encourage participation in physical activity by all'. The vision of the Active Australia campaign was to have all Australians 'actively involved in sport, community recreation, fitness, outdoor recreation and other physical activities' (Australian Sports Commission, 1997: 5). Three goals were considered critical to the realisation of this vision: to increase and enhance lifelong participation; to realise the social health and economic benefits of participation; and to develop quality infrastructure, opportunities, and services to support participation.

Importantly, Active Australia was not an isolated initiative as many government programmes had previously been, but a cooperative attempt across a number of government departments to develop a common approach that aimed to increase participation in sport, community recreation, fitness, outdoor recreation and leisure. At the core of the Active Australia programme was the acknowledgment that participation in some form of physical activity would make Australians both healthier and happier.

The Active Australia programme was developed in consultation with the major industry sectors of sport, community recreation, fitness, outdoor recreation, health, and physical and outdoor education. As such, it recognised that sport and recreation participation opportunities were supported and delivered by a diverse range of providers, including state and local government, the private sector, voluntary community sporting groups, health promotion agencies, and schools.

At a practical level, Active Australia was a three-tiered program that provided for as many sporting, recreational and fitness opportunities as possible, in order to maximise both access and equity. The Active Australia framework consisted of three networks: Schools, Local Government organisations and approved Providers.

The Schools Network was committed to the provision of sport and physical activity that was fun, safe, challenging, rewarding and well managed, that had a focus on learning, and was linked to the local community. The Local Government Network recognised that local councils play a key role in the development and delivery of sport and recreation. Since they were often engaged in the planning of programmes and facilities for both organised and informal activity, local councils were in a perfect position to facilitate the linking of schools, clubs and organisations. Lastly, the Provider Network aimed to improve the standard and quality of sport, recreation and fitness clubs and organisations. These clubs and organisations had the opportunity to become a registered Active Australia Provider by adhering to the model, and establishing a working framework and quality standard. A Provider could then display the Active Australia logo, and link in with the other two networks that formed part of the Active Australia programme.

Social development

In 1997 the Minister for Sport established a sport injury and prevention task-force, which addressed a variety of safety and risk management issues in sport. The taskforce concluded that a much stronger injury prevention and safety management programme was needed. A series of guidelines were designed, and were implemented through a publication entitled *Sports-Safe Australia: A National Sport Safety Framework*. Resource packs were subsequently produced, and were disseminated to sport associations and clubs throughout Australia in collaboration with Sport Medicine Australia, the umbrella organisation for sport medicine professionals (Australian Sports Commission, 1998a).

A further initiative was taken at this time in response to growing concerns about the increasing incidence of anti-social behaviour in sporting clubs throughout Australia. Not only were there signs that some sporting associations and clubs had marginalised minority groups like aborigines, non-English speaking migrants, and the elderly, but there were also an increasing number of complaints about unfair discrimination and harassment. As a result, the Minister for Sport requested the Australian Sports Commission to design a number of harassment-free sport strategies that addressed the problems of homophobia, sexual abuse, and child protection in sport. Pilot education programmes were developed with NSOs, a number of harassment officers were trained, and a variety of educational and awareness packages were produced. At the same time, the Women in Sport Unit developed a series of handbooks that contained strategies for recruiting women and girls as coaches and officials (Australian Sports Commission, 1998a).

Community sport facilities

While the social development aspects of sport policy had strong support, a proposal to resurrect the Labor Party's community, cultural, recreational and sporting facilities programme did not. In 1997 the House of Representatives Standing Committee on Environment, Recreation and the Arts examined the possibility of designing a dedicated programme to fund sporting and recreational infrastructure. The Standing Committee produced a report entitled *Rethinking the Funding of Community Sporting and Recreational Facilities: A Sporting Chance*, which contained a detailed history of Commonwealth Government assistance to sport facility construction, a critical analysis of the current situation, and recommendations for future government action. While the Committee found that there was large unmet demand for sporting and recreational facilities, it did not think a grants programme was the best way of responding to this demand. The Committee agreed there was a case for directly funding disadvantaged communities, but did not think it should apply to all new community sport facility extensions. For these proposals, the Committee recommended the low cost strategy of 'assisting providers to make better use of existing facilities' (House of Representatives Standing Committee on Environment Recreation and the Arts, 1997: xv). The Committee went on to note that while government funding of sporting facilities contributed to improvements in sport performance, enabled greater participation in competitive sport, brought economic gains, and 'fostered community bonds', they were 'not a prerequisite for mass participation in physical activity' (House of Representatives Standing Committee on Environment Recreation and the Arts, 1997: 28).

Sport as industry

At the same time as it was developing its anti-harassment policies the Commonwealth Government was also formulating a detailed policy that focused on the economic benefits that sport could generate. A significant initiative took place in 2000, when the minister of sport, Jackie Kelly, launched the *Game Plan 2006* policy (Department of Industry Science and Resources, 2000a). *Game Plan* used Australian Sport International (ASI) as the foundation to generate more export income by assisting the overseas operations of coaches, sport scientists, sport medicine providers, sport goods suppliers, event management companies, and sport education and training providers (Department of Industry Science and Resources, 2000a). This policy was in part aimed at getting the AIS to become more self-sufficient.

The second initiative involved a comprehensive statement that linked sport to tourism. This statement culminated in the formulation of a *National Sport Tourism Strategy* in 2000 by the Department of Industry, Science and Resources. The major theme threading its way through the strategy was that Australia's strong international sporting image and major sport events, was a major motivating factor in bringing international visitors to Australia. In short, high-performance sport was seen to be a major tourism drawcard (Department of Industry Science and Resources, 2000b).

In general, the Howard Government consolidated the policy initiatives undertaken by the Hawke and Keating Governments while watching over a fall in funding. First, the Commonwealth Government commitment to the Sydney 2000 Olympics continued right up the Games. Second, it provided continuing support for NSOs and their pivotal role in providing management infrastructure and strategic leadership. Finally, it expressed a growing concern about community participation and the need to develop programmes aimed at increasing levels of physical activity. The funding arrangement for sport during this period is listed in Table 6.1.

In summary, notwithstanding a fall in funding levels, the period 1996–2000 featured a strong drive to not only maintain elite sport support, but to also strengthen club sport and community participation. There was a growing concern that despite Australia's many international successes, and strong lead-in to Olympic Games, the nation was becoming less fit and less active. In other words, the anticipated participation flow on from young people wanting to model elite performers did not eventuate, and the accompanying social benefits were therefore unrealised.

The Active Australia programme aimed to remedy this problem, and was successful in increasing community awareness about the need to increase participation. The recognition rate of the AA logo or brand mark increased from 18 per cent in 1998 to 23 per cent in 2000, while just over 2,000 clubs and organisations, another 2,100 schools, and 20 per cent of all local government councils were members of the AA network. On the other hand, over the same period the participation rate for adults fell from 59 to 55 per cent (Australian Bureau of Statistics, 1999a). Despite a solid foundation of support, AA was

Table 6.1 Commonwealth Government funding to sport: 1996–2001

Year	Funding (AUS$ million)	Major developments and events
1996–97	146*	Active Australia Network introduced Atlanta Olympic Games
1997–98	99	'A Sporting Chance' recommendations on community sport facilities released
1998–99	99	Kuala Lumpur Commonwealth Games
1999–2000	108	Oakley inquiry into sport and recreation concludes
2000–2001	112	Sydney Olympic Games

* includes $50 million capital grant to Sydney Olympics

Source: Australian Sports Commission (2001a).

unable to sustain the level of community participation, let alone increase it. This was a disappointing policy outcome.

The Active Australia strategy was also complemented by programmes to enhance fairness and equity in sport associations and clubs. For the first time the Commonwealth Government, through the Sports Commission, aimed to systematically address dysfunctional aspects of sport organisations.

The third policy initiative during the first four years of the Howard Government was to maximise the economic benefits from sport by exporting our expertise and attracting more sport tourists. Sport was consequently more than a pastime, a crucial contributor to the nation's social capital, and a major source of national pride and self-esteem. As far as the Commonwealth Government was concerned, sport had also become an important industry in its own right, and by contributing economic benefits to the nation, justified government assistance. The Sydney Olympic Games were very costly. It drained the resources of the New South Wales State Government, dislocated the everyday lives of many Sydney residents, and relieved the Commonwealth Government of around $150 million, but also impacted positively on the Australian community. It attracted thousands of overseas tourists, confirmed Australia's reputation for staging high quality sport events, and enabled all Australians to bask in the reflected glory of Australia's outstanding athletic achievements.

The fourth policy initiative aimed to improve the information management systems of NSOs. To this end, SportNet, a Web-based registration and administration software tool for sporting bodies was put in place. It was primarily designed to assist sporting organisations in communicating with and managing their constituents. The ASC and Telstra, Australia's largest telecommunication company, collaborated to sanction SportNet as an aid to both grass-roots clubs and NSOs. This support was enhanced with an attractive rate that was designed to encourage NSOs and their constituents to take up the service. Hockey Australia was one NSO to become involved.

SportNet was designed to bolster clubs, associations and national governing bodies by providing them with online membership databases, email access, club websites, member access to records via the Web, online forums and communities, competition updates and club affiliation payments. In principle, SportNet enabled a club to enter member data online. This information would also be immediately accessible by state and national bodies as determined by the security arrangements in place. SportNet would therefore, in conjunction with club websites and email facilities, help national and state governing bodies to identify, profile, and target participants anywhere in the country.

There was little doubt that a database management tool such as SportNet could be enormously advantageous to the effective management and marketing of a sport. However, in the case of Hockey Australia, the implementation of the system did not yield the outcomes for which they had hoped. Specifically, a number of the technical features of the product were unreliable. This exacerbated the problem of lack of uptake and commitment from states, associations, and clubs. As a result, nearly three years after SportNet's introduction, Hockey

Australia sought to conduct a reappraisal of the database management needs of the organisation and its state and association stakeholders. Importantly, Hockey Australia recognised that the capacity for database and relationship marketing remained critical to their future activities. However, it was also sensitive to the political implications of making a second attempt to introduce a national database given the fact that several states were employing the SportNet system in part, while others had shown little commitment to changing from their own spreadsheet-based systems. The SportNet programme is currently under review by the Australian Sports Commission.

Olympic review: balancing the scorecard

In the aftermath of a highly successful Sydney 2000 Olympics, the Commonwealth Government, through the Department of Communication, Information Technology and the Arts, and Sport Minister Jackie Kelly, announced a new sport policy. The Government recognised the enormous public euphoria and national pride that followed from the Games, and consequently saw the value in continuing to support elite athlete development. In this context, it also noted the pivotal role played by not just the ASC and AIS, but also national sport associations and governing bodies. At the same time, the Government was committed to increasing the participation rate of Australians. Despite the relative success of the Aussie Sports and the Active Australia programmes, the sport participation rate only marginally increased between 1985 and 2001. There were still just over 45 per cent of adults who did not engage in any form of sport or physical activity (Australian Bureau of Statistics, 1999a).

A further catalyst for achieving a better balance between high-performance support and grass-roots participation programmes was the 1999 report on national sport policy produced by the Sport 2000 Task Force. The report was titled *Shaping Up: A Review of Commonwealth Involvement in Sport and Recreation in Australia*, and was chaired by Ross Oakley, a former chief executive officer of the AFL. The Sport 2000 Task Force recommended that there be a major change in government priorities and that more resources be put into participation activities (Oakley, 1999). For most of the 1980s and 1990s only 10–15 per cent of total Commonwealth Government spending was allocated to community sport and participation programs (Adair and Vamplew, 1997; Houlihan, 1997; McKay, 1986; Oakley, 1999). Although state and local governments had traditionally focused their funding on community sport, the Task Force believed that not withstanding Aussie Sports and Active Australia programmes there was a need for greater national leadership in this area.

An integrated approach to policy

As a result, four inter-connected policy goals were consolidated under the policy name of *Backing Australia's Sporting Ability: A More Active Australia* (BASA). Sports Minister Kelly launched the policy in early 2001. The first policy goal ensured that athletes, including those with disabilities, could continue to success-fully compete at international level. This involved coach education programmes, athlete welfare and training, and sport science support. The ASC continued to be the focal point for elite athlete support through managing the operations of the AIS and its 26 residential sports, and allocating high-performance funds to NSOs. At the same time, the ASC would coordinate the elite sport activities in the satellite centres, and link with the state sport academies. The primary aim was to maintain Australia's high-performance standards at Commonwealth and Olympic Games (Commonwealth of Australia, 2001).

The second policy goal aimed to enhance sport management structures and practices so that NSOs could deliver a range of quality sport services. To this end, NSOs were encouraged to secure additional revenue from non-government sources, use the Australian Sports Foundation to obtain tax-deductible funds, set performance targets, design better information technology systems, and generally improve internal efficiency.

The third policy goal was to create a sporting environment free from drug cheats, and ensure a level playing field where athletes can compete fairly. This tough on drugs approach involved a number of initiatives. They included supporting the ASDA and World Anti-Doping Authority, assisting NSOs to enforce anti-doping regulations, increasing the quality and frequency of drug testing for high-performance athletes, and using celebrity athletes to advocate drug free competition.

The final policy goal was to significantly increase the number of people partici-pating in sport right across Australia. This policy goal had a number of strands. The first was to encourage young people in general, and those in country and regional Australia in particular, to play organised sport. This is seen as vital for managing the alienation, community fragmentation, and social dislocation that many young people experience. The second strand was to increase membership of community sporting clubs and encourage the development of links with local schools and business. The third strand was to use the expanded club membership to build stronger pathways from local participation to high-performance com-petition. The final strand was to educate the sporting community about the value of sport, use community sport to develop a sense of fair play, mould the character and ethical standards of players, and use sporting clubs as a forum for eliminating harassment, racism, and sexism.

Funding implications

In backing this vision for sport the Commonwealth Government allocated on average, AUS$132 million a year for each of the four years from 2001 to 2005. The high-performance programme was allocated an average of AUS$103 million for each year, the tough on drug policy was allocated AUS$7 million, and the *More Active Australia* policy was allocated AUS$22 million. The sport management enhancement policy had no ear-marked funds, but in practice used some of the high-performance and *More Active Australia* allocations.

Table 6.2 Commonwealth Government funding to sport: 2001–2005

Year	Funding (AUS$ million)	Major developments and events
2001–2002	123	BASA policy launched
2002–2003	135	Manchester Commonwealth Games
2003–2004	150	Rugby World Cup in Sydney
2004–2005	132 (estimate)	Athens Olympic Games

Source: Australian Sports Commission (2001a).

At first glance these funding arrangements suggest that the Commonwealth Government aimed to strike a more reasonable balance between elite and community sport development. However, they also reveal growing concern over declining player registrations in some sports, and a drop off in club membership. The *More Active Australia* funding clearly aims to not only increase participation, but also consolidate the club structure of Australian sport, and consequently build the stock of social capital that resides in these organisations. Finally, the funding arrangements indicated that the Commonwealth Government wanted to continue the fight against performance enhancing drugs, and create a sporting culture that values fairness, equity and social cohesion. These aims have serious social benefits attached to them, but they are also notoriously difficult to secure. A summary of the Howard Government funding arrangements for the BASA policy is provided in Table 6.2.

Concluding comments

The years following the election of the Howard Government were marked by a strong focus on strengthening relationships between national sport organisations and their constituent clubs (Australian Sports Commission, 1999b). The fall in volunteer numbers and participation levels in some sports was a serious cause for concern, since the community sport club, together with the state and national governing bodies, had always been recognised as the foundation of the Australian sport system. At the centre of current government policy on sport was the belief that the strength of elite sport is in large part a function of the health of community sport. That is, the more players and officials there are in club sport, the more likely it will deliver talented young athletes to the elite sport area. The Commonwealth Government also suggested that community sport clubs could be used to engineer changes in social values and behaviour.

This period also marked the Commonwealth Government's serious intention to integrate sport more effectively into Australia's political economy. This involves two core themes. The first theme, which has been recycled with every change of government since 1972, involves sport being seen as the great national unifier, and the vehicle for building not only our national self-esteem, but also our international reputation for excellence. The second theme involves sport being recognised as an important industry, and a means of generating employment, building community infrastructure, attracting international tourists, and stimulating economic development.

To a large extent both aims have been met so far. Australia continued its domination at the Commonwealth Games and secured 206 medals at the 2002 Manchester Games, which was 41 more than the host country England, and 92 more than Canada. The Australian cricket team won the 2003 World Cup, and the Australian netball team maintained its word champion status. In addition, Layne Beachley won her fifth world surfing championship, and Alisa Camplin finished first in the aerial ski world championships. While the Australian rugby union team was defeated by England in the 2003 World Cup final in Sydney, there was no dispute that the six-week tournament had been a tourism bonanza for Australia.

However, these successes hide a number of challenges and problems facing Australian sport in general, and the Commonwealth Government minister for sport in particular. These challenges and problems will be addressed in the next section of this book by examining a number of contemporary cases and policy initiatives.

Part III
Practice

7 BASA: themes and assumptions

Background issues

As was noted in the previous chapter, in 2001 the Commonwealth Government introduced its new sport policy, which was titled *Backing Australia's Sporting Ability: A More Active Australia* (BASA) (Commonwealth of Australia, 2001). Like earlier sport policies, BASA aimed to strike a balance between elite, or high-performance sport, and community sport development. The policy formulation process was particularly challenging, since two opposing factors had to be dealt with. First, *Shaping Up* effectively recommended a much larger allocation of funds to community sport, local clubs, and programmes aimed at getting more people involved in regular physical activity. Second, Australia's success at the Olympics showed what could be done when funds were given to high-performance sport, and how this success generated a great sense of national pride and self-esteem.

BASA themes

When Jackie Kelly launched the Commonwealth Government's post-Olympics sport policy, she focussed on four primary goals.

The first policy goal was to ensure athletes could continue to successfully compete at international level. BASA identified coach education programmes, athlete support and further research in sport science as essential to achieving this goal. Furthermore, the Australian Institute of Sport would continue to be the centre for elite sport development. The central aim of this policy goal was to maintain Australia's high-performance standards at Commonwealth and Olympic Games.

The second policy goal was to enhance sport management structures and practices, in order that NSOs are able to deliver a range of quality sport services. NSOs were encouraged to secure additional revenue from non-government sources, use the Australian Sports Foundation to obtain tax-deductable funds, set performance targets, design better information technology systems, and generally improve internal efficiency. The central aims of this policy goal were to increase the professionalism of Australia's national sporting system and to ensure that the elite sport feeder system was appropriately maintained and developed.

The third policy goal was to create a sporting environment free from drug cheats, and ensure a level playing field where athletes can compete fairly. This tough-on-drugs approach involved a number of initiatives. They included supporting the ASDA and World Anti-Doping Authority, assisting NSOs to enforce anti-doping regulations, increasing the quality and frequency of drug testing for high-performance athletes, and using celebrity athletes to advocate drug-free competition. This policy goal had three complementary aims. The first aim was to increase the transparency of Australian sporting structures in relation to drugs. The second aim was to increase the national and international public's confidence in the Australian sporting system, and the final aim was to protect the credibility of athletic competition essential to the Olympic sports that are predicated on the notion 'higher, stronger, faster'.

The final policy goal was to increase the number of people participating in sport right across Australia. This policy goal has a number of strands. The first was to encourage young people in general, and those in country and regional Australia in particular, to play organised sport. This was seen as vital for managing the alienation, community fragmentation, and social dislocation that many young people experience. The second strand was to increase membership of community sporting clubs and encourage the development of links with local schools and business. The third strand was to use the expanded club membership to build stronger pathways from local participation to high-performance competition. The final strand was to educate the sporting community about the value of sport, use community sport to develop a sense of fair play, mould the character and ethical standards of players, and use sporting clubs as a forum for eliminating harassment, racism, and sexism. The overarching aim of this policy goal was to increase the number of people in Australia's club or organised sport system.

Translating policy into strategy

In 2002 the ASC translated the BASA policy into a four-year strategic plan (Australian Sports Commission, 2002a). The ASC plan effectively conflated the BASA four-pronged policy into two core objectives with an array of cascading strategies and programmes.

The first objective was to sustain an effective national sport system that offered improved participation. In order to achieve this objective the ASC identified a number of strategies. It wanted to first, use Active Australia partnerships and targeted NSOs to increase the number of young people playing competitive, club-based sport. It then wanted to improve participation pathways for women, the disabled, and the indigenous. It also wanted to improve the management of sport organisations by educating sport managers about the benefits to flow from effective planning, a strong information system, good leadership, and effective risk management. It finally wanted to support the education and accreditation of coaches and officials, help establish sport cultures that marginalised discrimination and harassment, and assist sport clubs to broaden their revenue base.

The second objective was to achieve excellence in sport performance. A number of strategies were set in motion to achieve this finely honed objective. The primary strategy was to provide selected NSOs with the funds to deliver programmes that ensured international sport success. This strategy was linked to the performance enhancement programme of the AIS that included not only access to high quality coaching and sport science, but also career education and counselling. The ASC also wanted to provide targeted assistance to athletes who were likely to perform well at subsequent World Championships, and Olympic and Commonwealth Games. Finally, the ASC desperately wanted to eliminate drug cheats by a process of coercion, education, and the use of sporting champions and role models to promote drug-free sport.

Underlying values and assumptions

Each of these above policy goals and strategies were underpinned by a number of values and assumptions. Some of these values and assumptions have been clearly articulated, while others are implied in the discussion supporting each policy goal. The assumptions underpinning the emphasis on elite sport development in BASA are linked to the issue of national unity. That is, funding for elite sport and high-performance sport is important because it improves Australia's international competitiveness and enhances its international sporting standing. This will contribute to a strong sense of civic and national pride, which will, in turn, lead to greater social cohesion and national development.

The core assumption underpinning the aim to increase the professionalisation of sport management in BASA is that a well-managed sport organisation will not only support the development of talented athletes, but also provide a springboard for local and community sport development. At the local level this will strengthen the club system, and thereby assist in attracting more members, players, and volunteer officials. In other words, better-managed sport organisations will assist in building the social capital of both national and regional sport communities.

The core assumption underpinning the attempt to create a level playing field in Australian sport in BASA is that athletes should not be allowed to obtain an unfair advantage over others. It follows that since certain drugs can improve performance, they should be banned from all sporting competitions. It is therefore critical that Australia continues to fund and manage its vigilant regulations and dope-testing regime.

The assumptions underpinning the attempt to increase sport participation in BASA are a little more convoluted in that there are a number of interlinking relationships that involve physical and emotional health benefits that provide positive outcomes for both individuals and society. The primary assumption is that greater levels of participation will enhance the fitness and health levels of the community, and give people a stronger sense of self-worth and personal identity. Other complementary outcomes include the building of social cohesion and the strengthening of community relationships. In short, having more people engaging in organised sport will improve community health and welfare. A secondary assumption is that sport is a public good and generates many external benefits. As such, it should be available to everyone. This means that barriers to participation should be minimised. These barriers include the high cost of joining clubs, purchasing equipment, and and travelling to venues. Barriers also involve the failure to accommodate all levels of ability, a tendency to discriminate on the basis of age, gender, race and class, and a perpetuation of a culture that overvalues aggression and winning.

The strategic thrust of BASA

At first glance, BASA appears to mark the winding down of the Active Australia campaign. The Active Australia programme, launched in 1996, was the first concerted attempt to link local government, schools, and private providers. These three networks represented the primary agencies that provided Australians with the opportunity to participate in structured or unstructured physical activity. Importantly, the Active Australia programme focused on the provision of opportunities for physical activity, rather than limiting itself to structured club sport. BASA represents a distinct policy shift.

The emphasis on the provision of opportunities for physical activity has been replaced by an emphasis on encouraging Australians to return to the club-based sport system, as a way of increasing participation. In BASA a policy goal is to significantly increase the number of people participating in sport right across Australia. Importantly, this policy goal focuses on participation in organised sport, rather than participation in unstructured physical activity. In other words, BASA assumes that we will be better off as a nation if people join clubs and play their sport in a more structured setting.

The distinction between physical activity and organised sport is an important one, and was discussed in detail in Chapter 2. While all sport involves some degree of physical activity, not all physical activity takes place in a sport setting. For example, most of the walking, cycling, and swimming activities take place in an informal setting. On the other hand, tennis, cricket, and netball participation take place in a highly structured situation. While sport is an important vehicle for increasing levels of physical activity, there is no direct relationship between sport participation and physical activity levels. It is possible, for example, for physical activity levels to increase while sport participation falls. Similarly, an increase in sport participation can be associated with a fall in the level of physical activity.

There are many community benefits from having a physically active nation. At one level, it is comforting to find that over the last 20 years the number of people engaging in regular physical activity has marginally increased. According to an Australian Bureau of Statistics survey in 1999, the proportion of Australians participating in regular physical activity has increased from 54 to 58 per cent, although a 2002 survey commissioned by the ASC set the figure at more than 70 per cent. This can be put down to the many promotional campaigns, and a number of health scares associated with poor diet and sedentary lifestyle. On the other hand, this increase in activity levels has done little to make Australians trimmer and healthier. For example, just over 55 per cent of Australian adults are currently overweight. In contrast, the figure for 1980 was only 35 per cent (Oakley, 1999: 60). At the same time, there are many health benefits associated with physical activity. Active people are less likely to suffer from heart disease, breast cancer and diabetes, and less likely to smoke cigarettes (Oakley, 1999). There is also convincing evidence that people who are physically active, but not super fit, are more emotionally stable and less likely to suffer the debilitating effects of depression.

Thus, there is a significant challenge for Australian society that arises from BASA. It acknowledges the necessity of increasing the physical activity of the Australian people, and understands the community health benefits that are likely to follow. However, it does not see unstructured, informal activity as the preferred way of attaining these socially desirable outcomes. A major theme that threads its way through BASA is the notion that the best way to get more people physically active is to enhance the status, structural presence, and management of the club sport system. Importantly, there are a number of agendas and beliefs that drive this emphasis on organised, formal and structured sporting competition, and the move away from unstructured, informal and unorganised physical activity and recreation in the Government's 2001–2005 sport policy. These agendas and beliefs are discussed below.

Reasons for strengthening the sport club system

Most fundamentally, in BASA the sports club is viewed as a cornerstone of Australian society. It has not only provided the foundation for Australia's sporting success throughout the post-Second World War period, but has also been a pivotal place for community activity. In short, the sport club is a major contributor to the nation's sporting infrastructure and social capital, and is therefore worth supporting through ongoing financial assistance.

The BASA policy is also a response to Australia's increasing globalisation and social dislocation. The emphasis on strengthening sporting clubs reflects a fear that Australians are increasingly becoming more individualistic, distant and removed from their communities. In this respect the sporting club is viewed as a social and communal panacea. The sporting club, in BASA, is set to become Australia's social cement. Thus, the sport policy for 2001–2005 is not only about increasing participation but also about bringing people together to share their cultural diversity, administrative expertise, and sporting passions for the good of the community. In other words, it aims to broaden the social capital of the nation (Productivity Commission, 2003).

The BASA policy also views the sport club as an important socialising institution in Australian society. Sport clubs, associations, and leagues provide the opportunity for the Commonwealth Government to solve a diverse range of social ills. The alienation, depression, and social dislocation faced by young people, particularly in rural Australia, are serious social problems. There has also been a groundswell of opinion that many social problems and dysfunctional behaviour like binge drinking, vandalism, public graffiti, and physical assaults, would be in part resolved if sport clubs were re-configured as places that not only taught the skills of sport, but also socially desirable behaviour (National Centre for Culture and Recreation Statistics, 2001). This includes drug education, anti-harassment programmes, alcohol management policies, and notions of fair play, equity, and inclusiveness.

The BASA statement also tacitly accepts the view that a main impact of international elite sporting success is to encourage young people play specific sports in a competitive club setting. If we assume the claim to be at least intuitively valid, then it makes sense to provide good local facilities and coaching that captures the increased demand that might follow from international successes and the concomitant media exposure for the athletes and their sporting activity.

The club-based system is also supported as a method of increasing participation because a well-developed club system acts as feeder network for high-performance sport. In this respect, BASA suggests there is a link between the quality of people participating at the grass-roots level, and international success. Therefore even if it is conceded that elite sporting success encourages only a few more people to participate in physical activity, it can nevertheless be argued that an elite development pathway is essential for identifying and nurturing talented athletes. Thus, BASA explicitly supports an elite sport feeder system, which may be achieved independently of anything that broadens participation in physical activity.

While it is not explicitly stated, the Commonwealth Government seems to believe that funding for physical activity programmes through the ASC has reached the point of diminishing returns. That is, it is unlikely that the number of people who participate in regular physical activity will increase markedly in response to more promotional messages and community come-and-try programmes. BASA is more inclined to the view that the key to increasing participation lies with structured sport experiences in a club setting.

The BASA statement also implicitly suggests that allocating funding to participation programmes that increases public awareness or even expands sport facilities, is not politically expedient. First, the benefits of the funding would be difficult to prove, and relative to international success of elite athletes, they would be even more intangible. Second, the benefits of large-scale programmes to increase participation in regular physical activity may be realised in 5 to 15 years time, which is well beyond the political life of most Commonwealth Governments. As a result, it is likely that the government that implements the policy will not be the one to benefit from the results. Thus, allocating resources to physical activity provides very little immediate electoral currency.

In summary, the policies in BASA suggest that increasing the levels of participation through promotional activities is both too soft and too resource intensive. Alternatively, it may be better for informal physical activity to take care of itself through lifestyle change, the market, and the provision of local government leisure services. It also suggests that the Commonwealth Government believes organised sport offers a variety of physical, social, and even cultural benefits that cannot be realised by individuals participating in unstructured settings. In other words, the sport club is the preferred catchment for people wishing to play sport, and makes good economic sense since facilities and resources are currently in place to absorb any increase in demand. It may also be that the Commonwealth Government cost-benefit analysis suggests that more widely distributed clubs with a range of support facilities will increase participation rates most effectively.

What BASA does not address

However, the emphasis on club sport as way of attracting more members and players does not fit comfortably with how people see the place of sport and physical activity in their daily lives. The 1998–99 survey of Australian participation in sport and physical activity conducted by the Australian Bureau of Statistics shows that for many of the most popular Australian sports, the majority of people engaged with them in an informal way (Australian Bureau of Statistics, 1999a). Over 70 per cent of people who went fishing, running, swimming, and walking, did so informally and without any club support or organisation. For example, 96 per cent of all walking was done outside a club setting, while the rate was 92 per cent for swimming. The level of organisation for aerobics and golf was higher, but even in these cases more people did it on a casual basis. In the case of aerobics, just over 50 per cent of the participation was done informally, and for golf it was 56 per cent. The sports that had most of their participation done in a club setting were netball (80 per cent), lawn bowls (90 per cent), cricket (79 per cent), and basketball (64 per cent).

On the other hand, only 31 per cent of Australians engage in competitive and organised sport activities. While the male participation rate of 34 per cent was slightly higher than the female rate of 27 per cent, the most significant differences centred on age. Whereas 61 per cent of the 15–19-year-old age group played competitive and/or organised sport, the participation rate for 35–44-year-olds, and those over 65 years was 28 per cent and 18 per cent respectively. Clearly, older people are less inclined to play competitive sports.

Structured and organised sport programmes have only ever attracted a minority of the Australian population. Many people do not need a formal club structure or competitive environment when participating in sport and physical activity. This trend to informal sport has been evident since the 1970s. While the number of registered organised sport participants increased by 20 per cent between 1975 and 1999, Australia's population increased by more that 25 per cent (Oakley, 1999: 85). Moreover, whereas in 1980 the Confederation of Australian Sport represented 6 million sport participants, by 1999 its 120 member sporting bodies spoke for only 3.5 million members. In other words, in 20 years, the proportion of Australia's population affiliated to a sporting organisation fell from 40 to 20 per cent (Oakley, 1999: 18). To this extent then, most people taking up a sport activity have embraced a sport-for-all rather than a competitive sport philosophy. That is, they have made their experiences casual, unstructured, and by implication often low cost and inclusive. This is a healthy development. On the other hand, it also suggests that the traditional club-based structure is losing its appeal for some people. Clearly, then, *BASA* anticipates an undesirable decline in the number of players, volunteer administrators, coaches and officials involved in sport organisations, unless immediate action is taken to reverse this trend.

The above discussion highlights the dangers of only using organised club-based sport as the vehicle to increase participation levels. Put simply, focusing exclusively on club-based sport may alienate sections of the Australian population, thereby increasing the number of Australians who do not participate in regular physical activity.

Is there a place for informal sport policy?

This increasing preference for small-scale, informal, uncompetitive, time-compressed activities is the result of a number of factors. The first factor is the changing lifestyles of many Australians. Young people in particular are more inclined to choose their sport activity on the basis of how easily it can fit into their busy work and social life. To this end, any activities that can give a solid work-out without too much preparation or fuss are very attractive sport options. Aerobics, running and walking are good examples.

The second factor is the general fall in club memberships of all types. Australians are less inclined to join clubs and associations than they once were. Again, young people have constructed other ways of meeting their social needs. The falling membership levels of lawn bowl clubs is in large part due to this factor.

The third important influence is the positive impact of previous messages from the Aussie Sports programme and the Active Australia strategy. They have seductively told us that physical activity is not only fun, but is also good for our psychological and physical health. Moreover, it need not be competitive or costly, and can be easily and simply incorporated into our daily lives. This message easily connects with people whose time is scarce, or resources are meagre.

A fourth factor is that an overwhelming emphasis on structured, formal and organised club sport is likely to alienate or discriminate on the basis of age, gender, ability, culture, or religion. Put simply, not all Australians are attracted to club-based sport. The danger in moving away from a system that encourages people to access a variety of sport and physical activity opportunities is that they may stop altogether, rather than engage in club-based sport.

Concluding comments

The Commonwealth Government's 2001–2005 sport policy confirms that elite sport development is still the driving force, as it was in the 1980s and 1990s. Moreover, it also illustrates that despite the fact that Australia is now the second most obese nation in the world, increasing the proportion of Australians engaged in regular physical activity is not a high priority, as it was in the 1970s. Rather, the *BASA* priority is participation in organised sport, the contribution it can make to the building of social capital, its capacity to support elite development, and most problematically, its potential to capture more people who want to play sport and stay fit and healthy.

Parts of *Shaping Up* have been ignored in the design of *BASA*. The report recommended increased funding and resources be devoted to the area of physical activity and participation, yet the 2001–2005 policy contains no provision for this outside the club-based sporting structure.

The tone of *BASA* can easily lead the reader to conclude that Commonwealth Governments have found it difficult to decide just how to handle the problem of physical inactivity. The Commonwealth Government has correctly concluded that getting more people to be physically active involves more than a promotional message here, and a come-and-try day there. In the end, increasing levels of physical activity will be more the result of changing social conditions, subtle shifts in how people understand the relationship between their physical and intellectual selves, and how people incorporate exercise into their daily lifestyles. In short, the Commonwealth Government policy is underpinned by a belief that while an increased awareness about the benefits of healthy lifestyles may have a positive impact on activity levels, it is even more important to consolidate the sport club system.

The policies contained in *BASA* will most probably broaden the social capital of the Australian sport system, and certainly develop our high-performance sport. Its focus on club-based, organised sport is admirable in many respects, and it will ensure a clearly articulated feeder system for elite sport. On the other hand, it is optimistic to think that building up the club system will solve social problems, and broaden physical activity participation rates. It may even have difficulty in increasing long-term levels of participation in organised sport, since it has to deal with the trend to informal sport activity. Moreover, there are significant social forces that make organised sport an increasingly unattractive option for many people, and this social reality is likely to be a problem for *BASA* policy.

8 Elite sport development: targeting high performance

Background

This chapter examines the policies, programmes and funding used to identify athletic potential, develop young talent, train elite athletes, and maintain Australia's strong international standing in sport.

The Commonwealth Government's elite development policies exploded into the public arena in 1981 when the AIS was established at Bruce, a suburb of Canberra, the national capital. As indicated in Chapter 4, its primary goal was to assist elite athletes improve their international sporting performances. It began its operations with an extensive infrastructure comprising an athletic stadium, an indoor sports centre, outdoor tennis courts, a netball centre, 26 coaches and 150 athletes in eight different sports (Daly, 1991). Over the next two years a number of additional international standard facilities were established. They included a gymnastics training hall, a four-court indoor tennis centre, and an aquatic centre with both a 50 and 25-metre pool. By the beginning of 1985 indoor facilities had been constructed for weight-lifting, basketball and netball, and outdoor facilities had been constructed for soccer (Australian Sports Commission, 2003c). By any measure, the AIS was a handsomely funded sport training centre.

The reputation of the AIS was enhanced at the 1984 Olympics at Los Angeles when AIS athletes won seven of the 12 swimming medals for Australia, the AIS gymnasts were close to winning medals, and three AIS track athletes won medals. The consequent euphoria infected the Commonwealth Government, and John Brown, the minister for sport, announced a 60 per cent increase in AIS funding for the1985–86 financial year.

Under the direction of John Cheffers, the CEO of the AIS between 1984 and 1986, the AIS not only consolidated its Canberra facility, but also developed a strong network of regional elite training centres. Following the 60 per cent funding increase in 1985–86 budget, residential satellite centres were established in field hockey (Perth), squash and diving (Brisbane), and cricket and cycling (Adelaide) (Australian Sports Commission, 1998b: 2). In 1989 the Commonwealth Government merged the AIS with the ASC in order to first eliminate duplication, and second ensure greater accountability and transparency in the wake of the Cheffers incident in 1985. In Chapter 5 it was noted that Cheffers had presided over a spending explosion which produced a serious budget deficit. In his defence, Cheffers claimed that athletes could not produce their best performances in a constrained climate where economic rationalism overwhelmed innovation. In the meantime, the ASC confirmed that the AIS would continue to be the focal point for elite athlete development, and during the 1990s the Institute consolidated its activities and successfully delivered many international sporting successes (Australian Sports Commission, 1999a).

At the Sydney 2000 Olympics 315 of the 620 team members had been AIS scholarship holders, and 31 of the 58 medals were won by former or current AIS athletes (Australian Sports Commission, 2001a). Moreover, most of the members of the world champion teams in netball, rugby and cricket were former AIS scholarship holders. At the same time, the Commonwealth Government funded elite training programmes managed by NSOs, which included coaching support, and overseas travel and competitions.

AIS scholarship programme

The current BASA policy continues to support elite athlete development. In the 2003–2004 Commonwealth budget, AUS$116 million was allocated to improving sporting excellence, which included the operation of the AIS.

The AIS is organised around a number of functional divisions, the main ones being Sport Programs, Planning and Evaluation, Athlete and Coach Services, and Technical Direction. The foundation division of the AIS is its Sport Programs, Planning and Evaluation area. Elite development programmes are provided at both the Canberra site and the so-called satellite sites around the nation. Most of the programmes are residential (that is, they require athletes to live on a central site for the duration of the training programme), but some are based around various state institutes and involve daily commuting. Table 8.1 illustrates the different types of elite programmes available to athletes.

The residential programmes at the Canberra AIS site include archery, artistic gymnastics, athletics, men's and women's basketball, boxing, netball, rowing, men's soccer, swimming, men's and women's volleyball, and men's water polo.

The satellite residential programmes are not only held around Australia, but also overseas. Adelaide runs the men's cricket and track cycling, Brisbane offers diving and squash, Melbourne delivers the golf and tennis programmes, Perth offers men's and women's field hockey, while the road cycling is based in Italy.

All other elite sport development programmes are run on a dispersed basis where athletes may be located in a number of states, and programmes customised

Table 8.1 AIS programmes

Site	Residential and central	Daily commute and dispersed
Canberra	Basketball	–
Satellite	Cricket	Water polo

to meet local needs. Most of the athletes in these dispersed programmes are in part supported by their state sport institutes, which are administered from a central location. The Australian football programme is administered from Melbourne, the alpine skiing, rugby union, rugby league, women's slalom canoeing, sailing, and water polo programmes are administered from Sydney, the softball programme is administered from Brisbane, the sprint canoeing and triathlon programmes are administered from the Gold Coast, while the women's soccer programme is administered from Canberra.

The sport programmes are supported by a system of scholarships that are awarded to elite athletes around the nation. Athletes must submit an application form which is assessed by the appropriate national sporting body, who recommends to the AIS programme directors that an offer be made. The scholarships enable athletes to use all the facilities of the training facility, and obtain specialist coaching. Funds are also given to athletes for participating in national and international competitions. In the case of residential facilities, accommodation is provided at no cost to the athletes.

In 2003 the AIS supported 27 sports and offered scholarships to 627 students. At any one time there are 200 athletes on scholarship. It employs around 70 coaches and a core of sport scientists who offer world standard training, and coaching services. The 2002–2003 ASC grant allocation to AIS scholarships was AUS\$15.3 million, ranging from AUS\$1.1 million for each of cycling and rowing, to AUS\$275,000 for boxing and AUS\$250,000 for skiing (Australian Sports Commission, 2003a).

Sport science support

The Sport Science and Sport Medicine Unit has established an international reputation for innovation. It developed the ice jacket that was used at the Atlanta Olympic Games, it designed the ultra-light carbon fibre track cycle, and designed a high altitude training simulator. The Sport Science and Sport Medicine Division has also been in the vanguard of drug testing. Working in conjunction with the Australian Drug testing Laboratory, it developed a test for artificial erythropoitin (EPO) which was used by endurance athletes to improve their performance.

Talent search

The AIS also has a strong talent identification programme. The AIS recognises that Australia's relatively small population of 20 million severely limits the pool from which talented athletes can be secured and developed. It therefore makes sense to provide a way of locating and identifying young people with the physical attributes and aptitude to become elite athletes. To this end, the AIS in conjunction with NSOs and state sport academies has established a National Talent Search Program (NTSP). The NTSP has been divided into three stages or phases. In phase one, state talent search coordinators target secondary schools and with the assistance of physical education teachers conduct a battery of screening tests which signify students with outstanding athletic potential. The aim is to locate those young people who are very strong, very fast, very agile, very well coordinated, are bio-mechanically superior, and have a lot of endurance. In phase two, the abilities and aptitudes of students are matched with specific sports to ensure the best possible performance outcome. In phase three, students are invited to participate in a talented athlete programme, run by either the national sporting body or the state sport academy.

The talent search program originated in 1988 when the AIS rowing programme coaches undertook a national search for young athletes who had the attributes to become elite rowers. The programme was so successful that it was extended to include athletics, cycling, canoeing, swimming, rowing, triathlon, water polo, and weight-lifting as a fast track means of training young athletes for the 2000 Olympics (Bloomfield, 2003). Since then the talent search programme has been consolidated into an integrated initiative that combines AIS leadership with state academy screening of the athletic potential of school students. While the talent search programme has been accused of being overly mechanistic in the way it examines the potential of young athletes, it has delivered a number of successful outcomes.

The talent search programme brings to the fore the whole nature/nurture debate, and whether hard work and good coaching can compensate for an average athletic inheritance. According to AIS officials, the key to high achievement is a 'superior genetic foundation' (Drane, 2003: 72). In other words, the best coaching will take athletes so far, and the evidence suggests that a young athlete who is not in the top 50 per cent of athletic ability will never reach international standard. On the other hand, recent AIS experience showed that athletically gifted and multi-skilled sports persons with only limited structured sport experi-ence behind them can reach international standards with intensive and high quality training. For example, in 1993 Cycling Australia and the AIS developed a pilot talent identification project that focused on South Australian secondary schools. The project discovered a number of talented young cyclists, three of whom went on to become world junior champions. In particular, Alayna Burns gained seventh place in the 3000 metres individual pursuit at the Sydney Olympic Games. More recently Natalie Bale and Luke Morrison won medals at the world junior championships in rowing and kayaking respectively. Neither Natalie nor Luke had an extensive history in these sports.

ASC high-performance support

As the previous discussion shows, the AIS has a pivotal role in supporting the high-performance programmes of NSOs. The NSO high-performance programmes area is also supported by an ASC grant scheme that provides funds for high-performance sport programmes. The best funded sports are swimming (AUS$3.3 million), rowing (AUS$3.1 million), athletics (AUS$2.4 million), cycling (AUS$2.4 million), sailing (AUS$2.3 million), and basketball (AUS$2.2 million). The allocations are significantly lower for golf (AUS$440,000), judo (AUS$385,000), diving (AUS$370,000), badminton (AUS$155,000) ice racing (AUS$55,000), and fencing (AUS$30,000) (Australian Sports Commission, 2003a). The NSO high-performance programmes are the driving force behind the development of international standard sporting achievement. They combine scholarships, coaching assistance, sport science advice, access to international standard facilities, and exposure to elite level competition to optimise the athletes potential. While each NSO works within the funding guidelines provided by the ASC, they all have their own distinctive approach to high-performance development.

The Athletics Australia high-performance programme

Athletics Australia is one of Australia's most prominent sporting bodies. While it has a relatively low participation base, it has produced many internationally recognised athletes including Cathy Freeman, the 2000 Olympic 400 metres track champion, Jana Pittman, a world 400-metres hurdle champion, and Patrick Johnson, who is a sub-10 second 100-metres sprinter. It is relatively well funded, since it receives an annual grant of $3.6 million from the ASC, and a million-dollar sponsorship from Telstra, Australia's largest telecommunication company.

Athletics Australia prides itself on the nationwide spread of its high-performance programme. This has been achieved through a three-tier structure. First, the head coach is located in Sydney under the umbrella of the AOC. This allows him to work closely with the AOC, which is an important funding source leading up to the Olympic games. Second, the high-performance manager is located at the AIS in Canberra, and works closely with the AIS coaching staff. Finally, Athletics Australia provides financial support for the delivery of high-performance coaching and training programmes at each of the state sport academies. While this approach leads to a duplication of coaching programmes, it ensures a high degree of access and opportunity for elite athletes around the nation. Most of the high-performance funds support the employment of coaches, but funds are also used to support participation at international competitions, training camps, sport science, medical and physiotherapy services, and direct financial support for selected athletes.

The success of the high-performance programme is measured primarily by the number of athletes who achieve an international ranking. Athletics Australia had been frequently criticised for its inability to produce a solid base of top ten rankings. When compared to cycling, swimming, and rowing, Australian athletes appear to under-achieve. Athletic Australia officials defend its performance by noting that unlike cycling, swimming, and rowing, nearly every country in the world has a track-and-field programme. As a result, an athletics top-ten ranking should be weighted more heavily than a similar ranking in any other Olympic sport. However, this argument should not hide the fact that, on the whole, Australian track-and-field athletes struggle to attain and sustain international excellence.

The Archery Australia high-performance programme

Unlike athletics, archery is a minor sport in Australia, and has produced nothing approaching a national sporting hero. It goes virtually unreported until its appearance in the Olympics every four years. At the same time, Australian archers have occasionally achieved international success. There have been four individual world target champions, while in the team events Australia obtained fourth place in the Atlanta Olympic Games and first place in the 1998 world indoor championships.

Australian archers claimed media attention for the first time at the Sydney 2000 Olympic Games when Simon Fairweather won a gold medal. Fairweather's ground-breaking performance set off a chain of events that culminated in archery being invited to participate in the AIS elite athlete program. In effect, Archery Australia convinced the ASC that given appropriate support, archery could further enhance Australia's international sporting reputation. The ASC consequently established an archery training centre at the AIS in Canberra, and allocated funds for both AIS scholarships and a high-performance programme. In 2003, AUS$499,000 was allocated to the AIS scholarship programme, while AUS$310,000 was allocated to the high-performance programme. This additional funding had a number of important impacts on Australian archery. First, it allowed it to retain the services of its head coach, Ki-Sik Lee, who is one of the world's leading archery coaches. Second, by creating a strong archery infrastructure it provided a national focus for elite development. Third, the scholarships enabled a number of young archers to gain exposure to international competition, sustained high quality coaching, and ongoing sport science support. Finally, the high-performance funds allowed Archery Australia to appoint a high-performance manager who could coordinate the elite development programmes, establish a nationwide talent identification process around regional competitions and tournaments, conduct regular coaching camps, and manage a schedule of international competitions.

Since the 2000 Olympics a number of junior Australian archers have won medals at international competitions, and there is a strong feeling amongst Archery Australia officials that because of its inclusion in the AIS programme, Australia could achieve a top-five ranking by 2006. The archery case demonstrates that in an internationally competitive sport world, sustained success will only come with government support. In this case, the critical support came in the form of funding to support facility development, the establishment of a centre for training of elite competitors on a full-time basis, a systematic talent identification and development programme, and the appointment of world-class coaches on long-term contracts.

Funding high performance

When assessing the high-performance programmes funded through the Commonwealth Government sport development policy, the first thing to note is that there has been a continual growth in funding to national sporting organisations (NSOs) over the last 30 years. Whereas in 1980 NSOs were allocated just over AUS$3 million for sport development, by 1990 the annual grant (including AIS scholarships) to all NSOs had increased to nearly AUS$32 million. The

2002–2003 annual grant to NSOs was calculated to be AUS$65 million, with another AUS$4 million going to a variety of sport organisations that serviced athletes with disabilities. By any measure, and taking into account inflation, this constitutes a massive increase in Commonwealth Government funding of NSOs.

The other striking feature is that the money is not distributed evenly across the sports. Ever since the establishment of the AIS, a few sports have been targeted for additional funding. In 1981 when the AIS began its operations, basketball, gymnastics, netball, soccer, swimming, tennis, track and field, and weightlifting were selected for special attention. It was not immediately clear as to why these sports were chosen in preference to some other cluster of NSOs. Swimming and netball were clearly selected because they were sports in which Australia already performed well internationally, but the same could not be said of gymnastics and weightlifting. Neither was it clear why soccer was preferred over rugby union, rugby league and Australian football. The only sensible explanation is that the senior officials of these NSOs were better able to sustain their arguments for their sports being included in the top eight. In any case, all of the 153 available AIS scholarships in 1981 were allocated to these eight sports.

Throughout the 1980s there was a constantly changing set of funding priorities. In 1983 for instance, field hockey was the highest funded sport with an annual grant of AUS$235,000, followed by basketball (AUS$165,000) and athletics (AUS$150,000). The next best funded sports were cricket, Australian football, gymnastics, swimming, tennis yachting, and baseball with grants between AUS$100,000 and AUS$140,000 (Australian Sports Commission, 1996: 59–62).

In 1989 the ASC reviewed its sport priorities and decided to target the seven sports in which it could achieve the best results on the international sporting stage. Basketball, swimming, and track and field were retained, but netball, gymnastics, soccer, tennis, and weightlifting were omitted and replaced by canoeing, cycling, hockey, and rowing.

In 1990 swimming had replaced hockey as the highest funded sport. It received AUS$2.2 million from the Commonwealth Government, while the combined allocation for men's and women's hockey was AUS$2.1 million. Athletics had maintained its favoured status with a grant of AUS$1.9 million, as too did basketball, which attracted AUS$1.7 million of Commonwealth Government funds. The other sports to receive more than AUS$1million were cycling (AUS$1.3 million), gymnastics (AUS$1.1 million) netball (AUS$1 million) and canoeing (AUS$1 million). Non-Olympic sports, even though they had a strong participation base, were not favourably treated at this time. Cricket, which had many more players than any of the sports listed above, received AUS$610,000, rugby league obtained AUS$193,000, while Australian football, the nation's most popular spectator sport was allocated AUS$200,000. In contrast, volleyball and water polo, both of which had relatively low participation levels, received AUS$670,000 and AUS$750,000 respectively

(Australian Sports Commission, 1991). These anomalies were defended on the grounds that, first, professional team sports like cricket, rugby league, and Australian football were already financially secure and, second, funds should be targeted to sports that could produce international success. Despite these arguments, there was a groundswell of opinion that funding should be more inclusive.

The current position

Over the last 10 years, there has been a broadening of the NSO funding base for elite sport development. In 2002 there were nearly 700 scholarships spread across 26 sports. However, when the current funding arrangements for NSOs are closely examined it is clear that the distribution of funds is still directed mainly to a few high-profile sports.

The first point to be made is that not all sports are eligible for funding. Sporting bodies have to satisfy a number of conditions before they can be eligible to receive grants from the Commonwealth Government. First, they must be recognised as a sport. As was indicated in Chapter 2, the ASC defines a sport as any activity involving competition, the use of physical exertion, and the use of skill to achieve a result. Second, they must be seen to be the national governing body for a sport, and responsible for the national development of the sport. In addition, they have to satisfy a number of administrative and structural requirements. First, they need to be legally incorporated. Second, they must have an operable strategic plan that covers at least three years. Third, they must have produced an audited financial report for the previous three years. Fourth, they must have links with affiliated associations in at least four states. Fifth, they must have a doping policy that is consistent with ASC guidelines. Finally, they must belong to an international sport federation that is linked to the General Association of International Sport Federations (GAISF) or the IOC, or the sport must have been played in Australia for more than 75 years and have a significant number of participants. On the basis of these criteria, some 125 organisations are designated or recognised as NSOs.

However, only 80 of these recognised NSOs are eligible to receive grants from the ASC. To receive a grant for use in high-performance activities and elite athlete development, the NSO must demonstrate that it is internationally competitive, has a broad base of public and media interest, and that the world championships have an international profile. To receive a grant for community sport development, it must have a base of coaches and officials and organisational structures to deliver a development programme.

To increase the probability of funding, NSOs need to show that they have in excess of 2000 registered and active participants, have a history of international competition, belong to an international federation that has at least 25 active member countries, have achieved a top-16 result in a world championship, or have been played for more than 75 years in Australia with a sizeable participation base.

In 2002 the ASC funded 67 NSOs, which means that the remaining 58 NSOs were not funded. These 67 funded NSOs were allocated funds from a total pool of $65 million. However when the distributions are analysed it is clear that most of the recipients receive only a modest share of the total pool of funds. The bulk of the grants go to ten sports, as Table 8.2 illustrates.

Table 8.2 shows that the top ten NSOs, which accounted for 15 per cent of all recipients, attracted AUS$33 million, or 51 per cent of all grant monies. In other words, the remaining 57 NSOs, which accounted for 85 per cent of total recipients, received only 49 per cent of available funds. As indicated previously this skewed distribution can be largely explained by the Government insistence that funding be used to achieve the best possible outcomes. While the *BASA* policy is in part framed by the desire to increase participation, the primary goal is to achieve as much international success as possible. To this end, sports that have a high likelihood of producing world champions, Olympic Games medallists, and Commonwealth games medallists will be given the greatest support. This means there is a strong bias to, first, sports that are represented in the Olympics and, second, those Olympic sports that have a history of delivering top-five and top-ten finishes.

The bias towards a select number of Olympic sports is put into stark relief when participation rates are compared to funding levels. For example, swimming and hockey receive a combined total of AUS$8.8 million from the Commonwealth Government, 90 per cent of which goes to elite sport development. By any measure these funds have delivered significant international success. Both the men's and women's teams have consistently been in the world top five, while Australia's swimmers are only marginally less successful than the dominant USA team. However, both have only a moderate participation base of 132,000 and 332,000 respectively. Netball, in contrast, which is not represented at the Olympic Games, has a participation base of 533,000 and a Commonwealth grant of AUS$1.7 million. The differences between funding and participation are even

Table 8.2 Approved grants to selected NSOs 2002–2003 (AUS$ million)

Sport	AIS scholarship	High performance	Sport development	Indigenous sports	Total grants to NSOs
Swimming	0.99	3.3	0.11	0.025	4.39
Hockey	0.94	3.2	0.15	0.035	4.37
Rowing	1.12	3.1	0.080	0.0	4.31
Track and Field	1.02	2.4	0.14	0.055	3.58
Cycling	1.15	2.28	0.11	0.0	3.54
Basketball	0.93	2.22	0.20	0.035	3.38
Sailing	0.39	2.27	0.14	0.0	2.79
Soccer	0.96	1.23	0.14	0.035	2.36
Water polo	0.85	1.44	0.040	0.0	2.32
Gymnastics	0.95	0.99	0.20	0.0	2.14

Source: ASC (2003a), *Annual Report*.

more marked when sailing and water polo are examined. Both of these Olympic sports are well funded by the Commonwealth Government, receiving AUS$3.0 million and AUS$2.3 million respectively. However, only 88,000 people sail competitively while the participation level for water polo is no more than 30,000. Rowing is similarly favoured by a sizeable funding arrangement despite low levels of participation. Its AUS$4.3 million allocation makes it the third best-funded NSO, but it governs a sport with only 47,000 participants. Golf, on the other hand, has 655,000 players who participate in an organised setting, but can only attract AUS$1 million of Commonwealth Government funds. Tennis has 549,000 organised players, but only receives AUS$975,000 from the Government. Squash, in particular, is disadvantaged by its exclusion from the Olympic Games. Whereas its participation level of 118,000 is significantly higher than rowing and sailing, it can only secure AUS$832,000 from the Commonwealth Government.

Even where Olympic sport funding is examined, there are some interesting anomalies. Athletics has usually been one of the three or four best-funded sport organisations, but while it has produced some world class performers over the last 20 years, it has not been all that good at producing world champions or Olympic Games medallists. On the other hand, triathlon, which gained a place in the Sydney 2000 Olympic Games, but is not nearly as well funded as athletics, has been dominated by Australians over recent years. Whereas athletics received AUS$3.9 million in 2002, triathlon could only claim AUS$1.1 million from the Commonwealth Government. Water polo, which has around the same participation levels as triathlon, but not the same international profile, was able to secure a grant of AUS$2.3 million in 2002. Gymnastics has also been favourably treated over the last 20 years, and in the most recent grant allocation received AUS$2.2 million, making it the tenth-best funded sport in Australia. However, during the Sydney 2000 Olympic Games it claimed only one Olympic medal, and outside the Olympics, obtains only an occasional world championship medal.

The key to understanding the Commonwealth Government funding arrangement for sport is to view it as an exercise in both rational and value-based decision-making. At one level there is a clearly defined logic to the funding process whereby sports are targeted for their capacity to produce international successes and medals. At another level the funding process is infected by biases and preferences in which certain sports are seen to be more needy, deserving, or appropriate. The funding process is also influenced by the capacity of some NSOs to gain the ear of ministers and their advisors more than others. This use of rational and irrational decision-making suggests that future funding arrangements will shift in response to a number of factors. First, there will be changing views about the capacity of different sports to deliver an international profile. Second, there will be changes in the ability of NSOs to convince the Minister for Sport that their sport has untapped potential. Finally, there will be changing notions of which sports deserve additional support on ethical or equity grounds.

Concluding comments

It is very clear that ever since the AIS opened its doors to Australia's elite athletes there has been a strong bias to high-performance sport, and a low priority given to community sport. While this preference for elite sport development has been criticised for failing to address the disadvantages faced by women, non-English speaking migrants and aboriginals, it has produced many international successes over many years.

9 Community sport development: targeting participation

In BASA the Commonwealth Government notes that 'through the introduction of a major new participation program, the Government wants to see greater numbers of Australians participating in grass-roots sport, particularly young people. We want to see this achieved right across the country in rural and regional communities as well as in our cities' (Commonwealth of Australia, 2001: 3). Furthermore, BASA refers to the government 'supporting a fresh approach to grass-roots participation, involving partnerships between the Federal Government, national sporting organisations, local sporting clubs, schools and the business community' (Commonwealth of Australia, 2001: 6). The Government policy statement also includes the aim of having one million more registered sport participants by the end of the four-year period between 2001–2002 and 2004–2005 (Australian Sports Commission, 2002a: 6).

The Targeted Sports Participation Growth (TSPG) programme is the major component of the 'fresh approach' referred to in the BASA policy statement, and is the cornerstone of the Australian Sports Commission's (ASC) junior and grass-roots sport development agenda. The ASC have used BASA as a mandate to increase participation in organised sport, particularly at club level and within the primary and secondary school systems. However, the TSPG programme is not designed to increase participation rates in unstructured, informal or *ad hoc* physical activity. An ASC position statement on new strategic directions for the Active Australia programme confirmed the re-focused policy direction. It stated that while it had been successful in 'educating the community about the importance of regular physical activity for achieving physical, social and emotional health', an 'Active Australia' under BASA would be one in which the ASC was able to 'expand the reach and active membership of grass-roots sporting clubs and associations' (Australian Sports Commission, 2001b: 1). There are several aspects to this stronger focus on increasing organised sport participation.

Table 9.1 shows that the participation in organised sport increased between 1996 and 2002. According to the Australian Bureau of Statistics (ABS), the number of adults (18+) participating in organised sport increased by in excess of one million people during the period 1996–2002. As a result, the percentage of the adult population participating in organised sport increased from 26.5 to 31.4 per cent. The number of children (5–14) participating in organised sport

Table 9.1 Organised sport participation 1996–2002

Year	Participants (18+)	% of total	Participants (5–14)	% of total
1996–97	3,476,000	26.5	1,585,200	61.5
1997–98	3,780,000	28.3	1,588,400	61.1
1998–99	4,106,000	30.3	N/A	N/A
1999–2000	3,986,600	28.9	1,568,200	59.4
2001–2002	4,550,400	31.4	N/A	N/A

Sources: ABS, Cat. 4177 (1996–97, 1997–98, 1998–99, 1999–2000, 2002), ABS, Cat. 4156 (1997, 2003), ABS, Cat. 4901 (2000).

remained steady during the same period, although it should be noted that relative to adult participation figures, the percentage of the total number of children participating is very high (approximately double in the period 1999–2000, as illustrated in Table 9.1). Overall, these figures suggest that the Australian sport system has provided significant opportunities for all Australians to participate in organised sport activities. In this context, the BASA policy aim of one million more participants is ambitious. An increase of one million organised sport participants between 1996 and 2002 is an indication of the success of the system, rather than a clear policy problem.

However, the organised sport participation figures in Table 9.1 are only one component of the entire participation landscape. Table 9.2 shows that while the overall physical activity participation figures appear reasonably healthy (62.4 per cent of the population participating in sport or physical activity in the year prior to interview in 2002), in many respects it is an illusion created by the fact that a person need only participate once in a year to be counted as having participated in sport or physical activity. Table 9.2 shows that in 2001–2002 only 10.5 per cent of the adult Australian population participated in any form of physical activity two or more times per week, and that 8.4 per cent of people

Table 9.2 Physical activity participation 2001–2002

Category	Number	Adult population (%)	Total participants (%)
Total sport and physical activity participants	9,056,300	62.4	100.0
1–52 times per year	3,459,000	23.8	38.2
53–104 times per year	4,078,000	28.1	45.0
105 or more times per year	1,518,800	10.5	16.8
Total organised sport participants	4,550,400	31.4	50.2
1–52 times per year organised[*]	1,738,000	12.0	19.2
53–104 times per year organised[*]	2,047,680	14.1	22.6
105 or more times per year organised[*]	764,467	5.3	8.4

Source: ABS, Cat. 4177 (2002).

[*] Organised sport figures are calculated by using the ratio of organised sport participants : total participants.

that participated in any sport or physical activity were doing so two or more times per week in an organised sport setting. These figures illustrate that there is a sport participation problem, particularly given that significant health benefits can be gained from thirty minutes of moderate cumulative physical activity every day (World Health Organisation, 2003: 3).

The ASC strategic plan for 2002–2005 noted that there is 'evidence to suggest that Australians are moving away from organised sport, [and that people are] citing a lack of time, increased costs, risk management concerns and loss of interest [as reasons for this shift]' (Australian Sports Commission, 2002a: 5). The ABS figures support this conclusion. Of the 9 million people participating in physical activity, approximately 3.7 million walk for exercise, 1.6 million swim and 1.6 million participate in aerobics or fitness activities (Australian Bureau of Statistics, 2002: 3). These are all relatively informal and unstructured activities. In the context of the general trend of the statistics presented in Table 9.2, the BASA policy is a response to the serious lack of physical activity and sport participation in the Australian community. Only a limited number of Australians are participating in enough physical activity to deliver any significant physical or mental health benefits. This has serious implications for the health of the Australian population. At the same time, a pool of 764,467 people participating in organised sport two or more times per week is small, particularly relative to countries with larger populations such as China and the United States of America. This problem falls within the BASA and ASC's ambit and has implications for making 'sporting structures relevant into the 21st century' (Australian Sports Commission, 2002a: 5), as well as ensuring that there are enough young athletes to feed high-performance programmes and professional sport leagues.

The BASA policy shift away from physical, social and health outcomes and towards organised sport participation is also in part a response to the difficulties of measuring outcomes and justifying budget expenditure. It is difficult to measure how many more people are receiving a physical or emotional benefit because of increased physical activity, or determine the ways in which they benefit, or the scale of the benefit. The BASA policy and the TSPG programmes represent a strategic move towards the implementation of activities and programmes that can be evaluated more easily and effectively. Organised sport participation, because of the way in which people participate and the way sport clubs and associations manage their members, is easier to measure than participation in informal or unstructured physical activity. The increased and improved measurement ability in turn assists with the evaluation of programme outcomes.

Finally, the BASA policy shift is also a move back towards the original intent of the ASC. In section 6.1(c) of the *Australia Sports Commission Act* of 1985 and section 6.1(b) of the *Australian Sports Commission Act* of 1989, the objectives of the ASC are referred to respectively as 'to encourage increased participation sport' and 'to encourage increased participation and improved performance by Australians in sport' (Commonwealth of Australia, 1985, 1989). There is no reference in the objects and functions of the ASC acts of 1985 and 1989 to physical activity, and yet during the 1990s the ASC became increasingly involved in the provision of activities, resources and promotion related to physical activity. In the *ASC Act of 1989*, one of the functions of the Commission was 'to co-ordinate activities in Australia for the development of sport'. Given this function it could be argued that a healthy and physically active Australian population is central to developing and sustaining a successful sporting system, and that the ASC should therefore be responsible for physical activity development, whether it occurs while participating in sport or not. However, the BASA policy is a clear statement of the government's intent to re-focus the priorities and energies of the ASC on structured sport and shift away from large-scale involvement in the promotion of informal physical activity among Australians.

The TSPG programme

The TSPG programme, which exemplifies the re-focusing of policy, has a number of core features. First, the TSPG programme aims to establish a three-way partnership between government, business and sport, as referred to in the policy statement. The support for a partnership-based model of sport development in BASA was, in terms of the policy-process model previously discussed, not only an articulation of the policy statement, but also had significant implications for policy implementation and practice. Second, the program targets only a small number of sports with an established and extensive club infrastructure for special support, to grow their business by expanding active membership of clubs and associations. Third, the ASC works in partnership with the targeted sports to establish sustainable participation growth. Fourth, the targeted sports were required to establish a sound business plan to support their TSPG initiatives. Finally, the targeted NSOs must establish programmes that have support at the local, regional and state levels.

As referred to previously, the TSPG programme has been established by the ASC in partnership with 21 established sports: Australian football, athletics, basketball, cricket, cycling, gymnastics, hockey, lawn bowls, netball, rugby league, rugby union, sailing, softball/baseball, swimming, surfing, surf life saving, tennis, touch, volleyball and men's and women's golf. Each of the targeted sports has a sufficiently developed infrastructure to be able to implement programmes that will have a meaningful impact on the policy objective of increasing organised sport participation. Each of the sports has a distinctive national profile. In the case of Australian football, rugby league and rugby union, each have a professional league in Australia (in the case of rugby union the league is shared equally with New Zealand and South Africa). Athletics, basketball, cycling, gymnastics, hockey, sailing, softball/baseball, swimming, tennis and volleyball are all Olympic sports. Cricket is Australia's national sport, with a well developed but poorly attended national league (state competition), and netball has the highest participation rates of any organised women's sport in Australia. Lawn bowls has a high participation rate among older Australians, while touch has a very high participation rate among school-aged children, particularly in New South Wales and Queensland. Surf life saving has reasonably high participation rates and embodies Australian beach culture. Furthermore, safe beaches are an important management and leisure imperative for every level of government. In some respects, men's golf, women's golf, and surfing are anomalies. While none of these sports have organised sport participation rates to challenge the traditional club-based sports, each has a large pool of informal participants and latent members.

The TSPG programmes can be organised around three distinct categories, as illustrated in Table 9.3. Table 9.3 shows that many of the sports involved in the TSPG programme have opted to run junior clinics, of which the highly successful Auskick programme developed by the AFL is an exemplar. These junior clinics typically run for between six and twelve weeks, involve participation in modified games and provide children with promotion packs, including sporting equipment and sponsors' products. Far fewer sports in the TSPG programme, as illustrated in Table 9.3, have developed programmes within the junior school model, which is similar to the junior clinic model, but instead of the clinic being delivered at a club, the programme is delivered within school time at schools. Finally, as illustrated in Table 9.3, a number of sports have developed an adult membership programme.

The TSPG programmes have been funded to the value of approximately $11.5 million over a three-year period that began in 2002 (although the staging of the ASC investment and the roll-out of programmes means that the funding will likely be delivered over a five-year period to NSOs). Table 9.4 shows the allocation

Table 9.3 TSPG programmes by type

Sport	Program type		
	Junior clinic	Junior school	Adult member
Athletics	✓	✓	✓
Basketball	✓	✓	
Cricket	✓		
Cycling			✓
Football	✓		
Hockey	✓		
Golf (men's)			✓
Golf (women's)			✓
Gymnastics		✓	
Lawn bowls			✓
Netball			✓
Rugby league	✓		
Rugby union	✓		
Sailing			✓
Softball/baseball		✓	
Surfing	✓		
Surf life saving	✓		
Swimming	✓		✓
Tennis	✓		
Touch	✓		
Volleyball	✓	✓	

Table 9.4 TSPG funding

Sport	Funding (in $)
Football	1,000,000
Netball	950,000
Cricket	900,000
Athletics	700,000
Lawn bowls	700,000
Sailing	700,000
Surfing	700,000
Swimming	700,000
Rugby league	650,000
Rugby union	650,000
Basketball	600,000
Softball/baseball	450,000
Tennis	450,000
Surf life saving	400,000
Hockey	390,000
Gymnastics	350,000
Golf (women's)	275,000
Touch	275,000
Cycling	255,000
Golf (men's)	235,000
Volleyball	200,000
Total funding	11,530,000

of funding to sports involved in the TSPG programmes. NSOs with more highly developed sport development infrastructure and resources have benefited more than small organisations, which have neither the capacity to roll out large-scale participation programmes, nor the ability to contribute significantly to the policy goal of one million more registered sport participants. The larger NSOs also often have the greatest latent demand in the community, are able to deliver in regional and remote areas, and are often more able to spend valuable ASC funding in effective and productive ways.

As previously noted, the TSPG programmes have been designed as business partnerships. In general, this has meant that NSOs have been responsible for securing sponsorship for their sport development programmes. The value of the sponsorship to all TSPG programmes has been estimated at approximately $10 million, but only a few of the 21 targeted sports have secured sponsorships that could ensure the financial viability of their development programmes beyond the ASC funding allocation. The biggest beneficiaries have been those sports that have been able to demonstrate to prospective sponsors that a large market for their product exists. Thus, those sports that have a large participant base, particularly of school-aged children, are able to secure larger sponsorship deals from larger commercial organisations. Nestle promotes the Milo brand through the CA programmes, Electrolux promotes the Simpson brand of whitegoods to the mothers and fathers of children participating in the AFL programmes, Goodman Fielder promotes the Uncle Tobys brand through the Swimming Australia programmes and Coca-Cola is the major sponsor of the TSPG programmes conducted by Surfing Australia. Simpson's sponsorship of the Auskick programmes is AUS$4.4 million (Australian Football League, 2004), which began in 2002, although it is likely that Simpson would have sponsored the programme, with or without it being adopted by the ASC. It is estimated that Nestle's sponsorship of the CA programmes is equally significant, while the Milo brand has been associated with junior cricket development since 1992. Thus, the sponsorship of the football and cricket programmes represent the vast majority of external funding to all TSPG programmes, which would have occurred with or without the TSPG impetus. Thus far, the TSPG programmes have delivered variable outcomes in terms of producing sustainable long-term business partnerships. The goal of creating partnerships and encouraging business to invest in sport is a sound one, but it is clear that for some NSOs, the sport sponsorship and investment marketplace is daunting. Any comprehensive evaluation of the business partnership component of the TSPG programmes will have to wait until the ASC has allocated all its funding to the 21 TSPG sports and pulled back to observer status.

The ASC board approved the funding of the TSPG programmes based on the business plans presented by the sports and the ability of each sport to deliver members and participants. In many respects the ASC adopted a return on investment model for the allocation of funding to the TSPG programmes. Faced with the target of one million new sport participants in four years, the ASC resolved to fund sports and programmes with the ability to deliver on-the-ground level. Hence, the sports that gained most financially had the resources and infrastructure already in place, and were more advanced in their sport development thinking. Finally, as part of a new era of relationships between the ASC and NSOs, which included 'funding and service level agreements', the ASC regarded the TSPG funding as an investment, rather than a grant. Furthermore, it was made clear to the sport organisations involved in the programme that funding would be at its greatest in the first year of the programme, decrease in the second and third years, and that in the fourth year the ASC would remove itself, with the programme continuing as a long-term, sustainable business practice. NSOs were also informed by the ASC that after the third year of the programme, there would be no additional funding. It remains to be seen whether other targeted development programmes will be put in place, or whether sport development will be left to the respective NSOs as part of their annual ASC funding, delivered through the funding and service level agreements.

As illustrated in Table 9.4, the AFL was allocated AUS$1,000,000 from the TSPG budget to develop new markets for its Auskick programme. From 1995 to 2001 the Auskick programme almost doubled its participants from 47,402 to 94,404, and from 2000 to 2001, the year in which the AFL applied to the ASC for funding under the new TSPG programme, the participation rate increased by 18 per cent (Australian Football League, 2001: 71). As illustrated in Table 9.5, the

Table 9.5 AFL game development funding 1998–2002

Year	Funding (AUS$ million)
1998	8.6
1999	12.1
2000	15.2
2001	16.5
2002	17.7

Source: Australian Football League (2002).

AFL's funding of game development, which includes the Auskick programme, increased from AUS$8.6 million in 1998 to AUS$17.7 million in 2002. At the same time, the ASC funded the AFL-TSPG programmes at a level greater than any other sport, and more than men's golf, volleyball, touch and cycling combined. In 2002 the game development funding of the AFL exceeded the total allocated to the entire TSPG programme by in excess of AUS$5 million, although it should be noted that only a proportion of this amount is spent on the Auskick programme. The allocation of AUS$1 million to the richest sport organisation in Australia to extend its reach seems extraordinarily generous were it not for the ASC's return on investment model of funding allocation. In short, the AFL was allocated the greatest amount of funding for TSPG programmes because it demonstrated that it was more likely than any of the other sports to deliver a significant share of the one million additional organised sport participants. If the Auskick program continues to grow at the rate experienced over the 2000–2001 period, the programme will attract an additional 45,000 participants over a three-year period. The AFL demonstrated that it had the capacity to convert significant latent interest in football into active participation, as well the capacity to distribute ASC funding through its game development infrastructure, a feature that smaller NSOs often lack.

The following case studies examine a TSPG programme from each of the three categories identified in Table 9.3. CA runs the Milo Have-A-Go (MHAG) and Crichit junior clinic programmes to develop junior participation generally and girls participation in cricket more specifically, Gymnastics Australia runs school-based aerobics and gymnastics programmes, and Women's Golf Australia has developed the Play A-Around (PAR) programme to increase adult membership.

Case study: Have-A-Go and Crichit

The MHAG programme began in 1993, devised and delivered by Cricket Victoria, and modelled on the AFL's successful Auskick. The programme spread in an *ad hoc* fashion to each of the Australian states and territories, to the point that by the mid-1990s there were effectively eight different junior development programmes being run within the clinic model. The programme was given greater national emphasis when CA appointed a general manager for cricket development in 2000, and was enhanced by the subsequent strategic plan, increased staffing and increased funding to the area that followed (McAllion, 2003).

The MHAG programme is an introductory cricket programme for boys and girls aged 5–10 years. The programme runs for 12 weeks, with one session per week. It emphasises the acquisition of basic cricket skills in a fun and social atmosphere, as well as encouraging the development of fundamental motor skills such as catching, throwing, hitting, running, stopping, balance, and coordination. The MHAG programme has five primary objectives that inform its structure and delivery, which are to provide each child with: cricket skills; physical fitness; an understanding of cricket and strategies; social skills that promote acceptable behaviour and positive relationships; and attitudes and values that will encourage participation in and enjoyment of sport and cricket, as both a participant and a spectator (Australian Cricket Board, 2002: 5).

The TSPG initiative enabled CA to further streamline the delivery of MHAG, as well as develop processes and structures that would significantly increase the efficiency, coordination and reach of the programme. As a result of the TSPG funding, CA has been able to increase the number of participants involved in the programme, as shown in Table 9.6. From a base of 12,000 participants prior to the TSPG programme, CA has achieved growth of almost 150 per cent. As a result of the TSPG funding, CA has also developed, implemented and managed a national database and national equipment distribution network (McAllion, 2003).

In 2003 the MHAG programmes were run in 820 accredited centres throughout Australia, in both regional and metropolitan areas. Table 9.7 shows that CA has achieved an even distribution in terms of metropolitan and regional participation, particularly in the larger states of Victoria, New South Wales and Queensland. Regional participation accounts for approximately 48 per cent of the total MAHG participation.

Like the funding to the AFL for the Auskick programme, the ASC funding supported a strong existing programme. CA was allocated AUS$900,000 through the TSPG initiative, and yet the MHAG programme was, relative to other Australia sports, reasonably well developed and funded. Moreover, the programme had support from a sport development department within CA that was both well funded and staffed, unlike many other NSOs. Given this, and Nestle's financial support for cricket development in Australia through the Milo brand, the programme may have prospered without the TSPG funding. At the same time, CA and ASC agreed that the requirements of the TSPG funding,

Table 9.6 CA TSPG programme participation 2001–2003

Program	2001 participants	2003 target	2003 actual
MHAG	12,000	27,500	29,053
Crichit	N/A	720	298

Source: McAllion (2003).

Table 9.7 MHAG regional and metropolitan participation by state, 2003

State/Territory	Metro	Regional
Victoria	6,583	7,066
New South Wales	2,046	2,303
Queensland	1,480	2,131
Western Australia	2,142	829
South Australia	1,541	676
Tasmania	320	966
Australian Capital Territory	600	–
Northern Territory	300	70
Total	15,012	14,041

Source: McAllion (2003).

such as the business plan and increased accountability and reporting, resulted in increased professionalism, national coordination and programme quality (McAllion, 2003). On balance, CA was funded primarily because it had the infrastructure and resources to deliver the increased participation figures required to meet the BASA target. In particular, the regional and metropolitan participation figures illustrate that CA has been successful at extending the reach of its participation programmes into regional areas, an important tenet of the BASA policy.

The second and much smaller programme developed and implemented by CA as part of the TSPG initiative was Crichit, an eight-week (one session per week) clinic for girls aged between 10 and 13. Prior to the implementation of Crichit, there were no formal opportunities for girls to play cricket after participating in the MHAG programme (McAllion, 2003). Because of a lack of under-age girls cricket competitions, once a girl reached the age of 10 her only option would be to play in one of the lower grades of senior women's cricket. This was clearly an unenviable situation, both for the skill and social development of girls playing cricket, and the retention of female players. Research conducted by CA indicated that not only were 10 per cent of MHAG participants girls, but only 10 per cent of these participants continued playing cricket after they were too old for the mixed sex clinics (McAllion, 2003). Hence, Crichit was developed by CA to partially fill a serious development gap in women's cricket.

Prior to Crichit, men's cricket clubs had been asked to offer programmes for girls, in order to increase the number of participants and develop an untapped market, but the response was to do nothing, or do something poorly (McAllion, 2003). In contrast, Crichit is a programme targeted specifically to girls, with paid coordinators, structured lessons plans with modified activities for skill development, venue quality guidelines, an emphasis on fun and social development, and specific marketing and branding targeted at young girls (pink posters and pro-motional material). In 2003 the programme was piloted in selected centres in Victoria, New South Wales, Queensland, Tasmania and the Australian Capital Territory, primarily in metropolitan areas. As only 298 girls participated (see Table 9.6), approximately 41 per cent of the target, the programme has yet to be implemented fully, and the growth of the programme during 2004–2005 will be a more accurate reflection of whether it is sustainable in the long term.

Case study: Gymskools and Aeroskools

In 2001, Gymnastics Australia (GA) presented a business plan to the ASC, as part of the TSPG programme. GA placed an emphasis in the plan on managing the gymnastics network (Gymnastics Australia, 2001). The implementation, development and success of the Gymskools and Aeroskools programmes formed a large part of this network. The mission of these TSPG programmes was to 'significantly increase the number of children and youth participating in Gymnastics through increased active membership', but perhaps more importantly, the vision of the programmes was to create 'an expanded, cohesive and diverse delivery network providing quality gymnastic activities across Australia through partnerships' (Gymnastics Australia, 2001: 8).

Gymskools, which began in 2002, is a gymnastic programme run in schools and gymnastic clubs for primary-school-aged children (4–12). The programme is delivered by Kidskills Australia, a private provider, on a fee for service basis. In 2001, two school-based gymnastics providers were invited to express an interest in becoming a business partner in the GA-TSPG programme. Kidskills Australia was selected as the approved business partner, and GA subsequently became a shareholder in the business, as part of the TSPG agreement. GA agreed to invest AUS$225,000 over a three-year period into Kidskills Australia through the Gymskools programme, subject to the programme meeting annual performance targets (Gymnastics Australia, 2001: 42).

The Gymskools programme consists of three main sub-programmes: Funtastic Gymnastics, emphasising basic gymnastic skills, teamwork and confidence; Safe Landings, designed for students to learn and apply safe landing skills; and Display, designed for older children, incorporating gymnastic skills, safe landings and sport aerobatics and culminating in a 'display'. Each of the above programmes is run over a 5–10-week period, depending on the length of the school term and individual school or club requirements. The fourth sub-programme is a One Day Fun Day, which incorporates elements of each of the three larger programmes, and enables schools to sample the Kidskills' product before committing to one of the intensive programmes.

As shown in Table 9.8, prior to the Gymskools programme, the Kidskills Australia programmes had 10,000 participants. By 2003 the participants had increased by slightly less than 100 per cent, although this figure was significantly less than the original ASC/GA target of 29,320.

GA receives a financial return on each student that participates in the Gymskools programme through Kidskills Australia, its business partner, making it one of the more unique and successful partnership arrangements within the TSPG programme. GA has also established a good working relationship with its constituent gymnastics clubs, to either run the programme as part of their

Table 9.8 Gymskools participation: targets and actual

Year	Original target	Revised target	Participation
2001	N/A	N/A	10,000
2002	25,120	N/A	13,699
2003	29,320	17,640	19,259
2004	34,080	21,420	N/A

Sources: Gymnastics Australia (2001), Gymnastics Australia (2003a).

activities, or work within a school-based programme to encourage more school-aged children to become a member of a gymnastics club. Specifically, through Kidskills Australia, GA invites gymnastics clubs to send a representative or promotional material to the school on the final day of programme. This has increased the opportunity for children to articulate from the Gymskools programme into the formal and structured club setting. Finally, GA has sought to establish the support of gymnastic clubs through extensive consultation, and by avoiding areas where gymnastic clubs are already heavily involved in providing school-based programmes.

As part of the TSPG initiative, GA also established Aeroskools, a sport aerobics programme conducted in schools by teachers or qualified instructors. Whereas Gymskools was designed to cater for primary-school-aged children, the Aeroskools programme has been targeted specifically at secondary-school-aged children (12–18). In 2002, GA introduced the programme into South Australia, Western Australia, Victoria and Tasmania, and in 2003 it expanded to include New South Wales and Queensland. GA estimates that in 2003 approximately 6,500 students participated in the Aeroskools programme, and in excess of 1,000 competed in a GA-sanctioned state or national Aeroskools championship (Gymnastics Australia, 2003b: 5).

In order to participate in the Aeroskools programme, a school must register its interest with the national coordinator and purchase an Aeroskools kit, which contains a video illustrating each of the sport aerobics routines for each of the levels of difficulty, a CD containing all music necessary for the programme and a set of choreography notes to guide the teacher and students through the routines. Unlike the Gymkools programme, which is delivered by a third party, the financial return on the Aeroskools programme is to GA alone. GA also provides teacher in-service training, or qualified consultants if required by the school. Schools are encouraged to work with their students to develop a sport aerobics routine that can be entered into a state or national championship. GA held national Aeroskools championships in Melbourne in 2002 and 2003.

Case study: Play A-Around?

In 1999, Women's Golf Australia (WGA) conducted a series of focus groups with a total of 1,600 women aged between 20 and 45, all of whom fitted the

ABS criteria for a person who plays golf on a regular basis (more than 14 times per year). The purpose of the focus groups was to establish why large numbers of social golfers were not becoming members of private golf clubs (Mooney, 2003). At the time there were approximately 130,000 female golf club members, but approximately 250,000 women who were active golfers and not associated with a club (Women's Golf Australia, 2002: 1).

The WGA focus groups revealed that there were significant barriers to club membership for the majority of the social golfers. Of those interviewed in the focus groups, the majority were in a double-income relationship, but had significant financial responsibilities and debts, including a house mortgage, car loan, higher education debt, superannuation contributions and general family expenses. These social golfers viewed the entry fee to a private golf club as an expense that could not be justified, given the high opportunity cost and limited benefits that would accrue (Mooney, 2003).

The focus groups also revealed that these female social golfers perceived that golf clubs were 'rules driven, particularly with regard to dress, male dominated, hostile, unsophisticated and stifling – in fact places where they take all the fun out of playing golf!' (Women's Golf Australia, 2003: 1). It was also clear from the focus groups that there was a generation gap between the members of golf clubs and these young, female social golfers. Furthermore, these golfers wanted to play whenever and with whomever they wanted, rather than be dictated to by the time or playing constraints of a member-based club. In this respect, privately owned public courses are perfectly positioned to accommodate the needs of golfers who require their sporting activity to be time-compressed, casual, and convenient. The focus groups also revealed that these social golfers would not take up memberships at golf clubs if additional services and facilities, such as a crèche or tennis court, were provided. It was obvious that these social golfers were happy with their informal and unstructured relationship with the sport of golf and club membership was something to consider in later life when they had fewer financial and time pressures.

As a result of the focus groups, WGA began to formulate a plan to convert these social golfers into members. The TSPG programme subsequently allowed WGA to develop the concept more fully in conjunction with the ASC and its constituent state sporting associations. In 2002, WGA launched PAR at the Australian Women's Open. It was designed to convert 30,000 of the 250,000 social female golfers into members over a five-year period (Mooney, 2003).

In WGA's original business plan, the programme for increasing female golf membership was referred to as the Women's Golf Network (WGN). The WGN was subsequently recast and branded as PAR and a significant proportion of the starting capital was spent on developing the PAR brand, design work and a professional and far-reaching communications strategy (Mooney, 2003). Specifically, the principles of the WGN were retained, but the business was given a playful image to attract women between the ages of 18 and 45. As illustrated in Table 9.9, according to WGA, approximately 79 per cent of the social golfers fall within this age bracket. The print and Web-based

Table 9.9 Distribution of Australian female social golfers by age, 2001

Age	Golfers	Percentage
18–24	42,069	17
25–34	61,867	25
35–44	91,580	37
45–54	32,166	13
55+	19,800	8
Total	247,482	100

Source: Women's Golf Australia (2002).

advertising and marketing provocatively asks the question of women golfers: Do you Play A-Around?

The PAR programme aims to increase female golf participation in regional, rural and metropolitan areas, provide social golfers with membership to a national organisation and provide and promote structured social golfing opportunities. It does so by offering social golfers the opportunity to gain an official handicap outside the club system, a regular programme of social and competitive golf events, seminars on golf rules, etiquette and technique, discounts on clinics, lessons, golf equipment and services, as well as opportunities to play the best golf courses in Australia. The membership benefits are designed to appeal to the golfer who enjoys the social or networking aspects of golf and would like to improve their game.

The PAR programme had a starting capital of AUS$475,000. The ASC contributed AUS$275,000 as part of the TSPG allocation and WGA contributed AUS$200,000. In late 2003, PAR had approximately 1,500 members, each paying an annual membership fee of AUS$80. This represents an annual income of AUS$125,000. If WGA and PAR achieve the five-year target of 30,000 members, then it is clear that the PAR programme would deliver a significant financial return on the AUS$475,000 investment. As a non-profit organisation, WGA is legally obliged to retain and reinvest this money, which essentially means that if PAR is a success, the state golf associations will have more money to spend on golf programmes throughout Australia (Mooney, 2003).

It remains to be seen, however, whether the PAR programme will deliver as a relatively small commercial enterprise, or as a programme that significantly increases the numbers of female golf members. As it stands, the PAR programme is developing well and is able to provide its members with a range of benefits. What it is doing less well is delivering the members that the ASC needs to reach its target of one million more organised sport participants.

Sport or play?

In many respects the BASA sport policy was a clarion call for the ASC to not only consolidate its high-performance emphasis, but also re-direct its energies outside the high-performance domain into organised sport. Previously, through the Active Australia initiative, among other developments, the ASC had been drawn in to providing, resourcing and promoting physical activity and recreation. The BASA policy, in contrast, focused on organised sport rather than physical activity or informal sport activities. The policy freed the ASC to place an emphasis on structured and organised sport in the sport development arena. However the implementation of the policy has provided some difficulties, particularly in developing programmes and activities that conform to the strict definition of sport articulated by BASA.

The concept of defining sport was discussed in Chapter 2, including the notion that policy makers, sport analysts and participants have typically focused on its regulatory and competitive dimensions. However, the programmes delivered by GA, WGA, and CA all rely on children and adults being involved in structured play, rather than competitive and rule-bound sport. The Gymskools programme emphasises motor skill development and body awareness; the PAR programme is designed to encourage rather than limit the social element of the golf experience for women; while the MHAG and Crichit programmes, although they include modified games in which competition is possible, emphasise skill development and fun as a way of increasing and strengthening the total participant pool. Aeroskools is the only programme in which the competitive dimension is emphasised, although even this is an optional last step in the programme. In reality, the operation of the TSPG programmes discussed above suggest that it would have been more appropriate to set a goal of one million more Australians to be engaged in structured play and physical activity, rather than registered in grass-roots sport.

Despite the concern about deciding just what outcomes have been achieved, and the extent to which BASA's sport development targets have been met, the approach taken by NSOs within the TSPG programmes is a sound one. It makes sense to encourage skill development in a structured play setting, prior to children articulating into club-based junior and senior sport, in which the emphasis is on regulation and competition is far greater. The development of motor skills, ball awareness, coordination and confidence is essential to the development of specific sport skill sets, and the subsequent growth of grass-roots sport in general.

Concluding comments

The TSPG programmes aim to encourage new and innovative ways of seeing, developing and implementing sport development. The programmes have increased the levels of professionalism of NSOs, and made most of them aware of the importance of creating and maintaining sustainable business practices and industry partnerships. The TSPG programmes have clearly had a positive effect on management practices and processes.

The CA, GA, and WGA programmes referred to in this chapter have had tangible outcomes, and can legitimately be regarded as successful. CA has increased the participation in a junior clinic programme and established a new programme for female participation to ameliorate the problems created by a significant gap in development infrastructure and support. GA has entered into an innovative business partnership to deliver school-based participation programs and developed a new school sport programme to facilitate growth in one of the new gymnastics disciplines. Finally, WGA has developed and implemented a programme to convert social golfers into club members. As with all the TSPG programmes, the three referred to in this chapter have had varying levels of success, and a full evaluation of the impact of these programmes will probably not be able to be made until 2010, due to long-term nature of sport development. Furthermore, it is also unclear how many of the people who participate in TSPG programmes, particularly children, will articulate into regular, organised, competitive sport through the club system.

It is also clear that faced with a bold statement that one million more Australians would be involved in organised sport within a four-year period, and allocated approximately AUS$12 million, the ASC developed a programme that would best satisfy the quantitative demands placed on it. Sports that could deliver participants were targeted and funding was allocated on a return on investment model in which outcomes could be measured. The final evaluation of BASA will necessarily be made on whether the aim of one million additional organised sport participants is achieved, as dictated by the policy statement. It is unlikely that the programme will be evaluated on the basis of the quality of the activities, or the experiences of children and adults who engaged in the programmes. This would have required a vastly different conception of accountability than that which was articulated in BASA and the ASC strategic plan.

Politicians, bureaucrats and industry professionals might consider that the debate about how sport is defined revolves around a typically academic and esoteric set of distinctions, yet in the case of the TSPG programmes these definitions are central to the evaluation of BASA's outcomes. Based on the three case studies presented in this chapter, it is possible to conclude that the term 'structured play' better describes the TSPG activities than does the term 'sport'.

The BASA target of one million additional registered, organised sport participants may be viewed as a grandiose dream, or alternatively, a necessary panacea to low participation rates. However, there is no dispute that the policy is having a positive impact on the overall health of the Australian sport system. The time frame in which the ASC had to implement the participation policy goal perhaps does not adequately account for the length and complexity of the sport development process. In the end, though, the TSPG programme has resulted in the consolidation and expansion of existing programmes, the development of innovative new programmes, and an increased awareness about the importance of systematic planning, business practices and self-sustainable funding.

10 Junior sport development: participation programmes and player pathways

Background

Through the policy platform expressed in *BASA*, the Commonwealth Government has clearly indicated its support for junior sporting programmes and initiatives. The BASA policy states that 'our aim is to see more sport played at the grass-roots level, particularly amongst school-aged children and in rural areas' (Commonwealth of Australia, 2001: 6). This policy flows on from the *National Junior Sport Policy: A Framework for Developing Junior Sport in Australia* first released in 1994 under the guidance of John Faulkner, the then Federal Minister for the Environment, Sport and Territories (ASC, 1994). Most notably, the policy identifies a junior sport development model, which emphasises the importance of customised activities for junior participants of different ages. It was also one of the first serious attempts to encourage modified competitions, rules, and games for juniors. While junior sport development is pivotal to the future health of Australian sport, cultivating junior participation is troublesome for many NSOs. In particular, they must combat a leisure market where opportunities to spend discretionary leisure time are plentiful, and where many attractive options are sedentary in nature. Moreover, the last five years have ushered in a new series of modified sport activities, designed specifically to promote junior participation. Most recently the ASC has facilitated the introduction of additional programmes and the expansion of many existing ones, through their TSPG programme. The TSPG programme, which is administered through NSOs, was examined in detail in Chapter 9.

The purpose of this chapter is to examine a range of junior participation programmes developed by NSOs in their endeavours to both provide the platform for the future growth of their sports, and discharge their funding obligations to the ASC as specified by the BASA participation policy. In this chapter, the key elements of a junior player pathway programme are drawn out by examining a range of successful initiatives across a variety of sport, and conflating the range of approaches to a set of best practices. In several instances, the relationship between the junior programme and the sport's player pathways are illustrated.

The state of junior sport participation in Australia

The latest Australian Bureau of Statistics data revealed that in 2003 there were approximately 2.6 million children between 5 and 14 years of age living in Australia (ABS, 2003). Of this number, around 62 per cent, or 1.6 million, participated in sport outside school hours, which had been organised by a school, club, or association. Table 10.1 lists the sports with the highest levels of junior participation.

At first glance these figures seem quite impressive, but they should also be considered in the context of overall leisure patterns. For example, within the same group of children over the same period, 98 per cent watched TV or videos, 79 per cent accessed the Internet at home and 71 per cent played computer or console games.

It is also relevant to note that not all junior participants are involved in club-based competitive sport. For example, the highest uptake is provided by the AFL in the form of Auskick, an array of connected activities that aim to give the participants an exposure to the basic skills and rules of the game. In 2002, approximately 110,000 juniors were enrolled in an Auskick programme of the 184,000 juniors participating in the sport. It might also be worth noting that ABS figures rarely match up with those provided by NSOs, the former more conservative and the latter, at times, notoriously optimistic and inflated. Somewhere around 10–15 per cent variance can be expected.

As the sport industry expands, there are strong levels of competition among different sports which is attracting young players away from well-established Australian sports such as football, rugby league and union, soccer, netball, tennis, swimming, hockey, basketball, and athletics. For example, there has been a growth in individual and 'extreme' sports and activities such as skating (in-line and skateboards), martial arts, BMX, rock climbing (mainly indoor), and variations of surfing and skiing.

The modified games model

Many of the most successful junior participation programmes have been devised as modified sport. The idea and practice of modified sport has been around since the 1980s, and has received two major boosts since, the first coming from the 1994 national junior sport policy, and the second from the TSPG programme

Table 10.1 Junior sport participation in Australia

Boys		Girls	
Soccer	22% or 301,100	Netball	18% or 233,000
Swimming	16% or 213,600	Swimming	17% or 225,500
Australian football	14% or 184,200	Tennis	8% or 100,100
Tennis, cricket, basketball	9% or 128,300	Basketball	7% or 88,900

Source: Australian Bureau of Statistics (2003) *Sport and Recreation: A Statistical Overview.*

emanating from BASA. As a philosophical approach, modified sport emerged from an acknowledgement that in many sports, playing surfaces, equipment, detailed rules, and structures that emphasise winning have all evolved to suit adults and, as a result, either discourage children from participating or diminish their enjoyment. Most modified sport programmes revolve around six key changes:

1   Playing surface dimensions are reduced.
2   Playing time is shortened.
3   Playing season is shortened.
4   Rule complexity is minimised.
5   Equipment is smaller and designed to minimise injury.
6   Emphasis on winning or defeating an opponent is lowered.

The following discussion highlights a range of modified junior programmes, including some of the most developed and well-established, some of the most popular and some of the newest.

Auskick

The AFL's Auskick programme is, like a number of other junior sport programmes sponsored by a business firm and its associated products. In this case, it is Simpson, a supplier of nationally branded white goods. The programme comprises a sequential series of activities that are targeted towards primary-school-aged children (5–12 years) and, importantly, their parents. Auskick is the most successful junior sporting programme in Australia, with more than 110,000 children participating nationally in 2003. The programme aims to recruit both children and families into Australian football, and is underpinned by two broad policy components. First, the Auskick programme is recognised as a graded, skill-based programme that sequentially equips participants towards competitions at a club and/or school level. Second, the Auskick rules and procedures are modified according to the varying developmental levels of participants, in order to maximise participation, skill learning, and development. All organisations that provide Auskick football are expected to meet these policy requirements by providing an environment that facilitates personal achievement, social cooperation, fun, and a sequential programme of skill-based teaching. Furthermore, providers are expected to deliver appropriate activities (including warm-ups, drills, games, Auskick matches), appropriately trained and accredited personnel (coaches, umpires, and officials) and ethical behaviour conforming to the AFL Code of Conduct for Participants.

With the emphasis on skill development, in Auskick sessions skills are taught using a teaching method known as the SPIR method (Show, Practice, Instruct, Reward), which is summarised below. The weekly coaching programme is typically structured to run for one hour and forty minutes, commencing with unstructured play with parents and friends and concluding with encouragement awards.

Show   Name the skill, demonstrate three times, provide a maximum of three
coaching points
Practice   Immediate practise in an appropriate activity
Instruct   Provide feedback on performance based on coaching points
Reward   Encourage and reward effort and achievement

Another important, and now, thoroughly copied dimension of the programme is
its 'pack', which contains an assortment of football-related materials provided to
participants upon enrolment. In 2004 the Auskick pack contained the following
items:

- Synthetic football
- AFL Auskick cap
- Backpack
- AFL Auskick drink bottle
- Interactive CD-Rom
- Giant AFL Poster Book features AFL stars.
- Simpson-branded AFL Auskick pencil case
- AFL Auskick bumper edition book comprising 132 pages of stories, games, and puzzles
- Membership Card – access to some AFL games
- Ten per cent discount to the AFL Hall of Fame
- Activity book – tips and activities for healthy eating
- Insurance cover and safety advice.

In addition to its two key policies, the AFL has articulated three core elements
which underpin the programme's success. These are fun and safety, parental as
well as child participation, and community-based management. The AFL
emphasises that enjoyment and safety are important ingredients for facilitating
skill development in this age group. Furthermore, the importance of parental
support is emphasised, with parents acting as coaches, coordinators, and volunteers.
Parental support is made possible through the AFL infrastructure, the simplicity
of the rules and procedures to follow, and specialised training. All parents, for
instance, are provided with a free orientation session at the beginning of the
year, whilst coaches, coordinators and other interested parents complete a Level
1 course to develop their understanding of AFL Auskick. Finally, the role of
local communities (e.g. clubs, schools, and centres) in the management and
ownership of Auskick programmes is highlighted, and facilitated through low
participation costs and volunteering.

A more recent addition to the AFL arsenal of junior development is the AFL
Sport Education in Physical Education programme, a school-based initiative, under
the guidance of a national youth coordinator. The Sport Education in Physical
Education Program (SEPEP) is based on a student-centred learning approach
where students coordinate and manage a season of sport, which exhibits parallels
with community sport. Students assume responsibility and ownership by taking

on roles (other than that of the player) such as a coach, umpire, committee member, or publicity officer. This learning environment allows students to develop social and cognitive skills along with the skills of Australian football. Critically, the SEPEP programme is supported by a sport education workbook/manual to be employed as a curriculum resource for use in school physical education programmes. In practical terms, this removes the onus of lengthy preparation from the school physical education teacher, and in so doing encourages them to introduce Australian football to students. In addition, teachers can meet the requirements outlined in the Health and Physical Education components of the State and Territory curriculum frameworks.

AFL Sport Education is therefore a curriculum model that represents a parallel to community sport, but is delivered through schools. It is designed for use in middle-level primary school through to early secondary school levels (years 4–10), the very location of some of the most powerful gatekeepers for sport participation. The programme is designed to encourage students to learn the skills of Australian football and benefit from the fitness outcomes of the sport. It also has the advantage of giving the students a better appreciation of other roles that are performed in community football environments. This means that it better prepares participants in the programme for the ongoing involvement in the sport in general, rather than only ever being involved as a player. In this sense, they are trained to be coaches and administrators rather than dropping out of the sport altogether. For example, during the season, students can not only develop their playing skills, but also learn other roles such as umpiring and refereeing, team management, coaching, captaining, sports journalism, public relations, and committee positions. Through the programme, there are also strengthened links to community sports providers and state sporting organisations. The AFL Sport Education model includes the following components:

- A season of sport (rather than units)
- Affiliation with a team (as players and in other roles)
- Student responsibility and ownership
- Formal competition with evenly matched, mixed ability for single sex or mixed gender teams
- A culminating festive event
- Celebration of the traditions and rituals of the sport
- Maintenance of records and publication of results.

A second major development introduced by the AFL is its Recreational Football initiative. AFL Recreational Football was developed to enhance retention amongst adults and young participants interested exclusively in fun. It is designed to provide an opportunity for all Australian football enthusiasts to enjoy participation in a game that is very similar to the traditional sport, but with some practical changes that lessens body contact and avoids congestion. For example, it is easy to play, is not as physically demanding, can be played by all ages and genders, and has an emphasis on fun and safety. It is a social sport designed for all ages and abilities. It can be played in a variety of settings, as its emphasis is on social rather than physical contact. This means it can be played at the local park or a more structured environment at a community club. The game is flexible in delivery and can be adapted to cater for the skills and needs of the participants. Little equipment is required. All of these characteristics expand the attractiveness of the sport to juniors and adults who have diminished interest in traditional version of the game.

The linking of modified, junior development programmes to player pathways for sport is pivotal to their ongoing success. In many recent cases, new programmes have been designed to bolster gaps in the pathway between school-aged players and serious junior participation members. Another motivation for junior participation programmes is to provide clearer pathways for players to advance through the higher levels of competition. Naturally, this can add substantial incentive to those junior players for whom the highest level of the sport contains heroes and glory.

The AFL junior pathway is identified in Figure 10.1, and highlights four possible stages through which players might proceed. Beginning with participation in the AFL's modified junior scheme, Auskick, players can progress to play with a junior club and penultimately in a youth team. Ultimately, should they persist, players can play senior football and a tiny elite will make it to the highest level of competition, the AFL. Some outstanding youth players in their late teens will be selected in elite representative squads which also eventually feed into the AFL competition. As an avenue for junior progression, the AFL junior pathway is highly developed with significant infrastructure. For example, players are aware that they can reach the pinnacle of the sport if they are sufficiently skilled. This provides an enormous incentive to talented young players with many AFL idols. However it can also provide a barrier to continuing participation, since, the majority of young players will not realise their dreams, and consequently be faced with a personal pathway that diminishes in appeal as it becomes more competitive.

Netball junior development

Under the custodianship of Netball Australia, netball remains the highest female junior participation sport in Australia. While like the AFL it enjoys the benefits of a traditional player base, it has also taken junior development seriously, culminating in the 2002 Netball Australia Junior Netball Policy. The document sets out the guidelines and philosophy for their junior modified activities, which channel participants through the sport's pathways. Specifically, the policy identifies seven objectives. These seven have at their core the themes of lifelong participation, skill and personal development, safety, equal opportunity to play, the cultivation of talent, and a commitment to integration and coordination throughout the pathway. Consistent with Commonwealth Government declarations on sport development, Netball Australia also acknowledges the importance of enjoyment, progressive development, specialisation, modified rules, and accredited coaches.

Figure 10.1 The AFL junior pathway.

Like all sports in Australia, although a national policy may be determined, the burden of action falls primarily to the state governing bodies. Only a handful of NSOs like the AFL, CA and Tennis Australia (TA), have the resources to employ development managers to either directly work with juniors in modified sport, or subsidise their employment on behalf of each state. As a result, the success of most programmes rests with the states. One of the leading state sporting bodies in Australia, Netball Victoria, has invested considerable resources and expertise in administering their junior programmes. For example, the player development pathways established by Netball Victoria, cater for participants who enjoy the game as a social outlet, as well as those who are aiming for elite achievement.

As indicated in Figure 10.2, the pathway progresses through nine steps, or levels of participation ranging from 5-year-olds to 17-year-olds. Each step is designed to sequentially develop skills and provide game experiences that are appropriate for each age. A brief summary of the focus of each step follows:

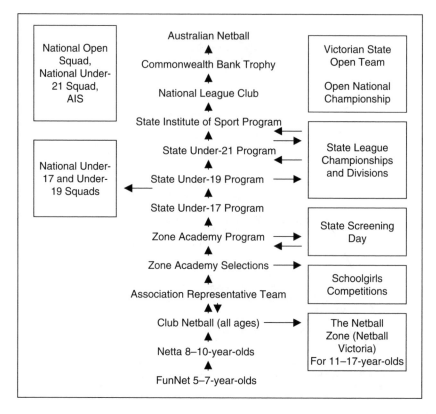

Figure 10.2 The Netball player pathway (via Victoria).

1   FunNet: Targeted towards 5–7-year-olds, FunNet is a programme that can be delivered by clubs, associations and schools, with support provided by the FunNet Program at Netball Victoria. FunNet aims to develop the movement and ball-handling skills that are required for step two (Netta), and for the game of netball in general.

2   Netta: For 8–10-year-olds, Netta further develops netball specific skills, and enables participants to put them into practice through modified rules games.

3   Club Netball: The Club Netball programme caters to all participants aged between 11 and 17 years. Clubs are affiliated to a netball association, and facilitate participation and development within the netball season. The beginning levels of club Netball include either the Netta competition teams or Under-11 Finals.

4   Association representative team: Involvement in an Association Team begins the pathway towards state and national league representation, through the Association Tournaments and developmental training sessions.

5   Zone-based association tournaments: In these tournaments associations compete for the opportunity to play in the Association Championship. The Zone-based Association Tournaments are one-day tournaments designed to highlight the junior talent within each Zone-based Association. Talent identification selectors attend the tournament and identify players in the 15 & Under and 17 & Under age groups for Zone Academy selections.

6   Zone academy programme: The Zone Academy Program fosters excellence, and provides players with the avenue towards Victorian Institute of Sport (VIS), State and National netball representation. The programme nurtures talented participants, team managers, coaches, umpires, and sports science personnel throughout Victoria.

7   Victorian State Schools Sporting Association (VSSSA) Schoolgirls and the Victorian State 17 & Under Squad: In conjunction with Netball Victoria, the VSSSA coordinates this programme, which is aimed to provide talented, under-age participants (aged 14 and 15) to compete in a school-based State Representative Team, at the National Schools Championships. The Victorian State 17 & Under Squad selects 25 out of 50 of the most talented participants aged 15–17 years in Victoria, identified through the Zone Academy Program. The squad trains in the lead up to final selection for the Victorian State 17 & Under Team.

8   Victorian State 17 & Under Team: Selection for the state team provides access to a thorough on- and off-court training regime, in preparation for the Netball Australia National Championships. Participants have the opportunity to be selected for the Australian 17 & Under Netball Squad.

9   Australian 17 & Under Squad and Victorian Institute of Sport (VIS):   Selected from the Australian 17 & Under National Championships, the Australian 17 & Under Squad comprises twenty talented netballers. Athletes attend a national training camp held at the AIS, and may be offered a scholarship to the AIS. The VIS programme for netball provides elite players, usually between 16 and 19 years of age, with the opportunity to realise their potential and work towards representing Victoria in State and National League netball teams.

Soccer, rugby league, and rugby union

Soccer, rugby league and rugby union's junior modified programmes are both similar to, and different from the Auskick programme. While soccer enjoys far greater junior participation numbers than Australian football (by virtue of its popularity across the country rather than being isolated to a few states), it has not been as successful in converting its massive junior player base into senior participation or elite success. The newly re-developed face of Australian soccer, the Australian Soccer Association, has embraced the need for junior development pathways for primary-school-aged children, but inherited the Rooball programme from their administrative predecessors.

Rooball was launched in March 2001 as the Australian Soccer Associations' junior development game for children of 6–10 years of age. Rooball aims to give young boys and girls more opportunity to participate in soccer, and develop skills from a younger age. The game is modified to maximise goal scoring and fun by using smaller fields with less players, simplified rules, modified equipment, and frequent interchange of players to enable all players equal time on field. The programme is divided into four groups, Under 7s and Under 8s (who play six-a-side game on a quarter of an adult-size field), and Under 9s and Under 10s (who play a nine-a-side game, on half an adult-sized field). The emphasis in Rooball is participation and fun for children and parents alike, and as a result the pressure of winning has been eliminated with no premiership points, semi-finals or finals conducted.

However, as soccer has historically suffered from a degree of fragmentation at the national level, the impetus for junior development has fallen to the states. For example, the Victorian Soccer Federation (VSF) has been running its Goalkick programme since 1997 for both boys and girls between 5 and 12, and is in operation in schools as well as regional and community centres. The programme is philosophically consistent with the ASC's junior sport policy and the chief elements of Rooball. It is based on several key policy principles. First, the focus of all junior sporting activities should be on enjoyable participation. Second, junior sports programmes should help to develop self-confidence and cooperative skills. Third, junior sport programmes need to acknowledge that there are different stages of development in children, and sport must be accordingly customised to each stage. Fourth, juniors vary in their acquisition of skills and physical development, and programmes need to account for this by, fifth, providing modified rules and, finally, de-emphasising competition.

The VSF offers its Goalkick programme in two stages. Goalkick 1 is for boys and girls from 5–12-year-olds while Goalkick 2 is a more advanced version leading more directly to game play and competition for 8–12-year-olds. Goalkick 2 is, incidentally, identical to the junior pilot programme conducted by Manchester United in the English Premier League. Goalkick runs for 75 minutes once a week for 12 weeks (for schools and community centres) or 16 weeks (for clubs). In 2003 the VSF celebrated the establishment of the 150th programme across the state. Although soccer enjoys enormous junior participation numbers in Victoria, the Goalkick programme only engages around 6,000 children every year.

The Australian Rugby Union (ARU) has established a similar junior programme with a set of tiered pathways designed to introduce new juniors into the sport gradually. Its philosophy is based on the view that modified pathways offer opportunities for children to develop confidence in their sporting performances. Under the banner of Junior Player Pathway Programs, the set of modified activities are focused on introducing the skills and tactical principles of rugby union to children between 5 and 12 years of age. Like Auskick and Goalkick, and the directives of the national junior sport policy, the critical dimensions of the rugby union model include fun, physical rigour, skill development, fair play, and safety. They have also been designed to account for the physical differences between adults and children, involving a reduced-size playing area, ball, playing duration, and the number of players.

There are three levels to the ARU junior player pathway. The first, Walla Rugby, is designed for players up to 8 years old, and offers the simplest and most basic version of the sport. No tackling is allowed and emphasis is placed upon fundamental skills such as running, passing, and catching. Mini Rugby is designed for children up to 10. It adds additional dimensions such as more free-flowing action, and introduces players to the contact aspects of the game, including the tackle, ruck, and maul. Midi Rugby is intended as the transition to the full version of the game. It focuses more on tactical dimensions while developing the physical elements of the sport in readiness for under-19 competitions.

The ARU junior player pathway is one of the most comprehensive in Australian sport. In addition to the three-tiered set of developmental versions of the game, the ARU have also introduced TryRugby, which provides an opening for boys and girls between 5 and 12 to become interested in getting involved in Walla, Mini, and Midi Rugby. TryRugby is run over six consecutive Friday nights and provides participants with rugby memorabilia including a backpack and ball, as well as plenty of encouragement to join Walla Rugby.

Not to be outdone, the ARL, the administrators of the NRL competition (changed from the ARL to NRL as a consequence of the resolution of the Super-league/ARL dispute) have developed a programme for junior development through a joint initiative of the Australian Rugby League Foundation and the ASC. Under the umbrella of the Kids to Kangaroos national development plan, the programme seeks to provide a pathway for junior players through to senior ranks. The first step comes in the form of the Smaller Steps programme, which introduces children to the game through a modified version. Like the ARU model, Smaller Steps leads to further programmes including Mini-footy, Mod League, League Tag, League Sevens or State-based junior competitions. These programmes complement the already robust school competitions that attract over 70,000 participants annually.

Have-A-Go Cricket

Have-A-Go, as described in Chapter 9, is CA's highly successful modified junior development programme for 5–10-year-old boys and girls. Like the other sport's programmes reviewed in this chapter, the Have-A-Go is specifically designed to combine participation with skill development. As the name suggests, fun and involvement are important philosophical elements of the programme. Have-A-Go is administered by clubs, associations, and schools as a pathway or feeder system for junior competitions at under-9s, under-10s or under-11s levels. The structure of the programme is inherently flexible, allowing for different clubs to customise it to their needs. CA also provides a detailed administration manual, videos, and promotional flyers to accompany the programme. In most states, development officers from the state association are available to attend one of the first sessions as well. The Nestle/Milo company is the major sponsor of this programme. Nestle also sponsors the TA junior player programme known as Milo Tennis.

Team athletics

Presently sponsored by IGA (Independent Grocers Association) a group of independent retail grocers, Athletics Australia has developed the Team Athletics Program, which adds a developmental focus to a sport that has been the beneficiary of substantial junior participation through the programmes run by the autonomous activities of Little Athletics. Team Athletics attempts to build on one of the sport's traditional weaknesses: its perception as an individual sport. In this case, the programme encourages parents to consider the team-building advantages of a programme designed for group interaction and to enhance the spirit of being involved rather than of personal achievement and winning. The programme focuses upon primary-school-aged children by developing in them the skill fundamentals that go along with running, jumping, walking, and throwing, as well as cultivating the requisite balance, agility, and coordination. Like many sports, Athletics Australia intends for the programme to be adopted by schools and, to that end, provides manuals and lesson resources for teachers. Team Athletics was one of the first programmes, along with Auskick, funded under the ASC's participation strategy. Around 4,000–5,000 children are engaged in the programme each year.

Go Swim

Australian Swimming Incorporation has introduced a 'Go Swim' programme with the intention of aiding children (6–11 years old) to make the transition from learn to swim programmes to either competitive or recreational swimming. The programme is sponsored by the Uncle Tobys breakfast cereal company, and aims to provide a safe, non-competitive environment where free giveaways are used to reward the children for their efforts. Again, like all modified programmes, 'Go Swim' is designed to fill a gap in the sport's player development pathway.

Aussie Hoops

Basketball Australia and the ASC launched Aussie Hoops in 2002 as a national programme for primary-school-aged children. Focusing on accessibility for children of all skill levels and physical characteristics, Aussie Hoops encourages social interaction and fun. Aussie Hoops is structured around four incremental stages of activity, beginning with school-based activity and moving through to versions of game play and competition. Like so many other junior programmes it has learned the lessons Auskick has taught. As a result, it attempts to close the gap between competitive junior club games and the more social or recreational side of the sport. In other words, Basketball Australia has recognised, in the footsteps of many sports before it, that there has to be a mechanism for primary school children to get involved in the sport without being thrown into the deep end of serious junior competition. Equally, if they do not wish to proceed into the more competitive world of the sport, they can transition more easily to social and recreational basketball. Another stalwart of successful programmes, those schools registered for Aussie Hoops receive manuals and coaching frameworks.

Concluding comments

This chapter highlights the elements of successful junior development policy initiatives that are characteristic of Australian sport pathways. Some sports possess inherent advantages and therefore can design simple and easy transitional programmes for children. For example, swimming and soccer do not need to be modified as much as cricket in order to encourage junior participation. Collision sports like Australian football, rugby union and rugby league have also had to severely modify and grade their programmes to suit the needs of young children. At the same time, it is possible to identify the common elements of successful programmes in the field of junior sport. These may be distilled into 10 features:

1   Modification: All successful junior programmes provide modified activities and games including the reduction of:

    • Playing surfaces
    • Playing time
    • Season
    • Rule complexity
    • Equipment.

2   Scientific coaching: The development of coaching theory has progressed to the point of embracing key principles associated with teaching motor skills to children. These principles are transferable across sports and should be the basis for coaching methods in modified junior sport programmes.

3   Incremental development: The most successful programmes have several sequential steps which reflect the awareness that stages of development in children are progressive.

4   Individuality: Most programmes contain an inherent flexibility that accommodates the fact that children of the same age may possess differing physical capabilities and skills, and will develop in a disjointed manner.

5   Participation-focused: All programmes are based on the development of confidence and cooperation, rather than competition and winning.

6   Customised: Better programmes, while broad in skill requirements, are also customised to the sport itself and are to some degree non-transferable, so that as participants develop they are encouraged to remain in the sport.

7   Flexible delivery: The best programmes can be modified to run smoothly in different environments including clubs and schools.

8 Parental involvement: Although many programmes do not offer a great deal for parents, the best provides mechanisms for parents to get directly involved.

9 Programme support: While most sports do not have the resources to provide development officers for every major area within a state, the provision of manuals containing instructions and guidelines for physical education teachers and other approved coaches greatly enhances a programme's uptake and duplicability.

10 Linkages to pathways: The best programmes play a clear and pivotal role in the sport's player pathway, to the extent that participants can track their involvement through to the elite level.

From a policy viewpoint, the programmes illustrated in this chapter highlight two important issues in sport development. First, they show how Commonwealth Government initiatives can be translated into action at the national and, subsequently, state sport organisation level. Second, this case also illustrates the reciprocal nature of sport policy development. While the Commonwealth Government has clearly defined policy that aims to increase junior participation in Australian sport, the innovation and development of the 'on-the-ground' programmes tends to come from the sports themselves, the principles of which become common features of government expectations. This case therefore demonstrates that as well as being a top-down process, sport policy can also often proceed as an 'emergent' or bottom-up process.

11 Management improvement in sport: performance measurement

Background

Sport organisations have recently been faced with a wave of accountability pressures instigated by the need to produce elite sport performances within rationalised sporting systems (Australian Sports Commission, 2003a). Increasing competition for funding has led to closer scrutiny of organisational expenditure. Added to this weight of improving the financial position of a sport organisation is the fact that revenue is strongly linked to the profile of its elite athletes and teams. While sports recognise the need to bolster their infrastructure, player pathways and community profile with well-directed investments, they are under immense pressure to demonstrate results. In short, the imperative is to achieve more with limited resources, and demonstrate that these scarce resources have been well-spent.

This efficiency and effectiveness imperative is reinforced by current Commonwealth Government policy and the distribution of funding through the ASC. BASA specifies the importance of cultivating excellence in sports management (Commonwealth of Australia, 2001). The relevant management improvement goal is the adoption of sound business and management practices by NSOs. To this end the following actions were articulated:

- Assist NSOs to deliver efficient and effective administration through management improvement initiatives.
- Set performance targets for NSOs with regular evaluations of progress towards achieving goals in elite sport, participation, fairness, funding, governance, and anti-doping.

In addition, in 2003 the ASC internal review report *Servicing Sport* explained the importance of ensuring that the level of ASC support and funding should be determined by an NSO's ability to contribute to the ASC's strategic outcomes. It is intended to provide performance information that will facilitate the monitoring and support of NSO's performance, while simultaneously augmenting overall management improvement. Some salient aspects of the new Funding and Service Level Agreement (FSLA) include:

- establishment of cross-ASC service teams to provide an integrated service to NSOs based on agreed needs and priorities;
- development of a single FSLA that would replace the existing Resource Agreement and replace/integrate all other existing agreements between the ASC and NSOs; and
- development of a performance reporting process that would be based predominately on NSOs' existing planning and reporting processes.

The BASA policy statement and the new FSLA system set the agenda for this case. Few Australian sport organisations have attempted to systematically develop a performance management framework beyond on-field sporting achievements. As a consequence, the ASC has been constrained in its ability to set up an Australian-wide model for gathering data from NSOs. However, among the NSOs that have more recently embraced the concept of developing a comprehensive performance management framework is Tennis Australia (TA).

TA is the governing body of tennis within Australia. Its chief responsibilities include promoting and facilitating participation in tennis at all levels, as well as the operation of national and international tournaments. The most prominent of these include The Davis Cup, The Fed Cup, The Uncle Tobys Tour and the Tennis Australia summer Circuit, which constitutes eight tournaments leading into one of Australia's most successful sporting events, The Australian Open. TA is generally regarded as amongst a handful of the best sporting organisations in the country, their reputation exemplified in this case by their preparedness to place their operations under a lens of analysis with the view of continual improvement and development. Recently, the Tennis Division of TA set about to construct a balanced system that accounted for both performance outputs (in terms of effectiveness) and the relationship between those outputs and organisational resources (efficiency). This process was funded by the ASC in explicit support of TA's desire to enhance their performance management in line with BASA policy. This case reveals the process carried out by TA and explains the results and implications of such a course of action (Westerbeek and Smith, 2003). In so doing, it highlights the dimensions of performance that need to be understood before constructing a sport-based performance management framework.

Performance management and TA

Performance management is an organisation's way of communicating, implementing and measuring their strategies. In commercial businesses, this revolves around a financial imperative. Sport organisations also seek to yield a return on their resource investments. However, the measurement of this dividend is not as narrowly focused as it is for a commercial enterprise. It may involve a financial outcome, but for non-profit sport organisations these resources are reinvested. Thus, governing sport organisations have to balance a range of goals that represent the needs of their constituents. These include improved sport infrastructure and participation rates, elite success, spectatorship, and public recognition. A performance management system monitors the acquisition of these sorts of goals, relative to their importance.

Tennis Australia's Tennis Division collected scores of micro-performance measures, but only a handful of those measures were considered representative of the division's macro performance. The outcome of the process was a performance framework that began the process of identifying the type, quality, and quantity of data sufficient to enable TA to determine the effectiveness and efficiency of its constituent departments. And in so doing, the gap between ASC's need to provide outcome measures for government, and TA's ability to provide outcome and output measures for the ASC were narrowed.

The work undertaken by TA in seeking to align outcomes and outputs is impressive. The Tennis Division, for example, has identified major objectives and has related key performance indicators (KPIs) against these objectives. Thus, for example, against an objective (effectively an outcome) of increasing the number of individuals playing tennis, it prescribes a 10 per cent increase in registered players and a 5 per cent increase in social players (effectively outputs). These required outputs were then passed to the Participation Development Department to be further refined and implemented. The weakness in the system was exposed when it was found that within the Tennis Division alone there were some 84 objectives and 253 measurable actions. The sheer scale of these numbers prevented the collection of appropriate quantitative data. Despite this, there is a comforting agreement between the requirements of the ASC expressed in BASA and the actions of TA.

TA structure

Prior to the development of a performance management framework, the Tennis Division comprised eight departments: Tennis Operations and Events; Men's Tennis; Women's Tennis; Juniors; Media and Public Relations; Coach Education; Participation Development; and Business Development. The Division employed one divisional director and seven departmental managers comprising a total of 32 staff members.

Table 11.1 presents an overview of the link between what TA as an organisation has set out to achieve, and how the Tennis Division complements this picture. This matrix shows where the Tennis Division contributes to the objectives of the organisation as a whole. In general terms, most departments fit within the bigger picture of the organisation, directly or indirectly setting performance standards that are a direct derivative of organisational performance measures.

It is worth noting that within the Tennis Division considerable effort has been invested in identifying and coordinating the operational activities of the different departments. This has been achieved mainly by developing a core objectives and measurable actions document for the period 2002–2005. Irrespective of the good intentions with which the document has been developed, and also acknowledging the potential value such a document can add to the operational

Table 11.1 TA and tennis division strategic and performance management relationships

TA Objective (key result areas)	Major objectives	Key performance indicators	Related Tennis Division Department	Major objectives	Key performance indicators
Australian Open	Biggest tennis event in Asia/Pacific region	Attendance Prize money TV Ratings			
Participation	Increases in players	Increase registered players (10%) Increase social players 5% Increase participation rate (frequency) 10% (disability) 10%	Participation development	Increases in players	Increase registered players (10%) Increase social players 5% Increase participation rate (frequency) 10% (disability) 10%
Player development	Strong player development programme	Three players in top 20 and 10 in top 100	Coach education	Coach development and quality improvement	Certified coaches Funding assistance to, e.g. member associations and endorsed coaching agencies.
			Juniors	Expand base of national competitive players	2 top 10 6 top 100 (boys) 4 top 100 (girls)
Representative teams	To be competitive and achieve international success	*Finishing position:* Davis Cup, Fed Cup, Olympics, Hopman Cup	Men's and Women's Tennis	Elite success	3 top 20 (singles) 10 top 100 (singles)

Department	Responsibility / Objective	Measure / Target
Men's and Women's Tennis	Elite success	3 top 20 (doubles) 2 top 50 (doubles) 6 top 100 (doubles)
Tennis operations & events	Develop and manage events (other than Aus. Open)	Number of event visitors TV ratings
Business development	Sponsorship acquisition, maintenance	Sponsorship and Naming rights Radio partner Print media partner
Participation Development responsibility		
All departments	Programme development	Funding assistance
Media & public relations	Promote players, sponsors, events, TA, AO	
Event Management (non-Aus. Open)	Continue reputation for excellence	World Team Cup, World Youth Cup, Marble Cup (veterans), Britannia Cup (veterans)
Tennis for disabilities	World leadership Promote programmes Increase participation rate	Increase participation rate 10% per annum
Membership partnerships	Communication and consultation Provide funding and resources Recognition of role	Distributed monies
Marketing and communications	Build image and brand Advertise programme and services Promote events	

efficiency of the Division, it is very easy to get lost in its micro-level details. For example, the plan incorporates 84 objectives and 253 measurable actions, to be coordinated by the departmental managers, and ultimately, by the divisional director. As will be shown, while departmental managers are guided by the document, they do not focus on the collection of quantitative data in relation to most of the objectives and activities because of limited time and optional requirements.

Ultimately, performance information that is collected is limited to a narrow range of performance areas that are deemed important by the Board of Directors of TA. This includes data such as junior and senior rankings, sponsorship relationships and their value, participation registration numbers and spectatorship and profitability of events. The Pareto principle (the 80/20 rule) applies to what is being measured and what is consequently evaluated in the Tennis Division. Eighty per cent of operational activity goes unmeasured because twenty per cent of activities are easier to measure and also seem to be driving the public perceptions of the organisation. In other words, the tennis public perceives the success of the organisation to be based on player rankings, and players' success overseas and in events such as the Australian Open and Davis/Fed Cup. In this regard, TA's crown jewel is media exposure and spectatorship at the Australian Open.

The key finding concerning how operational activities fit the rest of the organisation and how the measures are used to assess performance are that efficiency and output results of the Division are assessed on an overly narrow range of performance criteria. There is a range of operational activities that are critical to the success of the Division, but these activities only indirectly contribute to performance measures such as rankings and financial success of events.

Measuring financial performance

In measuring financial performance, measures of stock turnover and merchandise sales are used, together with balance sheet ratios. The KPIs associated with keeping on budget are clearly measurable, and there is the opportunity to undertake limited efficiency measurement. However, cost-benefit calculations cannot be performed for some of the larger-expenditure items such as travel, mobile phones, and credit cards. One obstacle to financial efficiency measurement is that for most of the programmes undertaken in the Tennis Division, there are few revenue outputs to measure against the resource inputs.

Measuring staff development

Performance management is undertaken for members of the Tennis Division via a professional development review. It is structured on the basis of a qualitative rating system. It has moved recently from a management by objectives style to a broader and less confronting approach designed by a workplace improvement team of managers. The new system is moving towards a competency-based approach, with what is known as a target-setting programme. In general, the system is moving more towards broad skills and competencies rather than results and outcomes. It is more difficult to see the links between individual performance and departmental goals with such a system. However, the new approach is underpinned by a strengthened staff development philosophy that better manages the needs of individuals. From this perspective, and considering the input of staff members in the new approach, it offers more scope for professional development than its predecessor. As most management-by-objective approaches to staff performance appraisal are limited in their ability to develop staff members as opposed to reward or punish them, the new approach is commendable. It should be understood that the approach is a personal development review rather than an individual performance appraisal. The change in system further underpins the importance of Divisional performance measurement.

Even outside the Tennis Division there is a sense that it is understaffed. This results in long hours, much travel and the use of trainees and volunteers. In particular, the junior and women's events are under-resourced. Time credits are used instead of overtime payment, but long hours and commitment are expected. In such a time-pressured environment, it is much harder to devote significant and structured time towards staff development. However, more training is being introduced in order to develop better succession planning despite relatively low turnover making advancement more difficult.

Staff members are assisted with training and professional development. TA offers education opportunities, and funds training courses where there are particular needs for staff members to be skilled in new areas. The new professional development review will aid this process.

Measuring operational performance differs widely across departments. For example, in one department fortnightly progress meetings are common, whereas in others few formal meetings take place. In some instances timelines are associated with each project whereas other projects are viewed as ongoing. Another issue is the difference in downtimes per department. The participation department receives little downtime as a consequence of its ongoing activities.

Measuring the success of events

Almost all staff members of the Division are involved in at least some tennis events. Operational activities are not limited to the dedicated department's 'tennis operations and events'. For example, as many as three non-event department managers assume positions as (domestic and international) tournament directors. From a tennis event perspective, the key objective is to provide events that are professional, world class and cost effective. This objective is hard to measure and the process is in someways arbitrary and subjective. For example, the International Tennis Federation (ITF) rates the success of the Davis Cup ties and makes a payment based on this judgement. The performance measures for this are known before the event leading to the construction of a checklist. There is a pre-tie and post-tie report. Core activities of the Events Department therefore revolve around the operation of the Davis Cup and to a lesser extent the Fed Cup. The ITF performance measures regarding the Fed Cup are not as prescriptive as those regarding the Davis Cup. Referees reports are provided as well. All events rely on the goodwill and input of volunteers. At many events, exit surveys from the public are undertaken. The biggest issue in regard to measuring the performance of events is the competing agenda of building elite tennis players versus the need to generate revenue through the Davis Cup in particular. For example, the players decide their preferred playing surface for the Davis Cup. The TA Board then must make a decision about whether this is an appropriate level of financial investment. They subjectively decide whether there is a return on ranking investment.

Other data that is collected are letters from the public and the players. Usually these are complaints. There is also typically a debriefing session with all staff members after the event in order to rate its success and to identify areas for improvement. Sponsors' feedback is also considered pivotal.

The Uncle Tobys tournament series of 26 weeks (what used to be the satellite and challenger series programme) revolves around minimising expenditure without compromising the quality of the events. More resources are needed but fewer are available. Thus, the Events Department is charged with finding better locations for the events where staging costs are diminished. They also seek to maintain a consistency between the tournament-hosting cities. On the other hand, the Davis Cup and, to a lesser extent, the Fed Cup are geared towards maximising net revenue.

Job turnover is low in events due to its popularity, even amongst staff members from other departments. Staff members are not concerned about the number of hours that have to be worked and carefully plan the documentation of activities into operations manuals. Events employees perceive that the Davis Cup largely determines how the Events Department is assessed. As a result, much of the work undertaken in lower profile events is not measured.

Measuring junior performance

The Juniors Department is faced with a number of rival imperatives that compete for their focus of performance attention. For example, the department works with state associations on around 80 tennis events but also supports the senior's tour and develops the level of junior elite players that will feed into the senior ranks. The latter can be expressed through international junior rankings but can also be determined by the numbers of elite juniors making it to the senior's tour.

The Juniors Department is charged with providing a strong competitive tournament environment with high participation numbers, a directive that overlaps to some extent with the activities of the Tennis Operations and Events Department. They also assume a range of elite player development tasks, some of which overlap with the Men's and Women's Tennis Departments. Success is measured in terms of the number of events organised and the number of juniors sent to play overseas (achieved within budget). The manager of the Juniors Department is also the Tournament Director of the Junior Australian Open.

Measuring participation

One of the main observations in regard to measuring participation development is that departmental goals are unrealistic. In an increasingly competitive sport participation market, combined with already excellent participation figures, it seems quite ambitious to seek an increase in participation of 10 per cent every year. Staff members argue that a more appropriate approach would be to pace participation growth against the available infrastructure, the quality of facilities and the size of the available population. A more realistic growth figure might be around a 3–5 per cent increase annually.

Participation programmes have been recently rationalised. This means that in the participation department, the 'new programmes mentality' had to be altered to one concerned with delivering quality with existing programmes. Some programmes were eliminated while others were amalgamated. However, an indigenous programme has been introduced as a result of support from the ASC.

The collection of participation data is more extensive than in any other performance area including comprehensive tennis club membership profiles. All research undertaken by the participation department is compiled in the facts sheet that TA produces. Data sources include a national sport survey by the Sweeney Consulting Group and the Australian sporting goods industry. States are also expected to return quarterly data sheets via their TA-supported development officers. Industry sources are also reviewed including sport-related journals and the ASC. The usefulness of the data sheets for performance measurement is compromised because of the time it takes to receive all necessary information.

Measuring media and public relations

The role of the Media and Public Relations Department and marketing in general in the Tennis Division is subject to much debate. This is largely because the TA marketing function is fragmented. The Marketing Department that resides in the Corporate Services Division is conducted to some extent independently from the Australian Open Division, and is also undertaken through the Media and Public Relations Department of the Tennis Division.

The Media and Public Relations Department was geographically separated from the Corporate Services Division Marketing Department, irrespective of considerable potential for overlap. Furthermore, in the Tennis Division there is also a Business Development Department largely in charge of all sponsorship acquisition and servicing. However, the Media and Public Relations manager views his department's main tasks to be promoting tennis players and achieving positive exposure for TA sponsors. He argues that 90 per cent of his department's time is spent on obtaining exposure for sponsors. While greater physical proximity will enhance leveraging opportunities for the Marketing, and Media and Public Relations Departments to work together, their ongoing separation constitutes an ongoing dis-economy of scale and an unnecessarily complex area to measure performance.

Much performance measurement in the Media and Public Relations Department is based on intuition. Although media monitors are periodically employed, mainly during bigger events that can justify spending resources on the expensive exercise of media monitoring, most performance measurement is done through an interpretation of achieved coverage. That is, has media coverage been achieved, was the coverage positive, and most importantly did the sponsors get positive exposure? The success of the department is substantially based on tennis personalities and is therefore at least partly uncontrollable. Successful coverage for sponsors is in part measured by the feedback received from interested patrties.

The Australian Open is the most effective media activity of all. This needs to be seen in the light of the TA mission, which revolves around creating greater numbers and better-quality tennis players. The Media and Public Relations Department's job is to maximise the chances of getting exposure to support that mission. This is done in a competitive environment in which hundreds of stories compete for publicity. Measuring performance in such an environment is an inexact science. Everything can be done correctly and yet may not yield any exposure because better stories win the media space. At other times, the department may get exposure with little effort. Broad performance indicators can be time/ space in print, time/space on air, clarity of the message, and sponsor feedback. Ultimately communications in the Tennis Division is about generating publicity, mainly from the perspective of servicing sponsors. However, there is no direct link to TA marketing, which represents a lost opportunity.

Measuring elite development success

The main objective of the operational activities that support elite players is to help them achieve improved world rankings. The Men's and Women's Tennis Departments seek to facilitate the growth of champions, increase tennis participation (play, coach, administer, etc.), help organise elite events, provide player services during the Australian Open (during which the Women's department manager is appointed to the role of Player Services Supervisor), and manage the Fed Cup team. The Men's Tennis Department has responsibility for Business Development as well.

The success of player development activities is principally measured by player rankings. Other performance benchmarks are more subjective and include measures such as skill improvement, development as a player, number of graduates from TA elite tennis programmes, and achievement of Davis Cup or Fed Cup status.

It is widely acknowledged that coaching support and education is vital to the success of developing elite tennis players. However, the development of coaches and the provision of coaching support is the responsibility of a separate department. According to one of the managers the most important means of performance measurement is the personal, day-to-day contact between players and department support staff members (or with the department manager personally). Department staff members cultivate an ongoing relationship with individual players to best meet their personal needs. However, the quality of this contact is subjective and difficult to measure in a standardised way.

The targeted athlete project (TAP) involves the selection of a number of high potential players who are subsequently supported and assisted by divisional staff members and coaches and scouts around the country. The key success factor to ensure TAP success involves a national network of people that can provide assistance and information where and when needed. In excess of 60 TAP players are monitored and supported by two departments.

Ultimately, the ranking goals that drive the elite departments are based on the (potential) quality of players that are available. Money does not guarantee high rankings, but lack of money can limit the department's ability to deliver optimal services to players. The second most important means of creating tennis champions is to offer competitive infrastructure close to home. This provides players with the opportunity to play in international tournaments without having to travel overseas. It has to be noted that most tournaments are loss-making entities, and might be better seen as investments in the development of world-ranked players.

In addition to these two success pathways are a number of programmes that are offered to athletes and their support staff, all aimed at developing their ability to manage the requirements of the professional game (i.e. mentor programmes, coaching programmes, and scholarships). Some skill-analysis tools such as Swinger, a device used to measure skill progression, can further measure player development, but this only constitutes a small part of the measurement of the overall effectiveness of elite programmes. These measures include international experience, all surface experience and off court media skills. Irrespective of the performance of the managers in this department, success is in the hands of the players.

Measuring business development

It is ironic that while sponsorship is one of the few areas of activity in the Tennis Division fully driven by a profit objective, and therefore has an important revenue raising capacity, it also has the fewest full-time staff members dedicated to it. Regarding business development, the core objective of the department is to develop packageable and saleable sponsorship products. In other words, whenever an opportunity to package communication benefits for a potential sponsor occurs, departmental staff members use their network to sell these opportunities. To have business development in one department further adds to the fragmentation of marketing activities throughout TA. Business is developed in a number of departments, sponsors are serviced in others, and if the event is big enough (e.g. Davis Cup), business development for the event is taken in-house into the Events Department (with assistance from the Men's Tennis and Business Development Department). There are no clear performance measures across all entities that have (assumed) business development roles.

Experience in packaging sponsorship opportunities and selling them is the main driver of sponsorship pricing strategies, and hence, income maximisation.

Departmental staff members know what the market is prepared to pay, and what established properties are worth, although there is no standardised approach to packaging and commercialising sponsorship opportunities. Because of the flat Tennis Division structure, decision-making about what could or should be the Division's sponsorship products is dependent on too many people and on too many different departments. There is a perception among staff members that if more resources are put into sponsorship packaging and commercialisation (within one department rather than across many), higher returns will be generated. By and large, success of business development is measured against the previous year's figures. There is clearly an expectation to grow sponsorship income every year.

A performance management framework

The performance model that follows is based on the Tennis Division's findings from desk research, interviews, the Tennis Division managers' workshop and a questionnaire distributed to all staff members in the Division. The model represents the dimensions of successful tennis management and development. It provides the core drivers of successful sport organisation. In the case of the Tennis Division, successful tennis operations is based on nine performance areas:

1   Establishing and maintaining excellent tennis infrastructure
2   Establishing and maintaining a healthy tennis participation base
3   Developing and retaining staff knowledge and skills
4   Developing and marketing tennis event products (event customers)
5   Developing and marketing tennis performers (elite customers)
6   Developing and marketing tennis business products (sport business customers)
7   Developing and marketing tennis consumer products (sport customers)
8   Creating positive impacts for all stakeholder groups (community)
9   Achieving positive financial results and providing support activities.

Figure 11.1 maps the logical progression of building a successful tennis business from its foundations (inputs) to a range of critical customer processes (throughput or transformation) to delivering final results to tennis stakeholders, including the TA Board, which carefully monitor the financial position of the organisation. It can be seen that the organisational vision and objectives are at the peak of the sport business structure, maintaining a clear strategic outlook over the competitive environment. Financial resources are reinvested in the Tennis Division from this strategic point of view.

Figure 11.2 describes the core strategic objectives in each of the new performance categories. These objectives assist in the determination of what should be measured in the future, and hence what are the KPIs in each of the performance categories.

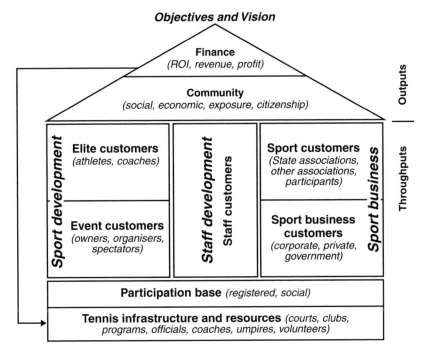

Figure 11.1 Building a successful tennis business.

Source: Westerbeek and Smith, 2003.

An overview of KPIs is presented in Figure 11.3. The KPIs provide a more precise and quantitative tool for tracking changes in the levels of performance.

Concluding comments

This case sought to explain the dimensions of performance management that TA needed to address in order to develop a performance management framework for the Tennis Division. The framework was based on current business literature, internal Tennis Division documents, interviews and a workshop with departmental managers, and a questionnaire completed by all members of the Division. This mass of information also reflects the performance dimensions of sport organisations generally, and its content specifically shows the areas that are critical to the success of the Tennis Division.

There were several noteworthy findings of the process that are relevant to other NSOs seeking to enhance their performance management systems and meet the BASA policy goals. First, there is a strong link between the strategic goals of TA and those of the Tennis Division. Second, while the goals of the Tennis Division's constituent departments are consistent, they are also voluminous, and

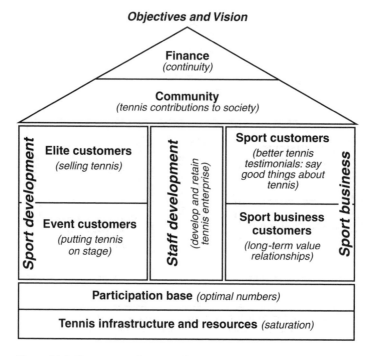

Figure 11.2 Strategic performance focus.
Source: Westerbeek and Smith, 2003.

lack focus due to an overemphasis on operational matters. Third, in terms of existing performance measures, the Division has produced a plan that outlines the objectives and actions to be taken by departments. The plan incorporates 84 objectives and 253 measurable actions, to be coordinated by the departmental managers. Fourth, while departmental managers are notionally guided by the planning document, the system often breaks down because they do not have time, or do not understand how to collect all the performance measurement data. Performance categories have subsequently been re-organised and re-focused in the light of the sport performance management system ratified by the Division during the review process. This is illustrated in Figure 11.3. The Division may be considered efficient in terms of its ability to convert its resources into outputs. However, it has been noted that some activities performed by the Division go largely unnoticed by the Board despite their importance to the performance of the Division as a whole. This can be remedied through the application of the sport performance management framework explored in this case, which demarcates the dimensions of divisional performance that are critical for success.

As a further consequence of the review and subsequent discussions, forums and planning seminars with staff, the Tennis Division introduced a streamlined

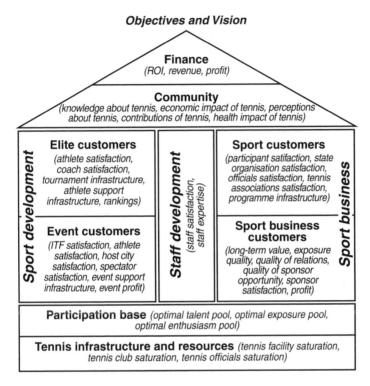

Objectives and Vision

Finance
(ROI, revenue, profit)

Community
(knowledge about tennis, economic impact of tennis, perceptions about tennis, contributions of tennis, health impact of tennis)

Sport development

Elite customers
(athlete satisfaction, coach satisfaction, tournament infrastructure, athlete support infrastructure, rankings)

Event customers
(ITF satisfaction, athlete satisfaction, host city satisfaction, spectator satisfaction, event support infrastructure, event profit)

Staff development
(staff satisfaction, staff expertise)

Sport customers
(participant satisfaction, state organisation satisfaction, officials satisfaction, tennis associations satisfaction, programme infrastructure)

Sport business customers
(long-term value, exposure quality, quality of relations, quality of sponsor opportunity, sponsor satisfaction, profit)

Sport business

Participation base *(optimal talent pool, optimal exposure pool, optimal enthusiasm pool)*

Tennis infrastructure and resources *(tennis facility saturation, tennis club saturation, tennis officials saturation)*

Figure 11.3 Examples of key performance indicators.

Source: Westerbeek and Smith, 2003.

structure, which recognised three complementary but discrete streams of tennis activity: elite tennis, events and growth or participation. Consistent with this improved performance management clarity, several structural relationships were shifted. First, the Events Department assumed responsibility for all junior, wheelchair and intellectually disabled events. Thus, the Junior Tennis Department was effectively relocated under the purview of Events, while wheelchair and intellectually disabled events were moved from participation. Secondly, the Participation Department took over responsibility for Coach Education and Facility Development, bolstering their role as key structural platforms in the success of tennis. Finally, the Men's Tennis Department stretched to include Business Development and its sponsorship and marketing responsibilities. In addition, the Division has consolidated its performance measurement to focus on between six and eight key objectives within each department. It has also embraced a renewed awareness of the performance interrelationships amongst departments.

In the future, the Division may choose to introduce some data collection systems. It is anticipated that this collection can be incorporated into daily operations without added work burdens. It is also clear that a conflated set of measures represents less work, and will allow the Division to chart all resource inputs into its programmes. These, in turn, will allow efficiency metrics to be developed. Efficiency metrics will express performance for each dimension as a relationship between inputs (resources) and outputs (KPIs). This can also lead to further understanding of the relationships between performance areas, such as the effects on participation of elite success. These actions represent a direct step towards excellence in sport management and an improvement in efficiency and effectiveness identified through systematic performance measurement. These actions are consistent with BASA policy that aims to assist NSOs develop more professional management practices.

Tennis Australia has demonstrated in this case, through their commitment to management improvement, that they deserve their reputation as one of Australia's pre-eminent sporting organisations, and represent a national body worthy of benchmarking.

12 Fair play in sport: drugs, discrimination, disadvantage and disability

The fair play ideal

The fair play concept has been an integral part of the sporting ethos. It has its roots in nineteenth-Century English school sport, where sport was seen as a vehicle for building character and leadership. It was quickly diffused to the public school system of colonial Australia (Stewart, 1992). It also became part of the amateur value system that underpinned sporting practice in general and the Olympic games in particular (Cashman, 1995). However, as indicated in Chapter 1, the amateur ideal was overwhelmed by the forces of commercialism during the 1970s and 1980s. More recently the fair play concept has been resurrected in response to drug use, the barriers faced by athletes with disabilities, discrimination, sexual harassment, and the ugly parent syndrome in children's sport. This chapter will address some of these issues through a selection of case studies that cover anti-doping policy, anti-harassment policy, indigenous sport policy and disability policy.

Anti-doping policy

There is a long history of sport players and athletes using drugs and pharmaceutical products to obtain a competitive edge over their rivals. The 1950s signalled a significant increase in the use of drugs to improve sporting performance. This occurred in response to the growing availability of amphetamines, that were used to stimulate the central nervous system, and the development of synthetic hormones, that could be used to increase muscle growth (Waddington, 2000: 115). Since then the use of performance enhancing drugs has become endemic. This is the result of sport becoming increasingly 'medicalised, professionalised, politicised and commercialised' (Waddington, 2000: 120–126). This means that athletes not only have a strong personal and economic incentive to gain a competitive advantage over their competitors, but also have a variety of customised and high quality drugs to choose from. In short, the whole performance enhancing drug area has become an industry.

Drugs-in-sport crises

During the 1970s and 1980s there was increasing evidence that many elite athletes were using drugs to improve their performance. The recent discovery of once confidential documents confirm that the amazing results of the East Germans at the Munich, Montreal and Moscow Olympics resulted from the skills of their biochemists as much as it did from the skills of their athletes. It was also an open secret that professional cycling in Europe contained a flourishing drugs market, and made a handsome contribution to the profitability of the pharmaceutical industry. During this period most Australian sport officials denied there was a local problem, and supported their claims with assertions that Australian athletes would not cheat anyway. These views were blown out of the water when the Four Corners current affairs documentary programme was broadcast in late 1987. In the documentary a number of coaches and athletes admitted that the AIS was effectively a distribution centre for a variety of steroids and other muscle building drugs (Houlihan, 1997). The international scope of drug use in sport was confirmed in 1998 when Ben Johnson, who won the 100-metres sprint at the Seoul Olympic Games, tested positive for steroids. No one could now deny that there was a serious international drug problem in sport. The Australian Government did not have a comprehensive drugs-in-sport policy at this time, although it supported the IOC anti-drug strategy. As was indicated in Chapter 5 the Commonwealth Government, through its sport minister, Graeme Richardson, launched a Committee of Inquiry in 1989 to be chaired by Senator John Black. The Black Committee found that drug taking was a problem in Australian sport, and included a number of athletes who had been scholarship holders at the AIS. The AIS denied it had a problem and cited its anti-drug policy and the fact that it had randomly drug tested its athletes since 1986 as evidence that it had the issue under control (Bloomfield, 2003). In 1990, following on from the Black Report recommendations, the Commonwealth Government established the ASDA.

Since then the Commonwealth Government has vigorously pursued what they see to be drug cheats, and in doing so, developed a broadly based anti-doping policy. The Commonwealth Government's Tough on Drugs in Sport (TODIS) programme was introduced in 1999, in part a response to another drugs-in-sport scandal. This time it was found that a number of high-profile cyclists were systematically taking a cocktail of drugs to improve their performance in the 1998 Tour de France. This led to an IOC inquiry which in turn led to the establishment of the World Anti-Doping Authority in 1999. Around the same time Werner Reiterer, one of Australia's best performed discuss throwers, published his autobiography. He not only alleged that drug taking was common amongst the Australian athletic community, but also admitted he had taken performance enhancing drugs in the run-up to the Sydney Olympic Games (Reiterer, 2000).

The Commonwealth Government subsequently reviewed the ASC sport drug programme, and followed up with its anti-doping policy of 2001. The BASA policy was underpinned by the belief that the use of performance enhancing drugs is unethical and unfair. Moreover, because it is also seen to be harmful to the heath of athletes, it should be made illegal. Indeed, there is now virtual worldwide agreement amongst sport officials that athletes who take drugs to enhance their performance should be banned from participating. This stance was defended on the grounds that doping is fundamentally contrary to the spirit of sport since it undermines values like respect for law, respect for self, fun and joy, health, honesty, character and education, excellence in performance, and community and solidarity (World Anti-Doping Authority, 2003: 3). In short, drug-users are cheats.

Current government policy

Under its current policy, the Commonwealth Government aims to stop doping practices in sport by the use of three measures. The first measure is to provide financial assistance to drug testing programmes. The second measure is to educate and inform athletes about the use of performance enhancing drugs. The final measure is to impose appropriate sanctions on athletes who have committed anti-doping offences. In support of these measures, the Commonwealth Government has utilised the services of the ASC, ASDA, the Australian Sport Drug Testing Laboratory (ASDTL) and the Australian Customs Service (ACS). A number of core strategies were then linked to these agencies.

In the first place, the Commonwealth Government, in association with the ASC, resolved that all NSOs receiving government funds must have a strict anti-doping policy in place. It is also expected that NSOs will provide sanctions of no less than two years for a first offence, and a life suspension for a second offence. At the same time, the Commonwealth Government has instructed NSOs to put in place mechanisms that ensure fairness and natural justice for athletes.

Second, ASDA has been funded to provide an effective and credible drug testing programme. ASDA has been operating as a statutory authority since 1990, and now has an annual operating budget of just under AUS$9 million. Around AUS$5.3 million (or just under 60 per cent) is provided by the Commonwealth Government, while the remainder comes from fees collected from sport organisations that contract ASDA services. The major contracting sport organisations are Australia's two largest sport leagues, the AFL and NRL. ASDA has 48 staff, and in 2002 performed just under 7,000 domestic drug tests, half of which were government-funded. Just over 70 per cent of all tests were conducted randomly, with no advance notice given to athletes (Australian Sports Drug Agency, 2002).

Third, the Commonwealth Government has encouraged ASDA to develop an educational campaign that gives athletes a concise and helpful knowledge of the Government anti-doping policy, and their obligations under the drug testing programme. The campaign involves extensive radio advertising, direct mail-outs to all elite Australian athletes, a hotline medication service, and the publication of a *Drugs in Sport Handbook*. The handbook lists all prohibited substances and all medications that contain banned substances.

Finally, Customs regulations have been strengthened by the imposition of heavy penalties for the importation of performance enhancing drugs. Most of Australia's NSOs have rules governing the taking of performance enhancing drugs. In addition, their polices have been designed within the framework established by the Commonwealth Government and the ASC.

Cricket Australia

Cricket Australia (CA), which has recently changed its name from the Australian Cricket Board (ACB), is one of Australia's largest and most powerful sporting bodies. CA has a detailed anti-doping policy, which it designed in 1998 in consultation with the ASC and ASDA. CA's policy was the first of any national governing body in cricket, and has been used as a benchmark for anti-drug policy in other cricketing nations. The policy has been applied to three cases, and in each the player was found guilty of drug use, and suspended from playing. Like the Commonwealth Government, and the ASC, CA condemns the use of performance enhancing drugs. In Clause 2.1 of its anti-doping policy CA states that 'the use of performance enhancing drugs and doping practices is contrary to the ethics of sport, and potentially harmful to the health of athletes' (Cricket Australia, 2003).

A detailed listing of performance enhancing drugs and doping practices are displayed under the heading of Prohibited Substances. The list of prohibited substances not only includes muscle-building drugs like steroids and drugs that increase the oxygen capacity of the blood, but also other drugs that can mask the existence of performance enhancing chemicals. These masking agents are referred to as Prohibited Methods.

The CA anti-doping policy states that it aims to prevent the above practices by first, 'imposing sanctions on players who commit a doping offence, second, educating its players about the whole drugs-in-sport issue, and finally, supporting the drug testing programmes of ASDA and other testing authorities' (Cricket Australia, 2003). Under the CA anti-doping regulations a player commits a doping offence if a prohibited substance is found in the player's body tissue, or the player takes advantage of a prohibited method. At the same time, CA acknowledges that players may be allowed to take a prohibited substance, or take advantage of a prohibited substance if they can demonstrate that the drug was used for therapeutic purposes, or that the drug was taken in exceptional circumstances.

The Shane Warne case

Shane Warne is one of Australia's greatest ever cricketers. At the end of 2003 he had played 107 test matches and taken 491 test match wickets at an average of 25.7 runs per wicket. He had also played 193 international one-day matches. In the minds of some cricket commentators he is the greatest leg-spin bowler of all time. He has been nominated as one of Wisden's five cricketers of the century. He is also a self-confessed larrikin, and a national sporting hero.

Shane Warne has also featured in a number of controversies and scandals. In 1994 he accepted cash from an Indian bookmaker in return for information on ground conditions. In 2001 he was accused of making obscene telephone calls when playing for Hampshire in the English county cricket competition. However these incidents paled into insignificance in 2003 when he was found to have taken an illegal substance.

Shane Warne has not only had to deal with an occasionally hostile media, but also serious injury. In the late 1990s he suffered a severe finger injury which side-lined him from first-class cricket, and then towards the end of the 2002 cricket season he dislocated his shoulder. He had major surgery in late December 2002, and it was thought he would be absent from the game for at least three months. However he made quick recovery after intensive rehabilitation, and resumed practice in late January 2003.

Coincidently, between December 2002 and January 2003, Warne was asked to give urine samples as part of ASDA's random testing programme for CA. His first sample was taken in early December just before he injured his shoulder, while the second sample was taken in mid-January immediately after he began post-rehabilitation practice and training sessions with his teammates. The samples were tested, and the second sample clearly showed a positive reading for Hydrochlorothiazide and Amiloride, two banned substances which act as diuretics. That is, they remove fluid from the body. While these drugs are prohibited for use by cricketers, they are available on a doctor's pre-scription from a chemist shop. In February 2003 Warne was advised by letter that the results of his sample were positive. In other words, his body tissues were found to contain banned substances, and he would have to attend an inquiry.

In line with CA's anti-doping policy, Warne was requested to attend a hearing of the CA Anti-Doping Committee, which comprised the Committee chair and two members. The hearing was scheduled for late February 2003. In his defence, Warne admitted he had taken Moduretic, a diuretic available on prescription. He also said that he was unaware it was a diuretic, and took it on the advice of his mother, who said it would get rid of excess fluid prior to a media conference he had agreed to attend. In evidence Warne said he took the tablet because he wanted to remove his 'double chin' before facing the media. In any case, he said he had only taken one tablet prior to the January drug test. He was also unaware that Moduretic was on the CA list of banned substances. In short, Warne was trying to convince the Hearing that his case should be treated as an exceptional circumstance in that he was unaware of the drug's status as a prohibited substance (Cricket Australia, 2003).

The Committee were unimpressed with most of Warne's evidence. Warne's statement that he did not know the tablet was a diuretic because the flaps of the tablet packet were missing was not convincing. He also made no attempt to contact the CA medical officers before taking it. Moreover, while Warne had attended a number of player drug education seminars, he said he learnt nothing about the diuretic problem, or the consequences that would arise from testing positive for banned substances. The Committee also concluded that the evidence given by Warne's mother was vague and unsatisfactory.

The Committee agreed that Warne was unable to establish a case that he should be treated favourably because of exceptional circumstances. On the contrary, the Committee concluded that Warne had acted recklessly and totally disregarded the possible consequences of his action. At the same time the Committee understood that there was not any evidence that Warne had taken steroids, and agreed that taking any number of Moduretic tablets would not enhance Warne's sporting performance. As a result the Committee decided to reduce the minimum two-year ban from cricket (under Clause 8.1 of the anti-doping regulations) to a one-year ban. This meant that Warne would lose one year of his AUS$500,000 contract with CA, as well as having his product endorsement potential diminished.

Warne did not appeal his sentence, which was not surprising in the light of a broad consensus that the penalty was not severe. It was also agreed that Warne's suspension had provided a strong wake-up call for other athletes, and sent a message that Australia is going to take drug code violations seriously. The Warne case also demonstrated that the Commonwealth Government anti-doping strategy was working, at least as far as cricket, Australia's national game, was concerned.

However, despite the vigilance of the ASC, ASDA, and NSOs like CA, there is still a nagging suspicion that performance enhancing drugs are still part of the Australian sporting landscape. The revelations of Werner Reiterer suggest that even when sport officials deny any drug taking, athletes will say otherwise (Reiterer, 2000). In 2003 it was revealed that a number of world-class track-and-field athletes were tested positive for the so-called designer steroid drugs, while some tennis players also tested positive for similar muscle-building drugs. While most of the allegations were denied on the grounds that the drugs must have found their way into legal food supplements, it is evident that the drug taking is still prevalent amongst many elite athletes. A thriving underground pharmaceutical industry is doing very nicely from the continuing need that athletes have to gain an elusive competitive edge over their rivals.

Anti-harassment policy

Australian sport has always contained a strongly masculine dimension. This is reflected in a sporting culture that both values physical aggression and marginalises women (Kell, 2000: 122). This type of culture is good for developing a competitive climate in which winning is crucial (Australian Sports Commission, 2000) and losing is shameful. However it also creates a climate where power and authority is used to threaten and punish vulnerable athletes. Moreover this power and authority is narrowly distributed, and for the most part held by senior officials and coaches. Athletes, on the other hand, have far less power and authority, and in most instances train and play within a rigid code of conduct and disciplinary framework.

Over the last 10 years a number of Australian sports have had to deal with various forms of harassment. This had ranged from bullying, in the case of Gymnastics, to inappropriate sexual advances in the cases of canoeing and swimming.

In 2000, in response to a growing concern that some sport officials and coaches were abusing their positions of authority by intimidating and sexually harassing young athletes, the Commonwealth Government instructed the ASC to develop a set of guidelines by which sporting bodies could address sexual discrimination and homophobia. These guidelines were formed within a general anti-harassment policy frame, and written up as an *Harassment-free sport* strategy (Australian Sports Commission, 2000). The strategy covers a range of discriminatory and harassment-type behaviours including homophobic taunts, the favourable treatment of heterosexual coaches and officials when compared with homosexual coaches and officials, unwanted sexual advances, the frequent use of abusive language, and transgender discrimination. The *Harassment-free sport* strategy also provided assistance on how sporting bodies could best implement a complaints procedure that not only enables grievances to be presented quickly and confidently, but also ensured that both parties were treated fairly, and given space to present their case without unnecessary duress.

The case of swimming

In 2002 the ASC consolidated its anti-harassment strategy into a Member Protection Program. Under this programme NSOs are assisted in developing a Member Protection Policy (MPP). The MPP is underpinned by the proposition that players, coaches, volunteer officials and administrators are entitled to a safe, welcoming and enjoyable environment. To this end, the MPP has two strands. The first strand is to protect the members of a sporting organisation from harassment, discrimination, vilification, and any other form of abuse. The second strand is to ensure that the right people are given positions of authority by undertaking screening and police checks.

Australian Swimming, the governing body for organised swimming activities, had been the focus of complaints of harassment over a number of years, and sought advice from the ASC on how it should proceed to ensure a safe environment for its members. It subsequently used the MPP as a foundation template for its own member protection policy. After extensive consultation, Australian Swimming produced a detailed MPP in 2002. The policy began with a statement about the need for guidelines that protect the 'health, safety and well being of all Australian Swimming members' (Australian Swimming Inc, 2002: 1). It went on to recommend the ways in which people can be screened for different roles and responsibilities in swimming associations and clubs. A strong emphasis was given to police checks on criminal offences in general, and sex offences in particular. The other major part of the Australian Swimming Member Protection Policy focused on harassment, which was defined as any 'offensive, abusive, belittling, or threatening' behaviour that was unwelcome and humiliating (Australian

Swimming Inc, 2002: 7). Sexual harassment was examined in detail, and ranged from offensive jokes and hostile comments about cultural practices, to threats against homosexuals and mocking a person's disability. There is also a detailed discussion of how a disciplinary tribunal should be designed, together with an appeals mechanism. In short, the Australian Swimming Member Protection Policy is a exemplar on how to implement a broad ranging but precise framework for ensuring a safe and protective sporting environment. In this case the ASC template has been the catalyst for effective policy development in the field of fair play.

Indigenous sports programme

There is no dispute that aboriginals are the most disadvantaged group of people in Australia. The heroic status of Cathy Freeman does not hide the fact that most aboriginals have limited access to modern sport facilities and services. This problem was not lost on sport policy makers, who have been examining the aboriginal sport issue since the 1980s.

As a result of consultation between the Aboriginal and Torres Strait Islander Commission (ATSIC), stakeholders of the Young Persons Sport & Recreation Development Program (launched in 1992 as a result of recommendations arising from the Royal Commission Into Aboriginal Deaths in Custody) and the ASC, the ISP was introduced in 1996. A management committee, comprised of the ATSIC Commissioner, a nominated ASC Commissioner and administrative staff from both ATSIC and the ASC, oversees the ISP, while the delivery of the programme is managed by the Indigenous Sport Unit within the ASC. The objective of the ISP is to enhance the quality of life for indigenous Australians and communities through using the vehicle of sport to promote healthy lifestyles and contribute to circumventing the social problems facing these individuals and communities.

The ISP is based on the principles of self-determination and self-management, with Aboriginal and Torres Strait Islander people working for Aborigines and Torres Strait Islanders, from the community level through to the management committee. As a result of partnerships with state and territory governments and ATSIC regional councils, the ISP employs approximately 50 sport development officers throughout Australia. These officers assist local communities to increase the participation of indigenous Australians in sport and physical activities, increase the number of accredited officials (referees, coaches, administrators), assist indigenous clubs and sporting organisations to coordinate their services and programmes, and to increase the awareness of the cultural diversity of indigenous Australians among non-indigenous sport administrators. The aim of these initiatives is to facilitate increased access and opportunity to sport facilities and resources (Brennan, 2004).

The ISP has also targeted 16 NSOs to support the programmes and strategies initiated by the development officers in each of the states and territories. In an attempt to ensure that the services and expertise of these NSOs are more accessible and inclusive of indigenous Australians, the ISP has encouraged the organisations to develop strategic partnerships with the development officers.

As a result of the partnerships a range of programmes have been put in place, all of which have a strong emphasis on providing educational and developmental infrastructure that fosters self-sufficiency and sustainability. For example, Swimming Queensland and indigenous sport development officers (ISDOs) have developed a swimming programme in the remote areas of the Gulf of Carpentaria, Murgon, and Cherbourg. The programme aims to encourage children to swim, conduct coaching and education courses within the community and establish a club and competition structure. Similarly, in Western Australia, Tennis Western Australia and ISDOs have developed a programme to develop junior tennis, in which members of five remote communities in the Kimberley region are trained as tennis coaches. In the Northern Territory, Basketball Northern Territory and ISDOs have designed a programme to establish club structures and competitions that have a direct affiliation with the mainstream governing sport body, educate interested community members and finally, include high schools with high indigenous populations in the inter-school basketball competition, as a way of increasing and improving junior pathways and development.

Disabled sport policy

Like indigenous sportsmen and women, disabled athletes have also been on the Commonwealth Government policy agenda for some time. Disabled sport policy is crucial to achieving fair outcomes, but it is also problematic. As the discussion in Chapter 2 illustrated, the purpose of policy is to set a direction; a collection of guidelines by which the Government translates values into action. Most times the policy is straightforward, but occasionally the writers of policy or that arm of government tasked with putting that policy into operation face a dilemma. It may relate to how or why the policy is being written, to how it is best expressed or to how, and by whom, it is to be measured. In the case of disabled sport, the ASC faces a dilemma in interpreting and implementing Government policy. First, it must interpret the policy knowing that whatever it does must comply with existing legislation, both Australian and international. Second, it may face either moral or legislative opposition in the way it implements its policy.

BASA policy on disabled sport is a case in point. In the Foreword to the policy statement, it is noted that it aims to cover 'all Australians' (Commonwealth of Australia, 2001: 7). This phrase is echoed elsewhere in the policy statement. In several instances reference is made to continuing support for the Paralympics and, in one instance, mention is made of AUS$15 million being set aside 'specifically for Paralympic Games sports and sports for people with disabilities' (Commonwealth of Australia, 2001: 5). There is one further instance of the policy being designed for 'all Australians regardless of culture, gender, race, capability, or age'. At the same time, there are two specific actions designated in the policy document in relation to disabled sport (other than the Paralympics) and which require the ASC to:

1   encourage the inclusion of athletes with disabilities into mainstream sporting programmes, where appropriate; and
2   ensure that grants to NSOs are structured to deliver . . . the mainstreaming of sport for people with disabilities.

We are left with two conflicting impressions from the BASA policy statement. On one hand, the policy is concerned with the special needs of disabled athletes, the special importance of the Paralympics, and the provision of funds for specialist organisations that service people with disabilities. On the other hand, the ASC wants to encourage disabled athletes to join in mainstream sports activities, and focus funding in a way that delivers this outcome.

Disability is defined as 'a physical or mental impairment, which has a substantial and long-term adverse effect on a person's ability to carry out normal day-to-day activities'. According to the Australian Bureau of Statistics (Disability and Disabling Conditions, 1998) around 19 per cent of the Australian population has a disability. In the Commonwealth *Disability Discrimination Act 1992*, it is against the law to treat someone unfairly or harass them because of their disability. Disability includes loss of physical or mental function, intellectual disability, loss of parts of the body, infectious and non-infectious diseases and illnesses such as multiple sclerosis and hepatitis C, malfunction, malformation or disfigurement of a part of the body, and learning and attention-deficit disorders including dyslexia. The disability may be a present or a past disability, may exist in the future or is assumed to exist (called an imputed disability) and the legislation is applicable, inter alia, in clubs and associations and in sport. Not only must BASA conform to the *Disability Discrimination Act 1992*, it is additionally covered by appeal legislation administered by the Human Rights and Equal Opportunity Commission.

In aiming to satisfy the provisions of the *Disability Discrimination Act*, BASA and the ASC have chosen to focus upon the intent of the Act. To this end the ASC has introduced a Disability Education Program (DEP) to support the promotion of a physically active lifestyle for all Australians including those with disabilities and has nominated greater grass-roots sports participation as a critical result area for people with disabilities. In addition, the ASC has provided grants under the Sports Excellence Program to National Sporting Organisations for People with a Disability (NSODs). These grants assist the NSODs in areas such as competition, the employment of coaches, talent identification and the development of aspiring elite athletes with a disability.

It is also clear that the ASC is required to undertake specific actions of encouraging the inclusion of athletes with disabilities into mainstream sporting programmes, and to ensure that grants to NSOs are structured to deliver the mainstreaming of sport for people with disabilities. Deaf Sports is a case in point. Under the Disability Act, the inability to hold a conversation with someone talking in a normal voice in a moderately noisy place, or the inability to hear someone talking on the telephone is considered to be a substantial disability. Under those criteria, the deaf, particularly the profoundly deaf, are considered disabled.

Deaf sports issues

Deaf Sports Australia (DSA) is a small NSO, representing the interests of deaf and hearing-impaired athletes throughout Australia. Throughout its almost 50-year history, DSA has represented deaf athletes, and with its help numerous deaf sportsmen and sportswomen have had the opportunity to represent club, state, and NSOs. Australians have been successful in both summer and winter Deaf World Games, and have been among the more successful competitors at the quadrennial Olympic Games for the Deaf. DSA's vision is that all deaf Australians will have the continual opportunity to participate in sport through the provision of efficient programmes, services, and information. There remains some doubt, however, that this vision is being fulfilled. Funds and lack of other resources discourage its early implementation. Many members lack knowledge of the services DSA can offer and more importantly, DSA possess limited and unreliable information about deaf athletes. It lacks data and system which would allow it to monitor the location of deaf people in Australia, their sporting interests, sporting clubs and organisations to which they belong or knowledge of their willingness to support an organisation such as DSA.

Under the *Disability Discrimination Act 1992* – Section 28, which relates to sport, it is 'unlawful for a person to discriminate against another person on the grounds of the other person's disability ... by excluding that person from a sporting activity'. It is not an unlawful discrimination, however, if the person is reasonably capable of performing the activities reasonably required in relation to the sporting activity, or if the persons who participate, or are to participate in the sporting activities, are selected by a method which is reasonable on the basis of their skills and abilities relevant to the sporting activity and relative to each other.

The DSA is adamant that deaf people should compete only against other deaf people and uses the Discrimination Act to support their position. In addition, they allege a moral prerogative for their viewpoint. On the other hand, the ASC believes that, provided deaf athletes can overcome some basic constraints in normal sport such as having competitors 'hear' the starting gun in athletics and understanding line calls in tennis, they can assimilate this disabled group into mainstream sport and comply with Government direction. After all, a deaf person is normally reasonably capable of performing the activities required in most sports. These different perspectives on deaf sport participation highlight the difficulty of implementing policy when it can be interpreted in a number of different ways. In deaf sports specifically, and disabled sports more generally, there is consequently an ongoing tension between the desire to compete amongst similarly disabled athletes, and the policy expectation that disabled athletes be encouraged to enter the mainstream.

The future of fair play

The Commonwealth Government fair play policies make it very clear that sport does not have an inbuilt or natural tendency to treat its participants fairly. In fact, there is a strong argument to support the view that sport is by nature unfair and discriminatory. For most of the time in twentieth-century Australia, women athletes were marginalised and aboriginals were abused in all sorts of ways (Booth and Tatz, 2000; Kell, 2000). Neither can athletes be guaranteed a playing field where no one player has an unfair advantage. The rampant use of performance enhancing drugs has only exaggerated this unfairness. The Commonwealth Government fair play policy is therefore a crucial mechanism for eliminating discrimination and abuse, controlling drug use, and generally creating a sporting culture that embraces fairness and equity. The policy is broad-ranging and eclectic, and has been for the most part enthusiastically received by NSOs across the nation. At the same time, there is still significant work to be done to eliminate inequity, discrimination, and cheating in Australian sport.

13 Regulating sport: the case of sport broadcasting

The scope of sport regulation in Australia

This book has for the most part focused on the ways in which the Commonwealth Government assists sport and guides its operation through the ASC. However, there are also a number of instances where the government has directly legislated to control the operation of a specific sport or sport-related activity. The most constrained sport in Australia is boxing which is regulated under detailed state government legislation. The legislation requires boxing promoters to undertake health checks on all boxers, and ensure a medical officer is in attendance. Boxers must also obtain medical clearance before they can enter the ring. The martial arts are also tightly constrained.

There are also a number of other important, if less direct, controls over the practice of sport. In Chapter 5, for example, there was a short discussion of legislative control over tobacco advertising and sponsorship in sport. There was also a brief analysis of sport broadcasting on pay TV. These controls over pay TV comprise the Commonwealth Government anti-siphoning policy.

The case of pay TV

In the earlier discussion of sport policy, it was stated that government policy can often seem, at best, ideological and, at worst, incomprehensible. It was also noted that policy had a rational side to it. In the case of the government anti-siphoning policy it was clear that when introduced it had a rational side to it. However, as time passed, the rational side quickly became ideological, and occasionally even slightly incomprehensible.

The origins of anti-siphoning rules

Part 7 of the *Broadcasting Services Act 1992*, empowers the Minister for Communications, Information Technology and the Arts to protect the free availability of certain types of TV programmes. He or she can, for example, specify an event the broadcasting of which, in the opinion of the Minister, should be available free to the general public. As a consequence of this, and as a condition of the licence granted to subscription TV broadcasting licensees, pay TV stations are not allowed to broadcast any event which the Minister has specified unless a national broadcaster (ABC and SBS) or a free-to-air commercial broadcaster (Channels 7, 9 and 10) has acquired the right to broadcast the event. Moreover, if a free-to-air broadcaster acquires exclusive rights to the event, the pay TV broadcaster is excluded altogether from live coverage unless the free-to-air broadcaster permits it (Australian Broadcasting Authority, 1992).

As a result of the power granted to the Minister under the *Broadcasting Services Act*, an anti-siphoning list of sport events deemed to be of national importance was proclaimed in 1994. Associated laws were created which gave free-to-air networks first access to the TV rights to these events. Should the free-to-air broadcasters decide not to acquire the rights offered, they are not compelled to do so. The broadcasters can simply make the decision to forgo those rights. Even in this event, however, a pay TV licensee cannot acquire the right to broadcast the event until either the Minister has exercised his discretion under the *Broadcasting Services Act* to remove the event from the anti-siphoning list, or, the event has been completed for at least a week at which time automatic delisting will occur (Australian Broadcasting Authority, 1996).

The objective of the anti-siphoning law is clear. It is to ensure that certain events are available to the whole viewing public by preventing pay TV licensees from acquiring exclusive rights to listed events. The current anti-siphoning list comprises domestic and international sporting events in 11 categories encompassing over 2,000 separate events in a variety of sports including cricket, tennis, golf, motor sports and the football codes. Included in the current list is every game in the AFL Premiership competition, every game in the National Rugby League Premiership competition, Rugby Union Test matches involving Australia, every match in the Rugby World Cup, every cricket test and one-day match involving Australia, the English Football Association Cup final, the Melbourne Cup, and a host of other sporting events.

The Minister has the additional power to add or remove events without reference to Parliament or legislation providing he/she forms an opinion on the need for an event or group of events to be available free to the general public. He/she is bound by no other criterion. The list has been amended substantially only twice since its creation, first to delist the 1994 Australia-versus-Pakistan test cricket and one-day series and then to list certain Rugby Super League events, and amendments to reflect name changes to the National Soccer League listing. At the same time, the Government has introduced anti-hoarding provisions which require commercial TV licensees that acquire the right to televise a designated event, but that do not propose to fully utilise that right, to offer the unused portion to the ABC and SBS for a nominal charge within a specified offer time. The national broadcasters must also offer unused portions of rights to each other.

Rational or ideological?

Ten years have passed and the policy remains. The question now is whether that policy may still be considered rational. For the answer to this it is essential to examine whether or not the fears proclaimed by the national broadcasters (the ABC and SBS) and the commercial free-to-air TV industry (Channels 7, 9 and 10) in 1994 when the policy was introduced were justified. It is important to consider what has changed in those 10 years and what the current situation is, and then we may be better placed to answer the question.

When the anti-siphoning law was introduced in 1994 it appeared to serve an excellent purpose, despite the fact that pay TV had yet to impose itself to any extent upon the Australian people. Indeed, Foxtel's cable service did not start until October 1995. Yet there was a palpable fear within the national broadcasters and free-to-air TV industry that pay TV would sweep all before it and, in the case of commercial free-to-air TV, garner the larger percentage of advertising revenue. There was a further expectation that major TV sports events would be siphoned from the free-to-air networks to pay TV. This fear was strong despite a US Federal Communications Commission Report in 1994 which found that notwithstanding the absence of anti-siphoning rules in the US there had been no migration of sports programmes to pay TV. It was a time when the three major Australian commercial broadcasters were suffering a profit fall, and the industry was under some threat. Advertising revenue had declined, and at least two of the commercial channels were struggling to stay afloat. The belief that pay TV would corner all the major sports events and thus deny sport to a large portion of the viewing population led to overwhelming support for the new law. In reality it was pay TV that suffered most. A prolonged period of turbulence and low pay TV subscriptions culminated in mid-1998 with the collapse of the Australis Media/Galaxy group. Nonetheless, when the policy underlying the anti-siphoning law was introduced, it had all the appearance of being in the greater national good and, therefore, quite rational.

Despite the belief that free-to-air commercial channels would lose access to advertising, this has not proved to be the case. In 2002 Foxtel secured only an estimated AUS$95 million in advertising revenue compared with AUS$2.2 billion taken in by the commercial networks. In fact, the majority of pay TV revenue came from subscriptions.

Over the past 10 years, having been granted monopoly access to the prime sporting events both in Australia and parts of the world, national broadcasters and commercial free-to-air TV might have been expected to embrace the prospect of televising all that they had been guaranteed. After all, that was the purpose of the policy and the law which they had so eagerly and so successfully sought. And yet in 2000, according to Australian Broadcasting Authority Chairman, Professor David Flint, 'ABA's investigation identified a number of events that [had] not received consistent free to air coverage. These [included] cricket matches in countries other than the United Kingdom, early rounds of the French Open Tennis Tournament, Australian Men's and Women's Hardcourt

Tennis Championships, and semi-finals of the Australian National Basketball League.' 'The anti-siphoning list aims to safeguard the interests of those in the Australian community without access to pay TV by ensuring free to air coverage of important sporting events', said Professor Flint. 'The rules were not intended to limit the enjoyment of pay TV subscribers to sports channels by reducing the amount of sport available on new services' (Australian Broadcast Authority, *News Release* 53/2001).

Flint's comments were appropriate. According to Foxtel, the anti-siphoning list has resulted in free-to-air broadcasters gaining exclusive rights to some 5,000 hours per year of live sport. And yet, of this, only about one-third of sport covered by the list goes to air live on free-to-air TV, and only around 40 per cent of the events are broadcast on free-to-air TV in any form. At one point, Foxtel complained that of about 650 hours of Wimbledon tennis covered by the list, only 12 per cent of those hours were broadcast on free-to-air TV in Australia during each Wimbledon tournament.

While recognising that free-to-air TV did not always wish to cover an event, the anti-siphoning law method by which the free-to-air channels could nominate events not to be covered and which could then be delisted by the Minister has proven to be cumbersome and difficult to operate. The reality is that by the time the free-to-air channels have taken their pick of the sports and decided what listed events they do not wish to cover, the pay TV industry has little time to apply to the Minister for formal delisting, and secure the TV rights. This has been the case, for example, with most Australian overseas cricket tours with the exception of the Ashes tours.

Pay TV, sport policy and economic viability

Contrary to original expectations, life has not been easy for pay TV during the past several years. *The Overview of Australian Pay TV* commissioned by Bloomberg Television, showed that during the period 1995–2002 the pay TV industry in Australia suffered eight years of financial losses and limited subscriber penetration. Losses amounted to around AUS$4 billion since 1995 and as at June 2002 there were still only 1.5 million subscribers in Australia (ANZ, 2003). As a result, the industry sought to introduce a series of radical measures. Among these changes, and with the approval of the Australian Competition and Consumer Commission (ACCC), it was agreed that market leader Foxtel and third-placed Optus could share a common programming platform.

At this stage it is worth noting that 25 per cent of Foxtel is now owned by The News Corporation Limited, 25 per cent by Publishing and Broadcasting Limited (PBL), and 50 per cent by Telstra Corporation Limited. Of these, Publishing and Broadcasting is also the parent company of Channel 9, a major free-to-air operator. In addition, Foxtel and second-ranked Austar compete head to head in only a few small national arenas and at the same time share a production company and an advertising sales operation. As a result, mutterings that pay TV is not competitive are bound to occur. Despite this concern, a number of former opponents of the Foxtel/Optus agreement now appear to be more welcoming of the accord. While the Confederation of Australian TV Stations remains opposed to the removal of the anti-siphoning laws, their position has been undermined by the relationship between PBL and Channel 9, and by a recent agreement between Networks 9 and 10, and Foxtel, to combine to secure the rights to Australia's most popular winter sport league, the Australian Football League, from Channel 7.

The anti-siphoning law not only applies to free-to-air or pay TV; it has a direct impact on sport itself. According to Rupert Murdoch, 'sport overpowers film and everything else in the screen-entertainment genre' (*Business Review Weekly*, 23 July 1999). There seems little doubt that sport drives subscription TV. At the same time, TV rights to sport are a major source of funding for sporting clubs and organisations. Indeed, the Australian Broadcasting Corporation (ABC) in its 2001 submission to the Australian Broadcasting Authority's (ABA) Review of Anti-Siphoning List commented that 'the cost of broadcast rights increased dramatically, [since the introduction of colour TV] beyond the amounts the ABC could afford, and [consequently] the number of hours and types of sport offered by the ABC has changed significantly' (Australian Broadcasting Corporation, 2001). TA echoed the views of many sporting organisations when in July 2003 it advised the Department of Communications, Information and the Arts that government and sport must 'engage in all measures which will enable a satisfactory investment and return for both the promoter and the television network, while ensuring the viewing public has access to premium events'. The opening of a more competitive market for sports TV rights can provide greater income opportunities for sporting organisations and players.

Today the broadcasting of sport has expanded considerably beyond the traditional media forms especially in relation to the Internet. Sport commentary is accessible on many websites while web TV allows enhanced visual coverage of sport on the Internet. Technology is itself making the original policy outdated.

In addition, an underlying consideration is that all government policies should be either independent or reinforcing. That is, either it should stand alone from other policy or it should be in general agreement with other policy. Yet, while the government policies on sport seek an increase in the number and quality of elite athletes, and a general increase in the total sporting population, the anti-siphoning legislation seeks to limit pay TV's ability to televise and popularise sport.

International comparisons

It should be pointed out that while Australia is not alone in its anti-siphoning legislation, the legislation is the most restrictive of any country. There is no such legislation in the US while in the United Kingdom and much of Europe, sport is divided into two anti-siphoning lists. In Group A are those events which must be offered to both free-to-air and subscription broadcasters on a non-exclusive basis, unless an exemption is granted, while events in Group B can be shown on subscription channels exclusively, provided edited highlights are offered to free-to-air broadcasters. In the United Kingdom and elsewhere in Europe where similar legislation exists, there are only a handful of events limited to Group A.

Concluding comments

Policy should not be forever. If conditions change, as they surely have over the past decade, then policy should be re-visited and recast. Pay TV is no longer the bogeyman it was thought to be in 1994, and in fact has faced many more financial and programming difficulties than free-to-air broadcasters. The original intent underlying the anti-siphoning legislation is indicative of policy that was once rational, and is now manifestly ideological and inconsistent.

Part IV
Evaluation

14 How can policy outcomes be monitored and measured?

Introduction

In April 2001 the Howard Government launched its new sports policy. While the government's ongoing commitment to sport is to be both praised and welcomed, its thrust is to encourage Australians to return to the club-based sport system rather than support them in undertaking unstructured physical activity. This is occurring at a time when the Australian population is ageing, participation levels in organised sport is falling, and public liability issues in sport are creating additional barriers to participation. While there is a concern that the BASA policy lacks a commitment to general fitness, and disenfranchises a host of unstructured and individual sporting activities such as walking, hiking, and fishing, it is clear that the Commonwealth Government's commitment is financially generous, and supportive of sport in general.

BASA provides a AUS$547-million investment in sporting activities over four years, an amount unprecedented in Australia's history. In providing this level of support for sport, the government articulates its expectations that NSOs will become more responsible and be held more accountable for a number of actions. They include integrating and managing their sport, achieving high-performance outcomes, building sound business management, producing participation growth, particularly among school-aged children including those who live in rural and remote communities. In addition, NSOs are required to work with government to escalate the fight against drug cheats.

As the Foreword to the BASA policy statement makes clear, Government policy on sport has twin objectives. The first is to assist Australian athletes to continue to reach new peaks of excellence. The second is to increase the pool of talent from which world champions will emerge (Commonwealth of Australia, 2001). To achieve its objectives, the government has listed 19 objectives which may be conveniently reduced to four primary goals. These goals are:

1   To support and strengthen national sporting structures so that Australian high-performance athletes have the systems and back up necessary to compete successfully at the international level.

2   To significantly increase the number of people, particularly the young, participating in sport across Australia including rural and regional communities.
3   To ensure NSOs adopt sound business and management practices.
4   To oppose the use of drugs in sport.

In nominating these goals, the Commonwealth Government, through the ASC makes clear that there are certain conditions and criteria applicable to the funding of sporting organisations. According to the CEO of the ASC, Mark Peters, those NSOs 'with a strong track record of sound management and competitive performance have few, if any, conditions or qualifications to their one-line appropriation [while] others may be monitored more closely or have their programs managed in association with [ASC] Commission staff' (ASC Media Release, 15 May 2001).

The difficulty in transferring government objectives and goals to NSOs is that it leaves government with few viable methods of determining the effectiveness of its own policies in achieving those objectives and goals. Essentially, all it can do is institute its own performance measurement programmes, and judiciously use secondary performance measures that are linked to NSO programme goals. In itself this is not entirely a bad thing. The role of government is to set strategic direction; to direct the course for others to follow. This is usually accomplished by stating general rather than detailed policy. Government, after all, is not required to be specific about detail. It is the role of the bureaucracy to implement policy and to measure its effectiveness. In the case of sport it is the ASC as the agency of the Commonwealth Government that is responsible for the delivery of the government's sports programmes, providing funds to NSOs for a range of purposes and for determining the effectiveness of those programmes. The ASC does not provide funding for state, regional and local sporting organisations or individuals. This is achieved through State Departments of Sport and Recreation.

The ASC as the intermediary between government and NSOs also has the difficult task of translating data collected from NSOs into information acceptable to government. In an ideal world, the data in the form of agreed outcomes and outputs would be the same for all parties. In a less than ideal world, agreement may appear to be in place but results rarely reflect such concurrence. The effect of differing outcomes and outputs is that sometimes it is hard to determine whether government policy is being achieved effectively and efficiently.

At this time, though, it is worthwhile explaining a few of the terms used by the Government in its policy statements and budget allocations to sport. This, in itself, is a cause of much angst among individuals and organisations. Some key terms are listed in Table 14.1.

The Government's sport budget

According to the ASC Financial Statement for the year 2003–2004, the total ASC appropriation in the 2003–2004 Budget is AUS$122.472 million. Additional estimates increased this amount to AUS$134.298 million and revenue

Table 14.1 Commonwealth Government budgetary terms and definitions

Term	Definition
Portfolio budget statement	A document which sets out the budget initiatives and explanations of appropriations.
Outcome	The (sometimes) intangible results or impacts on the community or the environment that the government intends to achieve.
Output	The goods and services produced by agencies on behalf of the government for external organisations or individuals.
Output group	To keep planning manageable, information on outputs will often need to be summarised or grouped for strategic management and external reporting.
Inputs	People, materials, energy, facilities, and funds that an agency uses in activities to produce outputs.
Accrual budget	Incorporates assets, liabilities, expenses, and revenues as well a cash receipts and expenditures. It focuses on all the resource implications of the strategic and operational plan.
Mission statement	A broad high-level statement of purpose for an agency. Relates to fundamental purposes. Should be a close relationship between these statements and planned outcomes.
Principal goals	Referred to as outputs in the PBS.
Strategy	Is the broad approach combining a variety of activities or actions, taken in order to achieve an objective.
Performance targets	Quantifiable performance levels or changes in level to be attained by a specified date.
Key job goals	The major outcomes of projects and activities that comprise a person's job and contribute to the objectives of the Section, Operational and Corporate Plans.
Programmes	Grouping of strategies or activities, which contribute to achieving an objective. Is divided further into sub-programs, components and sub-components.
Effectiveness	The extent to which programme outcomes match stated objectives.
Efficiency	The maximisation of outputs for a given level of resources, or minimisation of resources for a given level of output.

obtained from other sources further increased it to AUS$150.260 million. In turn, this money was appropriated to achieve two outcomes corresponding to the twin objectives nominated by the Commonwealth Government in its BASA policy document. Outcome 1, to increase the pool of talent from which world champions will emerge, has been allocated AUS$34.556 million while Outcome 2, assisting Australian athletes to reach new peaks of excellence, has been allocated AUS$115.704 million. Output and Outcome details are listed in Figure 14.1.

Included in Outcome 1 is an amount of $400,000 that is to be provided to the ASDA to continue the TODIS programme. Included in Outcome 2 is an amount of AUS$1 million to assist elite athletes preparing for the 2004 Olympic and Paralympic Games in Athens.

Outcome 1	Output 1.1
An effective national sports system that offers improved participation in quality sports activities by Australians. Total price: AUS$34.556 million Dept. approps.: AUS$29.943 million Revenue from other sources: AUS$4.613 million	National sports system development. Total price: AUS$34.556 million Dept. approps.: AUS$29.943 million Revenue from other sources: AUS$4.613 million
Outcome 2	**Output 2.1**
Excellence in sports performances by Australians. Total price: AUS$115.704 million Dept. approps.: AUS$101.355 million Revenue from other sources: AUS$11.349 million	National elite athlete development. Total price: AUS$115.704 million Dept. approps.: AUS$101.355 million Revenue from other sources: AUS$11.349 million

Figure 14.1 ASC budget outcomes (2003–2004).

As noted in Chapter 7, the ASC has developed a comprehensive Strategic Plan covering the period 2002–2005. It sets the directions for the ASC for that period and the broad framework and strategies that will allow the Commission to meet its statutory objectives and to achieve the outcomes that the government requires. Within that Strategic Plan the ASC has set critical result areas that link to the outcomes against which the Commission reports to the Parliament and to its stakeholders. In this respect the ASC prepares a Portfolio Budget Statement (PBS) similar to other agencies within the general government sector. The aim of the PBS is to provide sufficient information, explanation, and justification to enable Parliament to understand the purpose of each item proposed in the Appropriation Bills (Nos 1 and 2) and Appropriation (Parliamentary Departments) Bill. It should translate the information in the Bills into the related outcomes and outputs. The aim of the PBS is to allow readers to be able to draw clear links between the Appropriation Bills and the agency's annual report. In other words, is the money that is appropriated to an agency spent in the way the agency indicated and how can the Government be sure that is the case? The answer to this lies in the relevant performance information shown in the PBS and the agency's annual report.

Performance information is a critical tool for public-sector management and accountability. Public servants are governed not simply by their job specification or departmental rules but by legislation such as *the Financial Management and Accountability Act 1997* (FMA Act), which makes the agency's chief executive officers responsible for promoting efficient, effective, and ethical outcomes, and the Public Service Act 1999, which articulates the principles and values of the public service.

The task of translating data obtained from NSOs into a form which satisfies the government that the ASC is correctly undertaking its charter to translate a specified portion of government policy into action and result is made difficult by the fact that the ASC seeks to attain two very different results. The first of these results relates to its commitment to government to achieve two major tasks – that of assisting Australian athletes to continue to reach new peaks of excellence and to increase the pool of talent from which world champions will emerge – as well as several minor tasks such as administering the TODIS programme. As a consequence of this, the ASC under Output 1.1 (National Sports System Development) seeks to work with its key stakeholders to:

- provide integrated services and funding, based on their individual needs, priorities, and capacity to contribute to the ASC's objectives;
- provide specialised sport sector expertise and knowledge (e.g. high performance, governance, business management and planning, online education);
- develop strategies and programmes to improve recruitment of new participants, better management of clubs, accreditation of sport coaches and officials, and access to quality sport for target population groups;
- negotiate strategic partnerships to increase involvement in grass-roots sports;
- design, implement, and manage single funding and service level agreements (FSLA); and
- provide leadership in the areas of sport ethics and drug-free sports.

Under Output 2.1 (Elite Sport Development), the ASC seeks to:

- Work in partnership with NSOs and State Institutes and Academies of Sport to deliver high-quality sports-excellence programmes to ensure that Australian athletes excel at the highest levels of international competition.
- Lead and facilitate a nationally coordinated approach to the planning of high-performance sport for the 2005–2008 quadrennium, which aims to apply the collective resources of the ASC, the AIS and State Institutes and Academies in a coordinated fashion in order to achieve the maximum return in terms of elite performance.
- Work with NSOs to ensure anti-doping policies are developed and effectively implemented and to actively promote a sporting environment free from drug cheats.
- Strengthen the effectiveness of the AIS by maintaining its continuous improvement philosophy and by providing innovative and integrated support services to enhance athlete and programme performance.

The second result sought is to determine the effectiveness of the individual NSOs and the AIS in undertaking the tasks assigned to them by the ASC. The information sought here relates to how well the NSOs and the AIS help the ASC achieve its objectives.

The relationship between ASC, NSOs and the AIS is convoluted. There is within the government a model known as the purchaser–provider model. In its simplest form the Government funds or purchases services, for example government-funded welfare services. For most of its history, such government-funded welfare services have been delivered by monopoly government agencies and thus protected from competition between providers. However, for the past dozen years there has been an increasing trend to outsource the delivery of welfare services, that is, to purchase the activities of a service provider from outside the government sphere. The prime argument for this has been economic – others can provide services more cheaply than can government. In addition, it is believed that one of the key advantages of the purchaser–provider approach is that it entails an outcome orientation. However, as has already been realised at many of the government departments, measurable outcomes under the purchaser–provider model do not always incorporate all aspects of what is required to be delivered, and frequently competing bidders are unable to pre-specify the outcomes they will achieve. Now while we are not suggesting that NSOs fit neatly into the purchaser–provider model, it does in many ways act in a not too dissimilar manner.

Measuring the performance of NSOs

The ASC acts as a government agency and seeks to undertake a government activity, which in this case involves increasing the number both of elite athletes and of sports people in general. In this instance the ASC does not undertake the task itself but seeks only to act as administrator. This is comparable to many government agencies that utilise the purchaser–provider model. In the case of the ASC the task is even more difficult than might be expected because the providers in this case are numerous and very different. In many instances the provider is responsible for only a small component of the overall task. For example, TA, though one of the larger NSOs, has effectively contracted through the grant system to deliver certain programmes and services for the ASC. These tasks, however, make TA responsible primarily for only one comparatively small part of the ASC's Active Australia Program, an even smaller part of the ASC's Disability in Sport Program and for working in partnership with the AIS on the AIS Tennis Program, based at Rod Laver Arena in Melbourne. In some instances, such as the Tennis Over Australia Program (TOAP), the activity is a partnership between the ASC, TA and a commercial sponsor, in the case of TOAP, MILO. The ASC provides grants to about 60 NSOs for sport development activities. Of these a smaller number, some 20 sports have been identified as the best prospects for business growth over the next four years. TA is one of these. Under this system TA will receive additional funding support for participation growth programmes and will actively partner the ASC in delivering a programme of sustainable participation growth. Thus, the ASC will fund TA, in a pseudo purchaser–provider system, in an endeavour to help the government agency fulfil its government-imposed task.

From the perspective of TA, its government funding and its agreement with the ASC to undertake specified activities is only a small part of its overall funding and programmes. Separate from its activities for the ASC (yet frequently having a similar objective of attracting more people to tennis – as spectators and players), TA controls and runs a number of major tennis tournaments including the Australian Open, the Davis and the Federation Cups. Its activities also include a number of other partnership arrangements with numerous commercial sponsors as well as its own TAP. It is little wonder, therefore, that agreements and contracts between the ASC and TA are somewhat flexible and that there is often weak verification of outcomes and outputs. No matter how earnestly the ASC and TA seek to achieve agreement on outcomes and outputs there will always remain complexities and ambiguities in such an agreement. Equally important from the ASC perspective is the fact that TA represents a major sport and has no national tennis competitor.

The difficulties for the ASC do not stop with NSOs such as TA. If they did, then with time and goodwill both organisations could merge their required listings of outcomes and outputs and might achieve a workable arrangement. There are scores of NSOs working under some form of 'grant/contract' with the ASC. A few have a well-developed strategic plan similar to that of TA while many others are still coming to terms with the requirements imposed by modern management practices. In some instances this is a function of insufficient finance (with money often dependent upon the sport) or human resource power. In other instances it is simply lack of knowledge and the ASC is midway through a concentrated campaign to improve the management and the understanding of policy development within such sporting organisations.

In addition, each of the NSOs, in turn, works with state bodies and with individual clubs. Thus, the linkages move from federal government to the ASC, to NSOs, down to state organisations, and to clubs. And, not as rarely as might be imagined, policy can travel upwards and not simply downwards, and in the process translation often suffers. Because of this linkage, as either unde-viating or tentative as it may be, the government policy articulated in *BASA* may bear little resemblance to the outcomes and outputs sought by club office holders.

Government's measuring rod

In essence the problem is clear at the government level. Its sport policy involves the delivery of twin objectives or outcomes. The first is to increase the number of elite athletes, and the second is to increase the numbers playing sport. That task is passed to the ASC and again the objectives or outcomes are clear. In turn, that task is further devolved to the AIS in the case of elite athletes, and to NSOs in the case of elite athletes and for increasing the pool of sports participants. For the AIS, demonstrating performance measures including outputs against the required outcome is difficult but manageable. It has a much clearer relationship with the ASC than do NSOs. In the case of the NSOs the contract/grant agreed with the ASC might represent as little as 10 per cent of their income with the remainder coming from other sponsors. The question then arises of whether the NSO should apply a differing set of performance measures for that portion of its activities sponsored by the ASC against the remaining portion sponsored by other funding arrangements. The organisation, effort, and cost of complying with government-required performance measures may well diminish the attractiveness of receiving government funding. The funding received from government may then, in whole or in part, be passed from the NSO to state sports organisations, to individual clubs or be used in advertising or sponsorship. Where funding goes to state organisations or individual clubs that funding may again represent only a small portion of that organisation's or club's overall income. In microcosm this means that the state organisation or the individual club faces the same problems regarding the production of performance measures as those faced by the NSOs.

Concluding comments

Having determined some of the difficulties facing the ASC and NSOs, how then do these organisations proceed in order to ensure that all entities understand and fulfil the requirements associated with the implementation of the Commonwealth Government sport policy? Clearly, the process must start with the policy detail itself. It should be unambiguous and succinct, and should clearly specify the outcomes required. It should be set at the appropriate level and identify the relevant target group. Invariably, the focus of the outcome will be on the effect the government can have on the community, the economy, or the national interest. In the case of *BASA*, the policy to assist Australian athletes to continue to reach new peaks of excellence and to increase the pool of talent from which world champions will emerge fulfils the requirements just stated. The policy must also define the impacts or deliverables the government expects to achieve from the policy (outputs). In this instance the government not only specifies the outputs but also nominates what actions will be undertaken (for example, provides new and innovative support services to assist NSOs to achieve targets in both high-performance sport and significantly increased participation). In order to achieve successful outputs, the outcomes must be capable of being measured. Again this is inherent in the policy. It must also be remembered that the policy is not simply for its agency, in this case the ASC, or for general interest groups and sporting bodies, but is, in addition, required to advise the general public of the government's broad goals.

In turn, the agency tasked with implementing the government policy, the ASC, must determine the most appropriate organisation to service their requirement. This, generally, may be undertaken by long-term agreement, as with the AIS, by approaching an NSO directly or by requesting applications for grants. It may be undertaken at the national, state, or local level or it may be accomplished by setting up ASC-sponsored programmes such as those concerned with ensuring the adoption of sound business and management practices by NSOs. In setting up an arrangement with an external organisation, or indeed in-house, the ASC should require timely feedback on the performance of stated outputs and should design and agree in advance on specified performance measures. These measures, if they are to be valuable, must be easily understood, well-defined and cost-effective to collect, store, and manage. They must additionally be timely and appropriate. Standard definitions are also essential when comparing different NSOs, and within an NSO, specific demographic groups in the community such as youth, older people, people with a disability, and people with a non-English-speaking background.

There must be an understanding by the ASC that the outcomes it seeks are likely to be strongly influenced by factors that are beyond the control of the NSOs. Performance may simply be a factor of whether the organisation receiving the funding is part of the voluntary, commercial, or public sectors. Members, chief executives, and other office holders may have legislative or corporate responsibilities or may have limited responsibilities. As a result, outputs against outcomes should be accepted as being indicative rather than prescriptive. In addition there is the possibility of difficulties arising when seeking data from groups or individuals with a disability. Both the outcomes are achievable and those achieved can be affected by the differing environments in which organisations operate and the level of capability within an organisation. As a consequence, some form of quality control procedure needs to be introduced. Figure 14.2 shows the BASA funding flowchart for the years 2003–2004.

A factor difficult to measure relates to the effectiveness and efficiency of the various NSOs. Realistically, this task should be undertaken by the ASC or by an external agency commissioned by the ASC. Whenever government resources are used, government has a right to know how well organisations use those resources and what benefit the community derives from government expenditure on funded services.

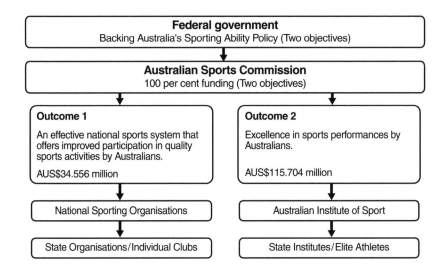

Figure 14.2 BASA funding flowchart (2003–2004).

Regardless of whether the relationship between the ASC and the NSOs is considered as a pseudo purchaser–provider agreement as suggested, as a grant against service agreement, or as a form of contract, there remains a necessity to establish a framework for performance measures and for quality control. Without such a framework the value of performance measures are limited and success against objectives becomes hard to determine. And if the success of objectives cannot be attained then the government runs the risk of being accused of wasting government funds. And that would never do.

15 What does it all mean?

Incremental or transformative?

Over the last 30 years there has been a massive change in the way the Commonwealth Government views the place of sport in Australian society. At the base level, there has been a dramatic increase in sport funding over the last 30 years in response to a number of problems and opportunities confronting Australian sport. In 1974 the Whitlam Government allocated AUS$7 million to sport development, which increased to AUS$13 million in 1981 when the Fraser Government set up the AIS. Since then the annual budget allocation has risen steadily, and it is now around AUS$150 million.

Current Commonwealth Government sport policy is multi-dimensional and, like the former governments, aims to strike an elusive balance between elite sport development, community sport development, and participation. Commonwealth Government sport policy can be conveniently divided into four strategic, but interconnected outcomes.

The first outcome aims to develop an effective national sports infrastructure by enhancing the management capabilities of NSOs in particular, and sport delivery agencies in general. Programmes are directed at improving coaching standards, the management skills of officials, the operation of NSOs, and the capacity of Australian sport to export its expertise.

The second outcome aims to improve participation in sport activities by Australians. This outcome has two strands. The first strand focuses on programmes to encourage more people to engage in competitive, club-based sport through its Active Australia and junior sport activities. The second strand focuses on programmes that assist marginalised groups in securing places in sport clubs and associations, and that also break down barriers to participation. These groups include aboriginals, people with disabilities, women, children, and older adults.

The third outcome aims to provide for continual improvement in the performances of Australians in international sport. In this case, programmes are directed at assisting NSOs to nurture talented athletes, enhancing the AIS scholarship programme, providing sport science support, and assisting athletes in managing their future careers.

Table 15.1 Commonwealth Government sport policy systems 2001–2004

Policy type	Key strategies	Program examples
Management improvement	Management training	Risk management and governance workshops
	Professional development	Coach and volunteer official development
		Designing performance measures
	Sport-Net	Information technology support
Participation	Active Australia	Street active clinics, after-school programmes
	Promotion	Sport expos, Active Australia Days
	Junior sport	Targeted 'kids' sport, Kids 'TRY' athlon clinics
	Indigenous sport	Coaching and participation programmes
	Social justice	alcohol education, women's sport
Elite support	AIS services	Scholarships, career and education support
	AIS facilities	Venues/playing fields, equipment, technology
	High performance	Elite coaching, sport science support
		Talent search and identification
		Seminars and workshops for young athletes
Fair play	Anti-doping	Tough on drugs
	Anti discrimination	Member protection policies
	Indigenous support	ISP
	Disabled support	Disabled support programmes

The fourth outcome aims to provide a climate and culture of fair play. The focus here is on not only drug control, but also eliminating discrimination and harassment, assisting indigenous communities, and dismantling barriers to disabled athlete participation. The breadth of the current policy arrangements is revealed in Table 15.1.

While many of the changes in sport policy have been incremental, there have also been a number of pivotal incidents and turning points that gave sport a new direction and the funds to make it happen. In particular, a number of funding increases were associated with changes in both the underlying values and policy priorities of the Commonwealth Government. These changing values and priorities are discussed below.

Whitlam's 'crash through'

The early 1970s signalled the beginning of a radically new approach to sport. For the first time since federation, the Commonwealth Government resolved to set a national agenda for sport. Whitlam's reformist government understood that sport was a public good and, using Bloomfield's report as a blueprint for change, argued that the allocation of more resources to community sport in particular would improve the social conditions of all Australians. The provision of additional sport facilities would not only give people the opportunity to accommodate a more active lifestyle, but also improve health and fitness levels, and promote community integration and social development. These were significant, if difficult-to-quantify, social benefits.

The elite development model

During the 1980s a dramatic escalation in funding accompanied the establishment of the AIS and ASC. Whereas in the 1981–82 financial year the government budget allocated AUS$13 million to sport, the figure had increased to AUS$32 million in 1985–86. The AIS in particular was a high-cost development. It not only involved the construction of many international standard training facilities, but also included a very sophisticated and costly sport science support network. AIS costs also escalated with the subsequent decision to establish satellite centres outside Canberra. In many respects the AIS initiative was controversial, since it shifted the focus away from grass-roots and community sport. However, both the conservative Fraser Liberal Government and the more reformist Hawke and Keating Labor Governments defended an essentially elite sport development policy on the grounds that high-performance sport, like community sport provided substantial social benefits. In this case, the benefits would come from the growth of civic and national pride associated with the anticipated international successes, particularly at the Olympic and Commonwealth Games, and world championships. It was also anticipated that the emergence of more internationally known athletes would enhance Australia's international standing. While there were still some claims that these successes would cause young people to emulate their heroes and join their local sport club, it has more recently been listed as a bonus in the light of flimsy evidence for the relationship.

Integrating sport's social benefits

During the 1990s, Commonwealth Government sport funding increased to support the preparation for the Sydney Olympics in 2000. Funding levels plateaued after the Howard Liberal Government was elected in 1996, but the Olympic effort was supported through to 2000. This emphasis on high-performance sport funding was justified on a number of interconnected grounds, although as indicated previously, some of these justifications had little supporting evidence. First, it was constantly stated that increased financial support for NSOs would improve their management practices, produce more specialised coaching, and enable athletes to gain more international competition. This in turn would improve their performance levels and enhance Australia's international sport standing. Second, these international successes would heighten Australian's sense of national pride. In an increasingly global world, sport was seen to be an important vehicle for developing a country's international standing. Third, it was expected that young people in particular would be inspired by the performance of Australia's high-performance athletes, and want to emulate these sporting icons. This would then lead to an increase in participation at the grass-roots level, a deepening of the pool of talented young athletes, an improvement in fitness levels, and a more health community. Fourth, Australia's reputation as a sporting nation could be used to secure more international business for local sport and leisure industry operators. Finally, there was a growing acknowledgment that since sport had become a global product, major sport events could be used to attract overseas visitors. The massive investment in the Sydney 2000 Olympics was defended on the grounds that it was not only great for Australia's international sports status and collective self-esteem, but would generate millions of dollars in foreign exchange through tourism.

The current position

The most recent Commonwealth Government policy statement, BASA, constitutes an attempt to integrate previous policy initiatives. It wants to balance its commitment to elite athletes with its desire to assist NSOs expand their sport development programmes and strengthen local sport clubs and junior sport programmes. It also aims to develop a more socially cohesive and ethical sporting landscape where drug-taking is contained, and where fairness and equity become integral parts of a sport organisation's culture. And, more generally, it wants to concurrently use sport to assist the nation's economic development. These are bold visions indeed!

Evaluating the outcomes

Australia has created a broad institutional structure for the delivery of sport. It comprises a combination of government departments and agencies, community-based clubs and associations, private not-for-profit organisations, and private commercial operators, which accounts for 13 per cent of total household expenditure (Australian Sports Commission, 2001b). It is supported by a network of 26,000 professional managers, more than 600,000 volunteer committee members, around 430,000 referees and umpires, 530,000 coaches and trainers, and finally nearly 400,000 volunteer officials and helpers. This has been accompanied by a continuing increase in Commonwealth Government assistance to the point where it has become the most influential player in Australian sport. Sport has been well and truly brought within the state sphere (Bryson, 1989). It has also become an industry. The metamorphosis from kitchen table to boardroom is nearly complete for many NSOs.

Lasting social benefits

The investment in elite sport development has also produced many inter-national successes. For example, Australia won 58 medals, including 16 gold, at the Sydney Olympics, which was well above previous medal tallies, especially when contrasted with Montreal Olympics in 1976, when the aggregate medal tally was five, with no gold. Australian athletes won 206 medals at the 2002 Manchester Commonwealth Games, which was a quantum leap from the 74 medals won at Edmonton in 1978. Moreover, the additional international successes of non-Olympic sports like netball, surfing, cricket and rugby demon-strate that the return from this investment has been considerable. By any measure, our international sporting successes have increased remarkably since the 1970s (Oakley, 1999).

The other lasting major benefit has been the professionalisation of sport's national governing bodies. A majority of these organisations, of which there are now more than 120, are efficiently managed and strategically aware of the development opportunities that exist in the wider leisure marketplace. At the same time, there are administrative soft spots in many of the smaller NSOs, and only 30 per cent of NSOs currently have full-time administrators.

Government investment in sport has also allowed Australian sporting bodies to export their expertise while managing events that attract many overseas visitors. The establishment of Sport Industry Australia, and the implementation of *Game Plan 2006* gave the Australian sport industry a greater international presence and stronger brand recognition (Australian Sports Commission, 2001b; Department of Industry Science and Resources, 2000a).

There is also some evidence that Australians' sporting successes have produced widespread civic and national pride. The record TV audiences for the 2000 Olympics, and the 2002 Commonwealth Games, and the large crowds who lined city streets to welcome them back to Australia were expressions of this collective self-esteem. The importance Australians' attach to international sporting achievement was confirmed at the 2003 World Rugby Cup, where even though Australia lost the final to England, the overall success of the event was celebrated throughout the nation.

When the last 30 years of government sport policy are viewed in aggregate, a number of themes and threads are evident. First, there are policies that aim to train elite athletes who can successfully compete internationally. Second, there are policies that aim to improve the management systems of NSOs. Third, there are policies that aim to leverage a variety of economic benefits from major sport events and the expertise residing in our sporting bodies. Fourth, there are policies that aim to manage the problems associated with the taking of performance enhancing drugs. Fifth, there are policies that aim to extend and improve opportunities for community participation, particularly among minority and disadvantaged groups. Sixth, there are policies that aim to build social capital through the support of community sport clubs and associations. Finally, there are policies that aim to create diversity and equity by changing the culture of sport organisations. However, as we suggest below, not all of these policy themes have been equally successful, nor have met the expectations that were set for them. These seven policy themes are listed in Table 15.2.

Problematic issues

Australians' sporting successes of the last 30 years have come at a significant cost. Indeed, the last 20 years of sport development has been accompanied by more than AUS$1 billion of Commonwealth Government funding, with most of it directed at elite sport and the larger NSOs. This investment in sport is most

Table 15.2 Commonwealth Government sport policy themes

Policy theme	Examples
High performance	AIS, athlete scholarships grants, elite coach education, talent search
Management improvement	ASC training programmes, grants for management improvement
Economic benefit	Sport Industry Australia, grants to mega sport events
Drug education and enforcement	ASDA, drug education programmes, testing
Community participation	Aussie sports, Aussie able, grants for junior development, targeted sport participation programme
Social capital	Volunteer training and recruitment programmes
Diversity and equity	Women's sport programmes, anti-harassment programmes, disabled and indigenous sport programmes

tangibly evident in the AIS facilities in Canberra, and the satellite centres around the country. One independent study estimated that between 1980 and 1996 it cost the Australian taxpayer approximately AUS$37 million to secure each Olympic gold medal winner. To put it another way, every medal won at the Olympics during that time involved an investment of AUS$8 million (Hogan and Norton, 1999). On the other hand, the relative scale of Commonwealth Government sport funding should also be put into context, since it represents only 0.07 per cent of total annual government expenditure.

At the same time, there is no evidence that 15 years of Commonwealth Government investment has dramatically increased the level of sport participation. We seem to have reached a sticking point in this respect. There are still more than 40 per cent of adult Australians who do not engage in regular physical activity (Australian Bureau of Statistics, 1999a). This is only a slight improvement on the 1974 figure of 48 per cent (Jaques and Pavia, 1976b). However there are some bright sports. The ASC has implemented a targeted sport participation programme that aims to attract an additional 1 million registered players. It has also developed programmes that aims to both promote the benefits of street sports like skateboarding and rollerblading, and secure more structures and facilities through consultation with state and local governments.

The participation rate for organised sport activities is even more dismal. Only 31 per cent of adult Australians regularly engage in organised sport, which is seriously below the 40 per cent participation rate for 1948 (Oakley, 1999). Despite Australia's global reputation for sporting excellence, and the media's constant promotion of Australia's international sporting heroes, people are less inclined to join sport clubs that they previously were. The idea that young people will swamp sport clubs waving a membership application form just because their favourite player wins an international competition has little empirical support. Neither will Olympic Games gold medals necessarily produce a wave of newly registered players. It should be remembered that only three Olympic sports appear in Australia's top ten participation sports (Australian Sports Commission, 1999b: 6). It will take a far more subtle and methodical approach to increase grass-roots participation in organised sport. In the current economic and cultural climate young people in particular have an explosive range of leisure activities to choose from. Sport no longer has the hold over people it once did, and many of its traditional values, its sometimes authoritarian culture, and frequently rigid dress codes, are seen as at best, silly, and at worst, oppressive.

And, neither has there been any improvement in the indicators of the physical health of Australians. Australia's international sporting achievements have not prevented the Australians becoming more obese. Australians are now the second most obese people in the world, second only to the United States. More than 50 per cent of Australians are overweight compared with 35 per cent in 1980 (Oakley, 1999). The government sports policy has clearly failed to keep the community fit and trim, although there are many countervailing forces contributing to greater inactivity. Web trawling, playing computer games, and attending cinemas, theatres and art galleries, are all valuable experiences, but are major distractions from sport participation. The ASC recently concluded that Australia faces a 'community health and fitness crisis' (Australian Sports Commission, 1999b: 31).

It is also difficult to demonstrate that the Commonwealth Government sport policy has created any additional social capital. If anything, there has been a fragmentation of sports clubs and leagues, and a consequent loss of social capital over recent years. This problem is acknowledged in the government's 2001 policy statement, and confirmed by recent changes in the level of player registrations. Between 1975 and 1998 the number of registered players increased from 3.2 to 4.1 million. This 22 per cent increase is, on the surface very satisfactory, but quickly loses its gloss when compared with the a 25 per cent increase in population over the same period (Oakley, 1999). A recent fall in volunteer numbers also threatens the social capital of sport clubs.

Moreover, there is insufficient convincing data that shows sport development strategies have built character, or changed the beliefs of players, officials, and fans about fair play and equity. So far there is little to indicate that sport policy has reduced juvenile crime rates and dysfunctional social behaviour. If anything, there is now an acknowledgement that sport club cultures have contributed to binge drinking amongst adolescents, and been the site for a number of sexual assaults and bullying incidents. Nor have Commonwealth Government sport policies had much impact so far on the elimination of alienation and social dislocation that runs through many communities. Indeed, there has been an increasing rate of depression in rural Australia over recent years.

Where to from here?

The last 30 years of Australian government sport policy has in many ways transformed the Australian sporting landscape. The local club and the state sport association still underpin Australia's sport system, but they have been effectively subsumed by high-performance sport institutes, professionally managed national governing bodies, and commercially driven national sport leagues. While the subsequent explosion in athletic standards allows Australia to claim that it is one of the best sport performing nations in the world on a per capita basis, there are many issues left unresolved. Drug abuse in sport is not fully under control, and some NSOs are still under-resourced and mismanaged. In addition, community sport is finding it difficult to recruit sufficient volunteers, participation rates have plateaued, and minority groups like aboriginals, some non-English-speaking migrants, and the disabled, are still disadvantaged.

But this does not mean Government money has been chronically wasted. Sport is a public or collective good, and provides significant social as well as private benefits, even when it focuses on elite sport programmes. As was previously indicated, these benefits not only include improved physical and mental health, the consolidation of social capital, and social integration, but also civic and national pride, an increase in tourism, and economic development. While there is a serious forgone cost, or opportunity cost in allocating so many scarce public resources to sport, the lack of any concerted resistance to the Commonwealth Government sport policy over the last 20 years suggests that it has strong public support. That is, citizens and voters seems comfortable having millions of dollars of federal taxes annually used to make a few privileged athletes even more privileged. Unless there is a taxpayer backlash it is unlikely that the Commonwealth Government sport policy will change dramatically in the immediate future. Indeed, in the light of our recent exceptional international sport performances, and the consequent feelings of collective pride and self-esteem, most Australians have given their unequivocal, if implicit, support to Australia's high-performance sport policy. Under the current sporting and cultural climate, any political party that includes a severe sport budget cutback in their policy platform will do so at their electoral peril. In other words, despite the concerns of critics that recent sport policy is biased towards the elite, and disadvantages ordinary players, minority groups, and community sport in general, it has a strong political logic that is linked to the social benefits it generates, and its electoral appeal.

While the social benefits from the high-performance policy area have met expectations, the benefits from the mass participation policy have not. In some respects community sport has declined as it faces falling registrations and volunteer support. This is still the Achilles heel of Commonwealth Government sport policy, although it should also be recognised that state and local governments have more direct responsibilities in this area. Nevertheless, community and participation sport has received significantly less Commonwealth funding than elite sport over the last 30 years, and has delivered fewer social benefits. It will be interesting to see if the current policy, which gives greater attention to mass participation, social integration, club and volunteer assistance, fairness, and equity, can reverse this situation. At the moment the Commonwealth Government is still searching for the right balance of excellence and participation (Australian Sports Commission, 2002a). At the same time, there is no longer any dispute that sport is an integral part of the Commonwealth Government policy mix, and can generate a significant array of social benefits. But it is also clear that some of the benefits are seriously under-realised.

Is there an alternative sport policy?

The continuing growth of Commonwealth Government sport funding is not only encouraging for sports' continuing development, but also surprising. In many advanced western industrial countries there has been a gradual shift away from a Keynsian welfare state ideology to a market-oriented ideology that aims to achieve less, not more, government intervention in economic affairs. This has been particularly evident in Australia, where de-regulation has been a constant theme since the early 1980s. For example, the Hawke Labor government introduced a floating exchange rate in 1983, and further deregulated the financial system in 1984.

There has also been a gradual privatisation of government services, which were exemplified in the sale of Qantas and the Commonwealth Bank to the private sector, and the partial sell-off of Telstra. In other words, state-owned enterprises were converted to profit-seeking public companies. This trend continued with the election of a more conservative Howard Liberal Government in 1996. The Howard Government was still in power in 2003. In fact, since the mid-1980s both Labor and Liberal governments have been underpinned by a neo-liberal ideology that aims to free up markets, reduce tax rates, dismantle trade barriers, eliminate government inefficiencies, and more generally privatise government business enterprises.

However, as we have shown, this neo-liberal ideology has also produced record levels of government spending on sport. Clearly, the Hawke, Keating and Howard Governments decided that additional resources should be put into sport because it represented a politically sound policy. That is, even though it did not neatly fit the ideology of neo-liberalism, it was seen to have strong electoral appeal. A number of national surveys confirmed that Australians enjoyed their status as not only a sport-loving nation, but also a very successful one.

At the same time, it is also clear that most of the funding has been directed to the elite end of the sport system. This was certainly not what the Whitlam Government of 1972–75 had envisaged when it laid the foundation for a broad-based Commonwealth Government sport policy. As indicated earlier, the Whitlam Government was a social democratic one. It aimed to increase spending on government services, extend the taxation base, strengthen government business enterprises, engineer progressive social change, and generally reduce social and economic inequality through income re-distribution and anti-discrimination laws. The Whitlam Government saw sport as a vehicle to achieve the final two aims in particular. Sport had the capacity not only to improve people's physical well-being, but also to extend and cement their social relations. In other words, it was seen to assist in building social capital and enhancing the leisure option of local communities. Whitlam's sport policy, unlike subsequent

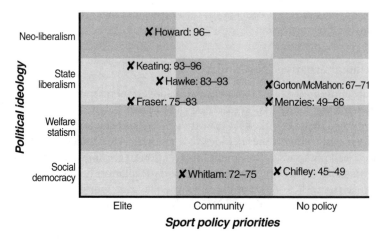

Figure 15.1 Sport policy priority matrix.

Commonwealth Government sport policies, focused on regional development and the provision of community sport facilities.

Our review of the last 30 years of Commonwealth Government sport policy shows that whereas both social democratic and neo-liberal governments believed that sport should receive government assistance, only the social democrats believed that most of the support should be directed to community sport. The policy differences are illustrated in Figure 15.1.

Figure 15.1 indicates that the alternative to current sport policy is best represented by a return to the Whitlam model that saw sport as a prime tool of social development, and as a means of achieving greater equality of sport ownership and participation. At the moment, a few high-profile Olympic sports receive most of the Commonwealth Government funding. In many respects the Whitlam model is socially desirable, and would assist in achieving many of the social benefits listed in the earlier chapters of this book. However, in the light of the widespread national pride that is generated from the resources used to ensure international sporting success, and the associated political kudos, the Whitlam model will be at best a secondary policy over the foreseeable future.

Final comments

Australian sport has gone through a major metamorphosis over the last 30 years. It has jettisoned its amateur values, attached itself to the corporate world, and professionalised its management structures and systems. At the same time the Commonwealth Government has progressively increased its financial assistance to sport and in many instances set the agenda for sport development. And this insidious government intrusion into what some people historically saw as a strictly apolitical institution has occurred during a period when government spent much of its time deregulating markets, withdrawing assistance to industry, and dismantling protective barriers. So how can this be explained? As hinted at the beginning of this book, the answer lies in the social benefits that flow from the practice of sport. While some of the benefits are more myth than fact, there are very substantial pay-offs from investing in sport, which is a particularly appealing proposition for neo-liberal governments. Moreover, as sport becomes commercialised and more professionally managed, the pay-offs become magnified. This occurs for a number of reasons. First, sport produces social benefits that arise from both participating and watching others participate. Second, the benefits can be both economic and social. Third, as sport becomes more commercialised it can more easily capture a mass audience and consequently spread the benefits arising from international sporting successes. The Olympic and Commonwealth Games, international tennis tournaments like Wimbledon, and international cricket matches generate a nationwide TV audience, and when Australians are victorious, feelings of national pride vibrate through the country. When a major international sport event is held in Australia, the benefit can be compounded with the flow of foreign exchange through tourism. In addition, while all this is happening, the daily pleasure and social bonding from community sport participation continues to flow. Successive Commonwealth Governments during the last 30 years increasingly understood that investing in sport would not only produce all these social benefits, but also consolidate their electoral appeal. The question is no longer should the Commonwealth Government invest in sport, but rather how much and where?

References

Adair, D. and Vamplew, W. (1997) *Sport in Australian History*, Melbourne: Oxford University Press.

ANZ (2003) *Australian Media Industry Landscape*, Melbourne: ANZ Banking Group.

Armstrong, T. (1987) Sport and recreation policy: will she be right? *Sporting Traditions*, May, 162–172.

Armstrong, T. (1988) *Gold Lust: Federal Sports Policy since 1975*, Unpublished PhD Thesis, Macquarie University, Sydney.

Australian Broadcasting Authority (1992) *Broadcasting Services Act*.

Australian Broadcasting Authority (1996) *Guide to Pay TV Anti-Siphoning Provisions*, Sydney: ABA.

Australian Broadcasting Corporation (2001) *Submission to the Australian Broadcasting Authority: Review of Anti-Siphoning List*, Sydney: ABC.

Australian Bureau of Statistics (1996–97) *Participation in Sport and Physical Activities* (Catalogue No. 4177.0), Canberra: Australian Bureau of Statistics.

Australian Bureau of Statistics (1997–98) *Participation in Sport and Physical Activities* (Catalogue No. 4177.0), Canberra: Australian Bureau of Statistics.

Australian Bureau of Statistics (1997) *Sport and Recreation: A Statistical Overview* (Catalogue No. 4156.0), Canberra: Australian Bureau of Statistics.

Australian Bureau of Statistics (1998–99) *Participation in Sport and Physical Activities* (Catalogue No. 4177.0), Canberra: Australian Bureau of Statistics.

Australian Bureau of Statistics (1998) *Survey of Disability and Disabling Conditions*, Commonwealth of Australia.

Australian Bureau of Statistics (1999–2000) *Participation in Sport and Physical Activities* (Catalogue No. 4177.0), Canberra: Australian Bureau of Statistics.

Australian Bureau of Statistics (1999a) *Participation in Sport and Physical Activity 1998–9* (Catalogue No. 4177.0), Canberra: ABS.

Australian Bureau of Statistics (1999b) *Sport Attendance Australia 1999* (Catalogue No. 4174.0), Canberra: ABS.

Australian Bureau of Statistics (2000) *Children's Participation in Cultural and Leisure Activities* (Catalogue No. 4901.0), Canberra: Australian Bureau of Statistics.

Australian Bureau of Statistics (2002) *Participation in Sport and Physical Activities* (Catalogue No. 4177.0), Canberra: Australian Bureau of Statistics.

Australian Bureau of Statistics (2003) *Sport and Recreation: A Statistical Overview* (Catalogue No. 4156.0), Canberra: ABS.

Australian Bureau of Statistics (2003) *Sport and Recreation: A Statistical Overview. Children's Participation in Cultural and Leisure Activities* (Catalogue No. 4156.0), Canberra, ABS.

Australian Cricket Board (2002) *Milo Have-A-Go Handbook*, Australia: Australian Cricket Board.

Australian Football League (2001) *105th Annual Report 2001*, Australia: Australian Football League.

Australian Football League (2002) *106th Annual Report 2002*, Australia: Australian Football League.

Australian Football League (2004) Australian Football League Website: www.afl.com.au, Australia: Australian Football League.

Australian Government (1983) *Sport and Recreation: Australia on the Move*, Canberra: Commonwealth Government of Australia.

Australian Labor Party (1996) *Sporting Partnerships: Election Policy Statement on Sport*, Canberra.

Australian News and Information Bureau (1962) *Sport: A Reference Paper*, Canberra: Commonwealth Government, Department of Interior.

Australian Olympic Federation (1927) *Australian Representation at Olympic Games: Note to Prime Minister Bruce, 14 November*, Canberra.

Australian Sports Commission (1986) *Strategic Plan: 1986/7–1988/9*, Canberra: Australian Government Publishing Service.

Australian Sports Commission (1990) *Strategic Plan: January 1990 to 31 December 1993*, Canberra: Australian Government Publishing Service.

Australian Sports Commission (1991) *Annual Report: 1990–91*, Canberra: Australian Sports Commission.

Australian Sports Commission (1994) *National Junior Sport Policy: A Framework for Developing Junior Sport in Australia*, Canberra.

Australian Sports Commission (1994) *Olympic Athlete Program: Making Great Australians*, Canberra: Australian Sports Commission.

Australian Sports Commission (1996) *Annual Report: 1995/96*, Canberra: Australian Sports Commission.

Australian Sports Commission (1997) *Active Australia: A National Participation Framework*, Canberra: Australian Sports Commission.

Australian Sports Commission (1998a) *Annual Report 1997/98*, Canberra:

Australian Sports Commission (1998b) *Excellence: The Australian Institute of Sport*, Canberra: Australian Sports Commission.

Australian Sports Commission (1999a) *Annual Report: 1998–99*, Canberra: Australian Sports Commission.

Australian Sports Commission (1999b) *Beyond 2000*, Canberra. Australian Sports Commission.

Australian Sports Commission (2000) *Harassment-Free Sport: Guidelines to Address Homophobia and Sexuality Discrimination in Sport*, Canberra: Australian Sports Commission.

Australian Sports Commission (2001a) *Working With Sport: Australian Sports and the Role of the Australian Sport Commission*, Canberra.

Australian Sports Commission (2001b) *New Strategic Directions for the ASC's Active Australia Program*, Canberra: Australian Sports Commission.

Australian Sports Commission (2001c) *Annual Report: 2000–2001*, Canberra: Australian Sports Commission.

Australian Sports Commission (2002a) *Strategic Plan: 2002–2005*, Canberra: Australian Sports Commission.

Australian Sports Commission (2002b) *Participation in Exercise, Recreation and Sport 2001*, Canberra: Australian Sports Commission.

Australian Sports Commission (2003a) *Annual Report: 2002–2003*, Canberra: Australian Sports Commission.

Australian Sports Commission (2003b) *NSO Online: Sport Recognition*, Canberra.

Australian Sports Commission (2003c) *The AIS at a Glance*, Retrieved 15 December 2003 from www.ais.org.au/overview.

Australian Sports Drug Agency (2002) *Annual Report 2001/02*, Canberra: Australian Government Publishing Service.

Australian Swimming Inc (2002) *Member Protection Policy*, Sydney.

Baka, R. (1984) Australian Government involvement in sport: a delayed, eclectic approach, in *Sport and Politics* (ed. G. Redmond) Urbana-Champaign.

Black, J. (1989) *Drugs in Sport: Interim Report of the Senate Standing Committee on Environment Recreation and the Arts*, Canberra: Australian Government Publishing Service.

Black, J. (1990) *Drugs in Sport: Second Report of the Senate Standing Committee on Environment Recreation and the Arts*, Canberra: Australian Government Publishing Service.

Bloomfield, J. (1973) *The Role, Scope and Development of Recreation in Australia* (The Bloomfield Report), Canberra: Australian Government Publishing Service.

Bloomfield, J. (2003) *Australia's Sporting Success: The Inside Story*, Sydney: University of New South Wales Press.

Bolton, G. (1990) *The Oxford History of Australia: 1942–1988*, Melbourne: Oxford University Press.

Booth, D. (1991) War off water: The Australian Surf Lifesaving Association and the beach, *Sporting Traditions*, 7, 135–162.

Booth, D. (2001) *Australian Beach Cultures: The History of Sun, Sand and Surf*, London: Frank Cass.

Booth, D. and Tatz, C. (2000) *One-eyed: A View of Australian Sport*, Sydney: Allen & Unwin.

Brennan, G. (2004) *Private Communication* (National Manager, Indigenous Sport Program).

Bridgman, P. and Davis, G. (2000) *The Australian Policy Handbook*, Sydney: Allen & Unwin.

Bruce, T. and Hallinan, C. (2001) Cathy Freeman: the quest for Australian identity, in *Sport Stars: The Cultural Politics of Sporting Celebrity* (eds D. Andrews and S. Jackson), London: Routledge.

Bryson, L. (1989) Sports, drugs, and the development of modern capitalism, *Sporting Traditions*, 6.

Caldwell, G. (1976) Sport and national identity, in *Sport in Australia* (eds T. Jaques and G. Pavia), Sydney: McGraw Hill.

Cameron, M. and MacDougall, C. (2000) Crime prevention through sport and physical activity, *Trends and Issues in Crime and Criminal Justice*, 1(6).

Cashman, R. (1984) *'Ave a Go Yer Mug': Cricket Crowds from Larrikin to Ocker*, Sydney: Collins.

Cashman, R. (1986) Sport, big business and the spectator, *Current Affairs Bulletin*.

Cashman, R. (1995) *Paradise of Sport*, Melbourne: Oxford University Press.

Cohen, B. (1980) *Sport and Recreation Discussion Paper*, Canberra: Australian Labor Party.

Colebatch, H. (2002) *Policy*, Buckingham: Open University Press.

Coles, A. (1975) *Report of the Australian Sports Institute Study Group*, Canberra: Commonwealth Government Department of Tourism and Recreation.

Commonwealth Government Sport Ministers Office (1989) *Media Release*, 6 December.

Commonwealth Government of Australia (1935) *Cabinet Paper*, 4 October.

Commonwealth Government of Australia (1941) *Parliamentary Debates* (Hansard), May–June.

Commonwealth National Fitness Council (1966) *Annual Report*, Canberra: Commonwealth Government.

Commonwealth of Australia (1985) *Australian Sports Commission Act 1985*, Canberra: Australian Government Publishing Service.

Commonwealth of Australia (1989) *Australian Sports Commission Act 1989*, Canberra: Australian Government Publishing Service.

Commonwealth of Australia (2001) *Backing Australia's Sporting Ability: A More Active Australia*, Canberra: Australian Government Publishing Service.

Confederation of Australian Sport (1991) *Sport Report*, Winter edition.

Confederation of Australian Sport (1991) *Sport Report*, Autumn edition.

Confederation of Australian Sport (1992) *Sport Report*, Spring edition.

Confederation of Australian Sport (1994) *Sport Report*, Winter edition.

Confederation of Australian Sport (1995) *Sport Report*, Autumn edition.

Cooke, A. (1994) *The Economics of Leisure and Sport*, London: Routledge.

Cricket Australia (2003) *Anti Doping Committee Hearing*, Melbourne: Cricket Australia.

Crowley, F. (1986) *Tough Times: Australia in the 1970s*, Melbourne: Longman.

Crowley, R. (1992) *Physical and Sport Education: Report of Senate Committee on Environment Recreation and the Arts*, Canberra: Australian Government Publishing Service.

Daly, J. (1991) *Quest for Excellence: The Australian Institute of Sport*, Canberra: Australian Government Publishing Service.

Department of Environment Housing and Community Development (1976) *Discussion Paper: Sport and Recreation Development*, Canberra: Australian Government Publishing Service.

Department of Home Affairs (1979) *National Fitness in Australia*, Canberra: Australian Government Publishing Service.

Department of Industry Science and Resources (2000a) *Game Plan 2006: Sport and Leisure Industry Strategic National Plan*, Canberra: Commonwealth of Australia.

Department of Industry Science and Resources (2000b) *Toward a National Tourism Strategy*, Canberra: Commonwealth of Australia.

Department of Sport Recreation and Tourism (1985) *Annual Report 1984–85*, Canberra: Australian Government Publishing Service.

Drane, R. (2003) Full medal racket, *Inside Sport*, December, 68–79.

Dunstan, K. (1973) *Sports*, Melbourne: Cassell.

Edwards, J. (2000) *Australia's Economic Revolution*, Sydney: University of New South Wales Press.

Edwards, M. (2001) *Social Policy, Public Policy: From Problem to Practice*, Sydney: Allen & Unwin.

Farmer, P. and Arnaudon, S. (1996) Australian sports policy, in *National Sports Policy: An International Handbook* (eds L. Chalip, A. Johnson and L. Stachura), Westport: Greenwood Press.

Francis, B. (1989) *Guilty: Bob Hawke or Kim Hughes?* Sydney: Bruce Francis Publications.

Gordon, H. (1962) *Young Men in a Hurry*, Melbourne: Lansdowne Press.

Gratton, C. and Taylor, P. (1991) *Government and the Economics of Sport*, London: Longman.

Guttmann, A. (1978) *From Ritual to Record: The Nature of Modern Sport*, New York: Columbia University Press.

Gymnastics Australia (2001) *Managing the Gymnastics Network*, Melbourne: Gymnastics Australia.

Gymnastics Australia (2003a) *Targeted Participation Growth Program: Gymskools – Final Report 2003*, Melbourne: Gymnastics Australia.

Gymnastics Australia (2003b) *Targeted Participation Growth Program: Aeroskools – Final Report 2003*, Melbourne: Gymnastics Australia.

Hamilton-Smith, E. and Robertson, R. (1977) Recreation and government in Australia, in *Leisure and Recreation in Australia* (ed. D. Mercer), Melbourne: Sorrett.

Harris, S. (1972) *Political Football: The Springbok Tour of Australia 1971*, Melbourne: Gold Star Publications.

Hartung, G. (1983) An interview with Federal Minister John Brown, *Sports Coach*, 7, 50–52.

Herald (1986) 9 June.

Hill, M. (1997) *The Policy Process in the Modern State*, Harlow: Prentice Hall.

Hogan, K. and Norton, K. (1999) *The Price of Gold*, Adelaide: School of Physical Education, Exercise, and Sports Studies, University of South Australia.

Houlihan, B. (1997) *Sport Policy and Politics: A Comparative Analysis*, London: Routledge.

House of Representatives Committee on Finance and Public Administration (1983) *The Way We P(l)ay: Commonwealth Assistance for Sport and Recreation*, Canberra: Australian Government Publishing Service.

House of Representatives Standing Committee on Environment Recreation and the Arts (1997) *Rethinking the Funding of Community Sporting and Recreational Facilities: A Sporting Chance*, Canberra: Parliament of the Commonwealth of Australia.

Hutchins, B. (2002) *Don Bradman: Challenging the Myth*, Cambridge: Cambridge University Press.

Hylton, K., Bramham, P., Jackson, D. and Nesti, M. (ed.) (2001) *Sport Development*, London: Routledge.

Interim Committee for the Australian Sports Commission (1984) *Report to the Minister for Sport Recreation and Tourism* (The Harris Report), Canberra.

Jaques, T. and Pavia, G. (1976a) The Australian Government and Sport, in *Sport in Australia* (eds T. Jaques and G. Pavia), Sydney: McGraw Hill.

Jaques, T. and Pavia, G. (1976b) Milk beneath the cream? in *Sport in Australia* (eds T. Jaques and G. Pavia), Sydney: McGraw Hill.

Jobling, I. (1987) Australian sporting heroes, in *Sport, Nationalism and Internationalism: A.S.S.A. Studies in Sport History: No 2* (ed. W. Vamplew), pp. 91–118.

Kell, P. (2000) *Good Sports: Australian Sport and the Myth of the Fair Go*, Annadale: Pluto Press.

Lalor, P. (2003) Drinking for Australia, *The Weekend Australian Magazine*, pp. 16–20.

Liberal Party (1996) *Encouraging Players, Developing Champions: Election Policy Statement on Sport*, Canberra.

Lindblom, C. (1959) The science of muddling through, *Public Administration Review*, 19, 78–88.

Lipsky, R. (1981) *How We Play the Game*, Boston, Beacon Press.

Loland, S. (2002) *Fair Play in Sport*, London: Routledge.

Long, J. and Sanderson, I. (2001) The social benefits of sport: where is the proof? in *Sport in the City: The Role of Sport in Economic and Social Regeneration* (eds C. Gratton and I. Henry), London: Routledge.

Mandle, W. (1976) Cricket and Australian Nationalism in the nineteenth century, in *Sport in Australia* (eds Jaques, T. and Pavia, G.), Sydney: McGraw-Hill, pp. 46–72.

Martin, S. (1989) *Going For Gold: The First Report on an Inquiry into Sports Funding and Administration*, Canberra: Commonwealth of Australia: House of Representatives Standing Committee on Finance and Public Administration.

Martin, S. (1990) *Can Sport be Bought? The Second Report on an Inquiry into Sport Funding and Administration*, Canberra: Commonwealth of Australia, Houses of Representatives Standing Committee on Finance and Public Administration.

McAllion M. (2003) Interview with Mark McAllion, Community Cricket Manager, Cricket Australia.

McKay, J. (1986) Hegemony, the state, and Australian sport, in *Power Play: Essays in the Sociology of Australian Sport* (eds G. Lawrence and D. Rowe), Sydney: Hale and Iremonger.

Mckay, L. (1991) *No Pain, No Gain? Sport and Australian Culture*, Sydney: Prentice Hall Australia.

Mooney M. (2003) Interview with Maisie Mooney, Chief Executive Officer, Women's Golf Australia.

National Centre for Culture and Recreation Statistics (2001) *The Social Impacts of Sports and Physical Recreation*, Adelaide: Australian Bureau of statistics.

Oakley, R. (1999) *Shaping Up: A Review of Commonwealth Involvement in Sport and Recreation (The Oakley Report)*, Canberra.

O'Connor, K., Stimson, R. and Daley, M. (2001) *Australia's Changing Economic Geography: A Society Dividing*, South Melbourne: Oxford University Press.

Parsons, W. (1995) *Public Policy: An Introduction to the Theory and Practice of Policy Analysis*, Cheltenham: Edward Elgar.

Pearson, K. (1979) *Surfing Subcultures of Australia and New Zealand*, University of St Lucia: Queensland University Press.

Prime Minister's Department, *Briefing Paper* (1935), Canberra: Commonwealth Government.

Productivity Commission (2003) *Social Capital: Reviewing the Concept and its Policy Implications*, Canberra: Commonwealth of Australia.

Putnam, R. (2000) *Bowling Alone: The Collapse and Revival of American Community*, New York: Simon and Schuster.

Reiterer, W. (2000) *Positive: An Australian Olympian Reveals the Inside Story of Drugs and Sport*, Sydney: Pan Macmillan.

Rickard, J. (1988) *Australia: A Cultural History*, London: Longman.

Salt, B. (2003) *The Big Shift: Welcome to the Third Australian Culture*, South Yarra: Hardie Grant Books.

Semotiuk, D. (1987) Commonwealth government initiatives in amateur sport in Australia: 1972–1985, *Sporting Traditions*, 3, 152–162.

Shelton, J. (1999) *'Life Be in it': From Incrementalism to Sharp Policy Reversals*, Unpublished MA Thesis, Parkville: The University of Melbourne.

Shilbury, D. and Deane, J. (2001) *Sport Management in Australia: An Organisational Overview*, Melbourne: Strategic Sport Management.

Sport Canada (1998) *Sport Participation in Canada*, Ottowa.

Stell, M. (1991) *Half The Race: A History of Australian Women in Sport*, Sydney: Angus and Robertson.

Stewart, J. (1999) *Public Policy: Strategy and Accountability*, Melbourne: Macmillan.

Stewart, J. and Ayres, R. (2001) The public policy process, in *Australian Handbook of Public Sector Management* (eds C. Aulich, J. Halligan and S. Nutley), Sydney: Allen & Unwin, pp. 20–35.

Stewart, R. (1984) *The Australian Football Business: An Economic Guide to the Australian Football League*, Kenthurst Town: Kangaroo Press.

Stewart, R. (1990) Leisure and the changing pattern of sport and exercise, in *Sport and Leisure: Trends in Australian Popular Culture* (eds D. Rowe and G. Lawrence), Sydney: Harcourt, Brace and Jovanovich.

Stewart, R. (1992) Athleticism revisited: sport, character building and Protestant school education in 19th century Melbourne, *Sporting Traditions*, 1, 35–50.

Stewart, R. (2002) Radio's changing relationship with Australian cricket: 1932–1950, *Sporting Traditions*, 19, 49–64.

Stewart, R. and Smith, A. (1999) The special features of sport, *Annals of Leisure Research*, 2, 87–99.

Stewart, R. and Smith, A. (2000) Australian sport in a postmodern age, in *Sport in Australasian Society* (eds J. Mangan and J. Nauright), London: Frank Cass.

Stoddart, B. (1986) *Saturday Afternoon Fever: Sport in Australian Culture*, Sydney: Angus and Robertson.

Telford, R. (1982) The Australian institute of sport: sport science and the talented athlete, *Sports Coach*, 6, 1–4.

The Age (2003) *Green Guide* (weekly supplements).

The Australian (2002–2003) *Media* (weekly supplements).

Toohey, K. (1990) *The Politics of Australian Elite Sport 1949–1983*, Unpublished PhD Thesis, Pennsylvania State University.

Vamplew, W. (1994) *The Oxford Companion to Australian Sport*, Melbourne: Oxford University Press.

Waddington, I. (2000) *Sport, Health and Drugs: A Critical Sociological Perspective*, London: E & FN Spon.

Westerbeek, H. and Smith, A. (2003) *Measuring Performance in Australian Tennis: An Efficiency and Efffectiveness Model for the Tennis Division*, Centre for Business Research, Melbourne: Deakin University.

Whitwell, G. (1989) *Making the Market: The Rise of Consumer Society*, Melbourne: McPhee Gribble.

Wind, H. (1960) The will and the way, *Sports Illustrated*, 23, May, 78–85.

Women's Golf Australia (2002) *Targeted Participation Growth Program: Business Plan*, Melbourne: Women's Golf Australia.

Women's Golf Australia (2003) *Play a Round Manual*, Melbourne: Women's Golf Australia.

World Anti-Doping Authority (2003) *World Anti-Doping Code*, Montreal, World Doping Authority.

World Health Organisation (2003) *Health and Development Through Physical Activity and Sport*, Switzerland: World Health Organisation.

Index